DEEP (Development Experience Exchange Partnership)
for the Vision of Vietnam

Vol. 2

Public Sector Reform for State Capacity and Sustainable Development in Vietnam

Written by Yeonseob Ha, Young Suk Jang, Hyun Joon Kim,
Yoon Jik Cho, Seungwon YU

YONSEI UNIVERSITY PRESS

DEEP (Development Experience Exchange Partnership)
for the Vision of Vietnam
Volume 2

Public Sector Reform for State Capacity and Sustainable Development in Vietnam

Written by Yeonseob Ha, Young Suk Jang, Hyun Joon Kim, Yoon Jik Cho, Seungwon YU

Published and Printed in the Republic of Korea
by Yonsei University Press.
50 Yonsei-ro, Seodemun-gu, Seoul, 03722, Republic of Korea
Tel: (+82-2) 2123-3380~2 Fax: (+82-2) 2123-8673 E-mail: ysup@yonsei.ac.kr
ISBN 978-89-6850-378-8 (94300)
978-89-6850-371-9 (Set)

The National Library of Korea cataloging in Publication (CIP) data for this volume can be found at the library's e-CIP homepage(http://seoji.nl.go.kr). and in the Korean Library Information System Network(http://kolis-net.nl.go.kr).
CIP Control Number: 2019053631

Table of Contents

CHAPTER THREE: Human Resource Management (HRM) Reform

Author : Yoon Jik Cho

Author : Yeonseob Ha

List of Figures and Tables

Figures

Tables

Abbreviations

General

ICT	Information Communication Technology
KDI	Korea Development Institute
KOICA	Korea International Cooperation Agency
MOHA	Ministry of Home Affairs
MOSPA	Ministry of Security(Safety) and Public Administration
NRC	National Research Council for Economics, Humanities and Social Sciences
NST	National Research Council of Science & Technology
ODA	Official Development Assistance
PAR	Public Administration and Performance Index
PAPI	Public Administration and Performance Index
PCI	Provincial Competitiveness Index
R&D	Research and Development
SCS	Senior Civil Service
SIPAS	Satisfaction Index of Public Administration Services
SOEs	State-owned enterprises
UNDP	United Nations Development Programme
VCCI	Vietnam Chamber of Commerce and Industry

CHAPTER One:

Institutional and Administrative Reforms

CPV	Communist Party of Vietnam
EPB	Economic Planning Board

FAGPE	Framework Act on Government Performance Evaluation
GII	Government Innovation Index
GOV	Government of Vietnam
ICT	Information and Communication Technology
IT	Information Technology
KCCP	Korea Commission for Corporate Partnership
KEDI	Korean Educational Development Institute
KIET	Korea Institute for Industrial Economics & Trade
KIST	Korea Institute of Science and Technology
KISTI	Korea Institute of Science and Technology Information
KOICA	Korea International Cooperation Agency
KRISS	Korea Research Institute of Standards and Science
LAN	Local Area Networks
ME	Ministry of Education
MEST	Ministry of Education, Science and Technology
MST	Ministry of Science and Technology
MOGEF	Ministry of Gender Equality and Familty
MOPAS	Ministry of Public Administration and Security
MIC	Middle-income country
MP	Master Program
NAPA	National Academy of Public Administration
NARS	National Assembly Research Studies
NATO	No Action, Talk Only
NPS	National Pension Service
OSS	One stop service
PCI	Provincial Competitiveness Index
PCNC	Presidential Council on National Competitiveness
PED	Planning of Economic Development
PMO	Prime Minister's Office
RAW	Readiness-Ability-Willingness
SEDP	Socio-Economic Development Plan
SEDS	Socio-Economic Development Strategy

SMBA	Small and Medium Business Administration
SME	Small and Medium-sized Enterprises
VILS	Vietnam Institute for Legislative Studies

CHAPTER Two:
Governance Reform

ACRC	Anti-Corruption and Civil Rights Commission
CPB	Citizen Participatory Budgeting
EGDI	E-government Development Index
KIPF	Korea Institute of Public Finance
MARD	Ministry of Agriculture and Rural Development
MOC	Ministry of Construction
MOH	Ministry of Health
MOIT	Ministry of Industry and Commerce
MOJ	Ministry of Justice
MONRE	Ministry of Natural Resource and Environment
NGO	Non-governmental Organization
PAC	Public Administrative Center
PSC	Public Service Charter
PSDAQ	Public Service Delivery Agencies
SIPAS	Satisfaction Index of Public Administrative Services
VAVN	Veterans Association of Vietnam
VFF	Vietnam Fatherland Front

CHAPTER Three:
Human Resource Management (HRM) Reform

ACWG	Anticorruption Working Group
BSC	Balanced Score Card
CPI	Corruption Perception Index
CPV	Central Party of Vietnam
EHRI	Enterprise Human Resources Integration
FEVS	Federal Employee Viewpoint Survey
FHCS	Federal Human Capital Survey
HR	Human Resource
HRM	Human Resource Management
IB	Integrity Bureau
KIPA	Korea Institute for Public Administration
MOHA	Ministry of Home Affairs
MOI	Ministry of the Interior
MPM	Ministry of Personnel Management
NPM	New Public Management
OPM	Office of Personnel Management
TAP	Transparent, Accountable, and Performing (Government)

CHAPTER Four:
Public Expenditure Management Reform

BARO	Budget and Accounting Reinvention Office
dBrain	Digital Brain
KDI	Korea Development Institute
KPFIS	Korea Public Finance Information Service
MTEF	Medium-Term Expenditure Framework
PEM	Public Expenditure Management
PIMAC	Private Infrastructure Investment Management Center
TFT	Task Force Team

EXECUTIVE SUMMARY:

PUBLIC SECTOR REFORM FOR STATE CAPACITY AND SUSTAINABLE DEVELOPMENT IN VIETNAM

Yeonseob Ha

Professor, Department of Public Administration, Yonsei University

EXECUTIVE SUMMARY:

PUBLIC SECTOR REFORM FOR STATE CAPACITY AND SUSTAINABLE DEVELOPMENT IN VIETNAM

This publication is the result of three-year long KOICA-funded joint research project by both HCMA and University Industry Foundation of Yonsei University called "DEEP (Development Experience Exchange Partnership) for the Vision of Vietnam". Professor Doowon Lee of Yonsei University served as the project leader (PL) of this three-year project along with a project manager (PM) assigned for each year's project. Dr. Kwang Woo Jun, the former Chairman of the Financial Services Commission of the Korean government also served as the Chairman of the Coordination nemCommittee of this project. We appreciate Dr. Jun a lot for his valuable advices and considerate supervision. Also, we appreciate Dr. Nguyen Xuan Thang, President of HCMA, for his devoted cooperation and support.

As the second part of this project, this report attempts to provide an analysis of Vietnam's public sector reform. The public sector has four ingredients; first, the public sector is essentially an institution. Second, the government itself is a governing mechanism. Finally, people and money are required to govern. Hence, the second year research focuses on these four aspects of the public sector; i.e. institutional and administrative reforms, governance reform, human resource management reform, and public expenditure management reform. Vietnam is recognized as one of most dynamic, fastest growing developing countries, particularly since the DoiMoi reforms were introduced in 1986.

While Vietnam still faces various challenges, the country has demonstrated high economic growth as a major middle-income country and has continued to build a springboard with which to leap toward high-income country status by accelerating the pace of economic growth, promoting inclusive growth, and enhancing the government's quality.

The research team is comprised of five Korean and seventeen Vietnamese researchers. The Korean researchers are Yeonseob Ha (Yonsei University), Yong Suk Jang (Yonsei University), Hyun Joon Kim (Korea University), Seungwon YU (Korean National Polica University), and Yoon Jik Cho (Yonsei University). The Vietnamese research team, who are led by team leader Le Quoc Ly (HCMA) and Hoang Van Nghia (HCMA), is comprised of both HCMA researchers and external experts. Tran Thi Thanh Thuy, Nguyen Thi Bao, Bui Phuong Dinh, Ngo Huy Duc, Nguyen Thi Thanh Hai, Le Van Loi, Truong Ho Hai, and Dao Ngoc Bau are the HCMA researchers. There are six external experts, including Truong Duc Thang (Office of the Government), Phan Ngoc Mai Phuong (the Ministry of Planning and Investment), Vu Xuan Nguyet Hong (the Ministry of Planning and Investment), Nguyen Thanh Trung (the Ministry of Science and Technology), Tran Van Ngoi (the Ministry of Home Affairs), and Dr Nguyen Ba Chien (the National Academy of Administration). The research team is organized as summarized below.

The theme of this second year research is closely related to the theme of Vietnam 2035, which includes a prosperous economy, creative people, and a just society. The three pillars of Vietnam 2035 are 1) economic prosperity with environmental sustainability, 2) equity and social inclusion, and 3) a capable and accountable state. The second year research is closely linked with the third pillar of Vietnam 2035, that is, creating a capable and accountable state.

Table P-1 Participants of PSR Research Team

<table>
<tr><th colspan="2"></th><th>Korea</th><th>Vietnam</th></tr>
<tr><td colspan="2">Project Leader</td><td>Doo Won Lee
(Yonsei University)</td><td>Nguyen Xuan Thang (HCMA)</td></tr>
<tr><td colspan="2">PSR Team Leader</td><td>Yeonseob Ha
(Yonsei University)</td><td>Le Quoc Ly (HCMA)
Hoang Van Nghia (HCMA)</td></tr>
<tr><td rowspan="4">Research Theme</td><td>Institutional and Administrative Reforms</td><td>Yong Suk Jang
(Yonsei University)</td><td>Tran Thi Thanh Thuy (HCMA)
Nguyen Thi Bao (HCMA)
Truong Duc Thang
(Office of Government)
Phan Ngoc Mai Phuong
(Ministry of Planning and Investment)</td></tr>
<tr><td>Governance Reform</td><td>Hyun Joon Kim
(Korea University)</td><td>Bui Phuong Dinh (HCMA)
Ngo Huy Duc (HCMA)
Nguyen Thi Thanh Hai (HCMA)
Vu Xuan Nguyet Hong
(Ministry of Planning and Investment)</td></tr>
<tr><td>Human Resource Management Reform</td><td>Yoon Jik Cho
(Yonsei University)</td><td>Le Van Loi (HCMA)
Truong Ho Hai (HCMA)
Nguyen Thanh Trung
(Ministry of Science and Technology)
Tran Van Ngoi
(Ministry of Home Affairs)</td></tr>
<tr><td>Public Expenditure Management Reform</td><td>Seungwon YU
(Korean National Police University)</td><td>Dao Ngoc Bau (HCMA)
Nguyen Ba Chien
(National Academy of Administration)</td></tr>
</table>

The expected outcome of the second year research is a so-called Transparent, Accountable, and Performing (TAP) government.

This study is composed of four parts: 1) Institutional and Administrative Reforms; 2) Governance Reform, 3) Human Resource Management Reform, and 4) Public Expenditure Management Reform. Ch. 1 discusses the principles, goals, and strategies of institutional reform and proposes the future direction of administrative reform in Vietnam based on the analysis of the Korean experience. Here, the term "institution" is not limited to market economy institutions, but refers to a more general framework of governing, that is, the rules of the game. Hence, this part discusses administrative reform such as the changes of incentive structures that face civil servants and the general public in Vietnam. Ch. 2 deals with governance reform with a special focus on the improvement of the state's capacity and accountability. A major roadblock to state capacity building in Vietnam is the fragmentation and commercialization of the state. In addition, limited citizen participation and the low quality of public services weaken accountability. Ch. 2 delineates key governance issues in Vietnam and provides the future directions of governance reform based on this diagnosis. Ch. 3 examines the current status of Vietnam's human resource management; this part basically proposes a sequential approach to HRM reform. The stabilization of career civil services is the most basic ingredient of HRM. For which management based on merit and the assurance of a high standard of administrative ethics are essential. Then, the Vietnamese government must prepare for evidence-based management. The final stage of HRM reform is the full-scale adoption of a performance management and position classification system. Ch. 4 also proposes a sequential approach to public expenditure management reform based on the analysis of Korea's so-called Four Major Fiscal Reform Initiatives that includes medium-term expenditure framework, top-down budgeting, performance management, and a digital budget and accounting system.

Table P-2 Structure of the Study

Ch. 1	Ch. 2	Ch. 3	Ch. 4
Institutional and Administrative Reforms - Vietnam's Status - Korean Experiences - Lessons and Policy Recommendations	Governance Reform - Vietnam's Status - Korean Experiences - Lessons and Policy Recommendations	Human Resource Management Reform - Vietnam's Status - Korean Experiences - Lessons and Policy Recommendations	Public Expenditure Management Reform - Vietnam's Status - Korean Experiences - Lessons and Policy Recommendations

Institutional and Administrative Reforms

Vietnam is an emergent country in Southeast Asia that is currently experiencing significant changes and growth. Its gross domestic product (GDP) per capita had grown rapidly since 1990, and the growth rate reached 6.4% in the 2000s. With the aim of accelerating overall reform, the National Steering Committee for Public Administration Reform (PAR), which was led by the Prime Minister, was placed within the central government and a steering board was set up in every ministry and province. However, the reform's scope remained limited and bureaucratic inertia has dragged down the reform process' speed and quality. The Vietnamese government resolved to break this impasse, and Vietnam's 2011–2020 Socio-Economic Development Strategy (SEDS) paid attention to several points, including structural reforms, environmental sustainability, social equity, and emerging issues of macro-economic stability. Sustainability is the most important quality of Vietnamese socio-economic development for moving to the next stage of national success. Only when economic growth is accompanied by social integration is stable, long term growth possible, which could be achieved by solving various social problems such as income inequality, regional disparity, corruption, and social conflict. National reform should be based on a long-term, balanced approach and driven according to careful, systemic plans. Reform plans require cooperative management, monitoring, and modification to ensure their effectiveness. South Korea presents a good model for Vietnam in that it has placed significant emphasis on balancing economic growth and social development regarding institutional and administrative reforms. Part I aims to draw lessons from investigating the dynamic changes in South Korea's policy paradigms and reform efforts. Part I analyzes successful and unsuccessful examples of the reforms that South Korea has employed over the last five decades to suggest guiding principles, goals, and strategies that would help Vietnam's reforms be effective; the results can be summarized as follows.

The guiding principles of Vietnam's institutional reforms should include three key components: (1) building an inclusive political system, (2) forming a stable and predictable government, and (3) enhancing fair economic and social orders. The goals of reforms should include that the government encourage citizens to participate in economic and social activities, form a stable and predictable administration by establishing and implementing credible rules and systems, and secure fair political, economic, and social rules. The government should set up guidelines for policy implementations and abide by them to reduce unpredictability.

The goal of Vietnam's institutional reforms is the pursuit of responsible and market-friendly reform. Aiming at quantitative growth, social integration, and stable, predictable social order will allow the nation to develop a new public management paradigm that can help achieve sustainable growth. Two strategies are required to realize this vision: (1) design institutions for inclusive growth and (2) establish a discipline for moderate and balanced institutional reform.

The simple pursuit of quantitative growth or greater efficiency is insufficient for the redesign of fair political, economic, and social order; institutional discipline must be established with moderation and balance to produce desirable outcomes. Vietnam ought to focus on reaching three sub-goals: fair distribution, the provision of equal opportunities, and quality and stable employment. In addition, the state and government should encourage their citizens' participation, establish executable and predictable game rules, and enhance the government's capacity to secure the consistent implementation of policies when establishing disciplines

Governance Reform

Good governance is a necessary condition of economic and social development. If developing countries wish to pursue sustainable progress, they must urgently establish principles for good governance and reform existing governance forms to remove barriers that hamper development. Part II outlines Vietnam's important governance reform agendas by reviewing their past and present governance reform initiatives. The Korean governance reform experiences that are relevant for Vietnamese governance reform are selectively introduced to develop policy recommendations for Vietnamese governance reform. The reformation of governance is ultimately aimed at establishing a sustainable governing system that will enable Vietnam to achieve the goals of Vietnam 2035. Part II looks at the State of Vietnam based on this theory of the state's functions in the market economy. However, it will not capture all the functions of state governance in Vietnam; rather it will look at the factors that hinder the effectiveness of the Vietnamese state's governance, as described in the report's scope, as follows.

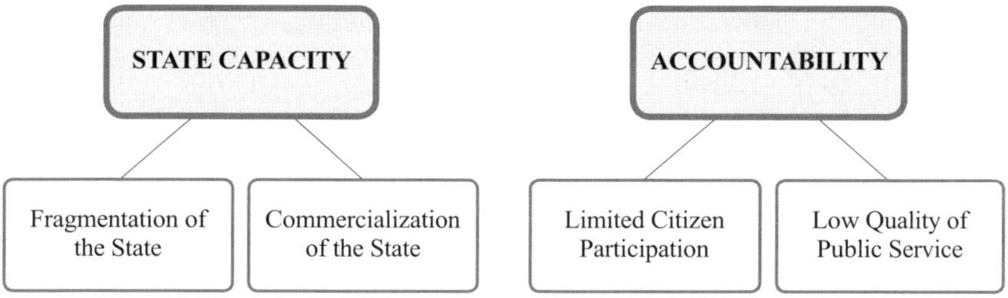

Figure A-1 Governance reform agendas adapted from the Vietnam 2035 report

One key issue that constrains the state's capacity development is the fragmentation of government authority. Striking a balance between centralization and decentralization of government power and responsibilities is particularly important when the state pursues economic development. However, Vietnam's current situation shows that too much power has been shifted from the central state to local authorities. Meanwhile , many local governments are heavily dependent upon support from the central government because they lack the financial capacity for self-sustainability. The pursuit of the balanced development of local government is necessary for the reformation of intergovernmental relationships in Vietnam.

One constraint that is often found in developing countries is that state-owned enterprises (SOEs) play key roles in the economy. The Vietnam 2035 report addresses that the state engages in the market directly through SOEs and the close links between the state and particular segments of the private sector have been strengthened. One accountability problem reported in the Vietnam 2035 report is citizens' limited voice and participation. Even though civic organizations are burgeoning in Vietnam, only state-sanctioned organizations are allowed to participate in policy processes. Presently, the state still plays a dominant role in providing public services around Vietnam. However, financial constraints and poor state management in the public sector mean that the services provided by the state generally fall short of citizens' needs. Improving the quality of administrative services for citizens and businesses is an important issue for enhancing the Vietnamese government's administrative accountability. When a new government was elected in June 2016, the new government's reform agenda was announced by the new Prime Minister for 2016–2020, who was committed to building an "incorruptive, development enabling, accountable and 'service' government." It is obvious that reform policies over the past few years have indicated the commitments of the Vietnamese government to trying to create favorable conditions for development and enabling good government in the context of a changing world.

Human Resource Management Reform

If one accepts that Vietnam 2035 is a critical vision statement for Vietnam, then reforms should focus on strengthening the three pillars: 1) economic prosperity with environmental sustainability, 2) equity and social inclusion, and 3) a capable and accountable state. Administrative reform efforts should be focused on the third pillar. Considering the fundamental concepts required to achieve the third pillar, the second year research team provides the concept of a "Transparent, Accountable, and Performing (TAP) government" that will helps to achieve 2035. The three values included in the acronym are quite familiar and have been discussed as critical factors to attaining high-quality governance. Although those values are not particularly new, that does not mean that most countries have successfully fully internalized and nurtured those values in their governance. Both developed and developing countries show room for improvement in actualizing those values; thus, by establishing a TAP government, the Vietnam government will have sufficient capacity to successfully achieve Vietnam 2035 with sustainability.

Full-scale, fundamental administrative reform was conducted in Vietnam with the launch of *Doi Moi*. The 1992 constitutional amendment positioned the congress and government as the core axis with the Communist Party (Seo & Im, 2013). Particularly for HRM, the enactment of Ordinance 25/CP of 1993 became the basic framework for the civil service system with a series of decisions by the Government Committee for Organization and Personnel (Moon & Hwang, 2013). The Ordinance of Cadres and Civil Servants was issued in 1998, and the Vietnam government made the rules of the whole HRM process more sophisticated by including recruitment, disciplines, retirement, leave of absence, training, etc. (Seo & Im, 2013).

Since the *Doi Moi* demonstrated fruitful outcomes, further major government reform efforts were shaped in 2001. The Vietnamese government launched a 10-year long-term plan for its reform called the Public Administration Reform (PAR) Master Program. that provided nine specific objectives: 1) Improving the administrative institutional system, regime, and policy; 2) Erasing and cutting off administrative procedures with red tape to reduce complicatedness; 3) Clearly identifying the functions, tasks, and responsibilities for organizations in the PA system; 4) The government's structure will be orderly appropriated; 5) Up to 2005, opportunities for decentralizing PA will be identified; 6) Up to 2010, civil servants will be professionals and modernized with a rationalized structure and size; 7) Up to 2005, civil servants' salaries will be reformed; 8) Up to 2005, financial mechanisms will be reformed in line with PA organizations and public services; 9) The civil service will be modernized (Can, 2013, p.111). Among these nine objectives, the sixth and seventh are directly related to HRM reform.

Particularly for HRM, the Vietnam government sought to reform HRM in the public sector even before the PAR Master Program. The major changes in civil service can be explained by three milestones. Milestone 1 was the 1998 " Issuance Ordinance of Cadres, Civil servants and Public employees." According to the Ordinance, personnel working in State-owned Enterprises (SOEs) are clearly separated from personnel working in bureaucracy. That is, the people working in SOEs are not regulated by the Ordinance. The Ordinance newly introduced both competitive examinations for the recruitment of new civil servants and public employees and examinations for grade promotion. Milestone 2 was the 2003 "Revision of Ordinance of Cadres, Civil Servants, and Public Employees." The revision of the Ordinance separated the management of public employees working in public service delivery agencies from the management of civil servants and cadres working at administrative agencies. Thus, two different laws were founded, the Law of Cadres and Civil Servants and later the Law of Public Employees. Another critical aspect of the revised Ordinance is the increased level of delegation. The revised Ordinance delegated the right to recruit public employees to become leaders/heads of public service delivery agencies based on work contracts. Finally, Milestone 3 included the "Issuance of Law of Civil Servants and Cadres 2008 and Law of Public Employees 2010." By this third milestone, a clear distinction consolidated between the management of civil servants and cadres and the management of public employees. The Law of Civil Servants and Cadres sought to combine the career system (closed system) and positioned system (open system), assure leaders' individual responsibilities, and enhance merit-based promotion.

When considering the achievements and remaining challenges of Vietnam HRM reform, one should consider how to make the current achievements more fruitful and sustainable and how to overcome existing challenges. The six HRM reform initiatives that will be introduced in the following chapter can further strengthen the Vietnamese HRM system . For example, the open recruitment system that the Korean government is using may provide some useful guidance for sustaining a diversified recruitment system that attracts talented people. The Korean government's performance evaluation system can also be a useful reference for the Vietnam government to further enhance civil servants' performance. The Performance Agreement that applies to high level officials in Korea can be considered as an alternative method of assuring the accountability of high-level officers.

Public Expenditure Management Reform

Even though public finance has played an important role in boosting growth in Vietnam, there are also many issues associated with the management of public expenditure. First, the structure of budget expenditure needs revamping. Recurrent expenditures accounted for a large proportion and tended to increase rapidly, from 52.2% for 2001–2005 to 55.2% for 2006–2010, and up to 63.5% for 2011–2015, while the proportion of investment and development expenditures gradually decreased from 31.2% in 2001–2005 to 28.8% in 2006–2010, and further to 23% in 2011–2015. Second, although public expenditure has increased rapidly, this increase has started having a detrimental effect on the economy. Third, the efficiency of public sector investment is inferior to that of the private sector; Vietnam's investment efficiency is lower than that of its neighboring countries. Fourth, the budget deficit as a share of GDP peaked at 6.90% in 2009 and has tended to decline in later years but remains at a high level; it averaged at 6.13% of GDP for 2006–2016.

In recent years, the Vietnamese government has gradually used the medium-term expenditure framework instead of short-term budgeting and moved from input-based budgeting to output-based budgeting. However, public expenditure management is not achieving the desired effect. There are several reasons for this: (i) fiscal discipline is not well established, (ii) Law on State Budget does not match the reality and the global trend of public expenditure management, (iii) lack of agency responsible for providing public financial information, (iv) Vietnam's economic growth model is not suitable, (v) statistical methods do not fit the general norms of the world; and (vi) lack of an effective mechanism for project management and monitoring.

PEM reform is strongly required in Vietnam to overcome the problems mentioned above. Various PEM reforms can be introduced or performed: Medium-Term Expenditure Framework (MTEF), Top-down Budgeting, Program Budgeting, Performance Management, Budget Coverage Expansion, Integrated Information Systems, The Rearrangement of Public Finance Statistics, Accrual Basis Government Accounting, Project Management (total cost management, preliminary feasibility tests, etc.). However, the Vietnamese government is not required to introduce or perform all PEM reforms simultaneously. A sequential approach to PEM reform is highly recommended in consideration of the administrative and institutional foundations of reform. Hence, it is necessary that the government prioritizes PEM reforms and analyzes related methods in depth. Korea has a long history with PEM reform and has introduced or performed almost all PEM reforms. Korea's trial and error can help the Vietnamese government prioritize PEM reforms and prepare actual introduction strategies and action plans.

CHAPTER ONE:

Institutional and Administrative Reforms

Young Suk Jang

Professor, Department of Public Administration, Yonsei University

Ⅰ. Introduction

Ⅱ. Guiding Principles of Vietnam's Institutional Reforms

Ⅲ. Administrative reforms in Vietnam: Learning from the Case of South Korea

Ⅳ. Conclusion

Ⅴ. Policy Suggestions

CHAPTER ONE:

ADVANCED HUMAN RESOURCE DEVELOPMENT FOR SUSTAINABLE GROWTH

I. Introduction

Vietnam is an emergent country in Southeast Asia that is experiencing significant changes and growth; it is interesting to see how Vietnam has achieved its development over the last 25 years. In 1986, *ĐổiMới*triggered the economic growth of Vietnam by initiating economic and political reforms that have transformed Vietnam from one of the poorest countries in the world to a lower middle-income country. Its gross domestic product (GDP) per capita had grown rapidly since 1990, and the growth rate reached 6.4% in the 2000s. This *upward* trend continued until 2015, when the country recorded a 6.7% GDP growth rate. The accelerated growth moderated itself during the first half of 2016, with the GDP expanding 5.5%, which is 0.8% lower than that during the same period in 2015. With regard to Vietnam's prospects heading towards 2035, the World Bank suggested that Vietnam's prosperity would be founded on three pillars: a modern rule-of-law State to be improved and renovated with regard to both quality and quantity, a fully developed market economy, and a highly developed democratic society in which the rule of law is the prime principle that governs societal interactions (World bank, 2016). In particular, the development of a "competent and accountable state" would be considered a decisive pillar of Vietnam's prosperity.

Much progress has been made in political and social arenas in Vietnam over the last quarter of a century; Vietnam's international status and strength have significantly changed from those of the past. The turning point in the history of the country's reform era was the Sixth Congress of the Communist Party of Vietnam in 1986. The decision by Congressto renovate the country was a revolutionary choice, shifting the country from **a centrally planned economy to a socialist-oriented market economy**. This is a historic transition in which, the Party and State of Vietnam left their historical legacy behind and developed a foundation for an era of socio-economic prosperity since the 1990s, with spectacular achievements that pulled the country away from a severe crisis and the brink of collapse. However, more effective measures are required for Vietnam to become further industrialized and modernized and for the Vietnamese people to gain a better quality of life. In fact, the 1997 Asian financial crisis revealed weak points in the public administration of Vietnam, and Public Administration Reform (PAR) became essential (Doan TrongTruyen, 1996). No Vietnamese policymakers denied the significance of harmonizing the nation's economic and administrative reforms, and so a public administration reform program was launched in January, 1995 by the Communist Party of Vietnam (CPV) and the Government of Vietnam (GOV) under resolution of the VIII Plenum of the Central Committee of the CPV. Some strategies were applied to rationalize the basic legal and regulatory structure of the public administration for two reasons: to reform all the administrative machinery and to improve the civil service with trained public servants (Martin & Nguyen Khac Hung, 2004).

The National Steering Committee for PAR, which was led by the Prime Minister, was placed within the central government and a steering board was set up in every ministry and province. The PAR was to include the reformation of the legal and judicial system, the organization and operation of the National Assembly, and various public enterprises. Although the initial results were quite productive in official quarters (International Colloquium, 1996), Vietnam still needed more creative and substantial legislation and regulations. The administrative procedures were upgraded and the 28 ministries of the central government were cut back to 23, while the nation also achieved a modest level of decentralization. Public enterprises leaned toward corporatization, which is interchangeable with "equitization" in Vietnam. The role of the National Academy of Public Administration (NAPA) was emphasized to keep pace with the newly developing market economy; the organization aimed to establish the foundation of various types of training.

However, the bureaucratic inertia and stiffness have dragged down the speed and quality of the reform process. The development and power of the central government are crucial in Vietnam, especially because the country "has developed a market economy within and around the state" and "there are virtually no limits to the domains of state responsibility" (Tonnesson, 2000). Given these remarks, it is not difficult to predict that the grand project of Vietnam is on the verge of failure due to its internal weaknesses. Even the officials who are in charge of the introduction and operation of the PAR process are often considered incapable and directionless. Their job is to monitor what changes will be effective among the range of models and the proposals of the development aid programs.

The Vietnamese government resolved to break through this impasse, and Vietnam's 2011–2020 Socio-Economic Development Strategy (SEDS) paid attention to several points, including structural reforms, environmental sustainability, social equity, and the emerging issues of macro-economic stability.

The government defined three "breakthrough areas" in the strategy: promoting human resources and skills development, particularly skills for modern industry and innovation, improving market institutions, and developing infrastructure (Mai May HtarPhwy, Bob et al., 2013; World Bank, 2016). The five-year Socio-Economic Development Plan (SEDP) for 2011–2015 paid particular attention to three critical restructuring areas in which state-owned enterprises and public investment could play crucial roles. The SEDP for 2016–2020 was approved in April 2016, and then some SEDP reform priorities were re-arranged because of slow progress. These reforms will be accelerated over the next SEDP for 2016–2020 to achieve the target value in the 10-year strategy.

It is natural to set ambitious goals after succeeding; the SEDP reported that the government set its sights on achieving a per capita GDP of US$ 3,141–3,261 by 2020. Its effect will be widespread and will lead to 6.5–7% annual growth over the next five years. Other ambitious projects were set by the SEDP to prepare for the continual decline of the poverty rate by 1.3–1.5% per year, to expand health insurance coverage to 80% of the whole nation, and to reduce the child malnutrition rate to below 10%. Sustainability was also addressed in the plan; this consists of keeping forest coverage at least 42% of total land, expanding access to clean drinking water to 90% of the rural and 95% of the urban populations, and other environmental goals such as waste management and pollution control. This plan clarifies the main issues: stabilizing the macro-economy, strengthening market institutions, and establishing infrastructure for the skilled labor force. The SEDP for 2016–2020 set nine main plans, including fast and stable economic growth, revising the growth model, and promoting competitive productivity.

The PAR journey has been through five stages started in 1975–1985, as a searching decade to re-position the role of the State and Government in rebuilding a nation(Thuy, 2016). Since the 1986 reform, the Party and the State of Vietnam have led and implemented Administration Reform programs, and their key tasks are to reform government agencies. A full-scale step was launched in 1986–1994 that initiated PAR. It was identified as the focus of the State reform in the period that followed, 1995–2001. The significant role of PAR and its activities were affirmed and carried out in an increasingly intensive manner, exerting strong impacts on society and becoming a driver of the renovation (*ĐổiMới*) course. The Prime Minister released Decision 136/2001/QD-TTg on September 17th 2001,to clarify that the Party and the State aimed for administration reform. Thus, the prime minister launched a fundamental legal framework for PAR activities at all levels and in all sectors during 2001–2010 that was the cornerstone of the administration reform at all levels and departments.

Based on an objective and serious review the achievements and shortcomings of the 2001–2010 PAR Master Program (MP), the Government promulgated the Public Administration Reform Master Program 2011–2020 (at Decision 136/2001/QD-TTg, dated September 17, 2001), which provided a legal framework for PAR strategy during the stage in which the country's industrialization and modernization was accelerated. In 2016, based on the review of the first half of the 2011–2020 PAR MP, the 2016–2020 PAR Plan was approved with the aim of accelerating the implementation of the MP during the second half, thus ensuring an accomplishment of PAR objectives and tasks during the second phase (2016–2020). In addition to the success of high policy level reform initiatives, as reflected in Socio-Economic Development Plans, PAR has also made considerable achievements at the level of local implementations.

Although a series of efforts at distinct levels have indicated that Vietnam has effectively continued a wide range of reform activities towards overall modernization, this remains necessary to maintain a more comprehensive approach, not only to achieve development agendas and objectives but also to establish a consistent and reliable system. South Korea would be a good model for Vietnam in that it placed great emphasis on balancing economic growth and social development regarding institutional and administrative reforms. This report aims to draw lessons from investigating the dynamic changes in South Korea's policy paradigms and reform efforts. This report provides valid lessons on how to make reforms more effective and suggest guiding principles, goals, and strategies that should be fully considered in institutional and administrative reforms in Vietnam by analyzing successful and unsuccessful examples in South Korea's administrative reforms. In the next section, we will first discuss what the general principles of institutional reforms should be that can lead to more successful administrative reforms in Vietnam. Figure 1-1 illustrates the overview of the report.

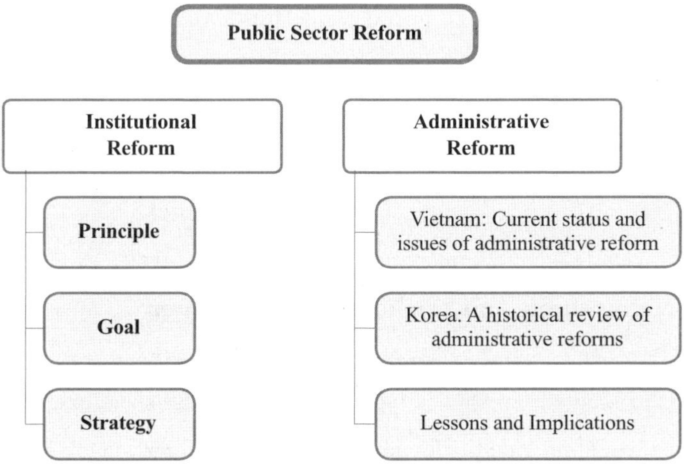

Figure 1-1 Overview of Institutional and Administrative Reform

II. Guiding Principles of Vietnam's Institutional Reforms

1. Building an inclusive political system

Establishing an inclusive political system can contribute to broadening the scope of social and political activities, thereby enabling a nation to uncover new sources of economic growth. After the 1980s, South Korea experienced democratization, and it was able to find new sources of growth such as in Information and Communication Technology (ICT) through that process. In case of young and emerging countries, it was essential that institutions, processes, and mechanisms were installed to support and promote national efforts to develop democracy (Association for Progressive Communications, 2009). Strategic use of and access to ICT not only has proven potential to bring about democracy but has also spurred innovative approaches to government services such as e-service portals and Home Tax Services in Korea. An inclusive political system that is properly equipped with ICT support would offer a wide variety of opportunities to discover and cultivate potential sources of growth in Vietnam.

2. Forming stable and predictable government

Establishing and implementing institutions that all social members respect and trust would provide the foundation of a stable and predictable government. South Korea's stable and organized administrative bodies have led policy implementations in a predictable manner, motivating its citizens to participate in social and economic systems. In the progress of regulatory reform since the 2000 OECD review, the commitment to a "participatory society" has made transparent regulatory regime shift from regulator-oriented regulation to user-oriented regulation (OECD, 2007). This effort has consequently raised awareness of and compliance with regulations among participants, leading to the stable policy implementation. In the case of Vietnam, excessive documents such as resolutions, decrees, and decisions from regulating bodies can impede effective policy implementation. There are calls for changes toward a broad-based foundation that can form a predictable government.

3. Enhancing fair economic and social order

"Trickle-down economics," which is a widely known primary factor that drives huge growth in South Korea, began to lose its efficacy with regard to long term development. Instead, the idea of creating a fair society has garnered strong support from citizens since Korea has experienced what an unbalanced economic structure and institutional setting can create. The Korean government supported the extensive growth of big business groups under the principle of trickle-down economics. While Korea accomplished rapid economic development alongside the huge success of big firms, new (and small) firms had fewer fair opportunities to participate in the market, which hampered fair competition and weakened the market economy. In the case of Vietnam, excessive administrative state intervention in economic activities was identified as an obstacle to economic development (Tran & Ngo, 2017). It is noted that the administrative bodies have failed to properly design a balanced business environment. Therefore, the government should reform the rules of the game to guarantee fair and equal opportunities to all business actors. Considering the global trends and the experiences of Korea, Vietnam must establish a fair economy and social order to accomplish sustainable development. After all, Vietnam's future success depends on three core pillars of reform: a modern rule-of-law state that is renewed both in terms of quality and quantity, a full market economy, and a high quality democratic society in which rule-by-law is taken as the leading principle that guides societal interactions (World Bank, 2016).

4. A Goal and Strategies for Vietnam's Institutional Reforms

4.1. Goal: A New Paradigm of Institutional Reform and Public Management

Goal	Pursuing responsible and market-friendly institutional reforms

Since the 1980s, Vietnam has pursued institutional reforms to construct a modified socialist system with elements of a market economy. This clearly indicates that Vietnam has joined the worldwide trend of creating a market economy that values efficiency and rationality. For the 2016–2020 plan, the country went forward and shifted its orientation from serving to enabling the government. The core missions of 2017 include developing institutions and legal policies, creating favorable conditions for business and production development, restructuring the economy, changing growth patterns, and boosting productivity, quality, efficiency, and competitiveness. Despite the emphasis on ensuring social security and calls for international integration, the orientation does not consider sustainable development. Earlier reforms might have allowed Vietnam to achieve a decent level of economic development, yet these are readily followed by negative side effects including corruption and regional disparity. From now on, Vietnam needs a different paradigm of institutional reform and public management as a mechanism with which to attain the goal of sustainable growth.

South Korea has also seen numerous adverse effects of the rapid growth, all of which have added to provoking various social conflicts. It has become heavily dependent on foreign countries in the capital and technology markets, and currently has the worst productivity imbalance among industries; its rapid growth has also increased the income gap and inequality. Many other nations have also suffered social inequality, poverty, and environmental issues that have led to economic slowdown. Against this backdrop, 17 Sustainable Development Goals (SDGs) were agreed in the 70th UN General Assembly in 2015. The agreement implied that global society was determined to discuss the matter of great concern to balance stable economic growth, social integration, and environmental protection.

Changes in its political, economic, and institutional orders are presumed to guarantee stable and sustainable social orders and social integration. Since economic policies with regard to rapid growth have inevitably impeded comprehensive development, a new model of inclusive growth should be addressed. The World Bank mentioned inclusive growth to show that the pace and pattern of economic growth should be interlinked and assessed together (OECD, 2014). The approach considers rapid economic growth necessary, but also sees that growth should be broad-based across sectors to ensure its sustainability. Thus, the government should seek measures that ease disparities in income, employment, and education to make the social integration and economic growth support mutual.

Traditional Economics

Focus on GDP as the key measure of success

Binary approach: either growth or equity

Focus on outputs (GDP per capita)

Attention to the average inequality (income gap)

Economics of Inclusiveness

Focus on material and non material living standards intergrated policies: growth and equity

Focus on outcomes (health, education, jobs)

Attention to different social groups and scales inequalities (income and well being)

Source: OECD (2015)

Figure 1-2 A Shift towards Inclusive growth

This report suggests ways to redesign an inclusive market economy and secure administrative capacity to achieve sustainable growth.

4.2. Goal: A New Paradigm of Institutional Reform and Public Management

Strategies	- Institution building for inclusive growth - The establishment of discipline for moderated and balanced institutional reforms

4.2.1. Institution building for inclusive growth

Inclusive growth is a type of growth that aims to both create new economic opportunities and ensure equal opportunities for all segments of a society (Ali & Son, 2007). Ianchovichina & Lundstrom(2009) suggested that fair distribution, provision of equal opportunities and protection in employment transitions are three major components of inclusive growth.

Fair distribution refers to the state in which the fruits of economic growth are distributed to the members of a society according to the rules that are agreed upon by the members. However, it does not mean that every citizen within a society should receive the same income. Rather, it means that the outcome of economic growth should be distributed based on their abilities and efforts. The mechanism induces participants to work hard for their own benefit.

Provision of equal opportunities means that all members of a society should be given equal opportunities when they meet certain criteria such as in education, work and other significant areas. Thus, it focuses on creating opportunities and making them accessible to all, regardless of individual circumstances. Providing equal opportunities entails a democratic decision making process so that diverse interests can be reflected in the redesign and reform of the system.

Employment stability refers to both the increase in employment and the improvement in job conditions and qualities. The overall progress among sectors and the following improvements in economic and social status of citizens have lead citizens to call for a better market environment, more decent jobs, and better life quality. If market conditions cannot meet citizens' demands, social conflicts may arise that harm the system. Vietnam is at this turning point on its path. The nation has recorded more than 6% average annual GDP growth since the mid-1980s and the unemployment rate has significantly decreased. However, the income inequality issue remains unsolved. Therefore, Vietnam should be concerned about fair distribution, the provision of equal opportunities, and job qualities in reforming its political, economic, and institutional systems.

4.2.2. Establishment of discipline for moderated and balanced institutional reform

Regarding the reform of a system, discipline plays an important part, since it cannot function properly without social agreement. If there is no social agreement, people may not observe established rules. Discipline refers to internalized rules (Barker, 1994) and the core mechanism that secures moderation and balance in the process of designing and adopting a system to achieve sustainable growth in the long term (Henry, 2013). Institutional discipline needs to be established with moderation and balance to produce desirable outcomes. Active social discourse that includes as many members of society as possible is of great importance for strengthening institutional discipline (Foucault, 1980).

Encouraging citizens' participation

Designing a system without encompassing all members of a society or at the cost of minorities can ruin the foundation of inclusive growth because it violates basic principles. In the process of designing a system, the participation of diverse members and the social agreement of participants should be guaranteed to ensure successful results from the rules. Therefore, the system must be designed in a way that can encourage citizens to participate and be better off in the long run.

Establishing the executable and predictable rules of the game

Regarding the aforementioned principle, if a newly designed system disproportionately encroaches on the benefits of some stakeholders or entails a huge cost, citizens may be inclined to deviate from it. No matter how well a system is designed, it cannot operate properly without the observance of its members. Therefore, the system should be designed in a way that people regard as both fair and reasonable.

Enhancing the government's capacity to secure the consistent implementation of policies

It is highly critical to that institutional predictability is maintained, as it is a core factor of a successful system. Predictability is related to how much members trust a system. Although a new system is designed based on broad social agreement, it still leaves substantial room for misinterpretation. The government should set up guidelines for policy implementations and abide by them to reduce unpredictability.

III. Administrative reform in Vietnam: Learning from the Case of South Korea

1. Current status and issues of administrative reform in Vietnam

Vietnam started administrative reforms in the late 1980s in an effort to build a socialist-oriented market economy and facilitate the country's far-reaching international integration. Thus, the Party and Government have paid increasing attention to carrying out required administrative reforms that have been designed to respond to actual needs at each stage of the country's development. A wide-ranging public administration reform (PAR) agenda (including notably the PAR MP 2001–2010 and 2011–2020, and the State Administration Reform Plan 2016–2020) have been implemented for more than one and a half decades. Clearly, despite great efforts to carry out those programs and plans, many reforms under the Public Administration Reform Master Program 2011–2020 remain incomplete, threatening the overall success of the master program and the success of many national development goals and reform agendas.

Along with Vietnam's far-reaching international integration, many fundamental reforms, policies, and legal and administrative reforms in particular have been conducted, which have allowed the country to become a middle-income country (MIC) by 2010. Nevertheless, further radical administrative reforms are required during 2016–2020 for the aforementioned objectives.

The history of administrative reform in Vietnam dates back to the late 1980s, following the adoption of the Party's renovation (*ĐổiMới*) policy at the sixth nationwide Party Congress in December 1986. The reform process can be divided into the four following stages, as shown in Table 1-1 below.

Table 1-1 History of Administrative Reform in Vietnam

Stage	The Reform Progress
1986–1994	This is the very first stage of reform in which the foundations of reform were laid out. PAR activities, although given attention, remained part of the overall state reform to enable the country to start its economic transition from a centrally planned economy to a market-oriented one. The most noteworthy step of reform during this period was the promulgation of Government Resolution 38/CP dated May 04, 1994 on the establishment of one step administrative procedures in handling the affairs of citizens and organizations. Along this line, the one stop service (OSS) mechanism was first piloted in Ho Chi Minh City and later in many other provinces and cities.
1995–2000	PAR was identified as the focus of state reform at the eighth Party Central Committee Meeting (VIIth legislature) in 1995. The significant role of PAR was affirmed and its activities were carried out in an increasingly intensive manner, exerting strong impacts on society and becoming a driver of the renovation (*ĐổiMới*) course.
2001–2010	The Prime Minister concretized PAR directions set by the Party and State by promulgating Decision 136/2001/QD-TTg dated September 17, 2001 approving the Public Administration Reform Master Program 2001–2010 in which the fundamental legal framework for PAR activities at all levels and in all sectors during the 2001–2010 period was provided.
2011 to date	Based on an objective and serious review of achievements and shortcomings from the 2001–2010 PAR Master Program (MP), the government promulgated the Public Administration Reform Master Program 2011–2020 (at Decision 136/2001/QD-TTg dated September 17, 2001), providing a legal framework for PAR strategy during the stage in which the country's industrialization and modernization accelerated. In 2016, based on the review of the first half of the 2011–2020 PAR MP, the 2016–2020 PAR Plan was approved with the aim of accelerating the implementation of the MP during the second half, thus ensuring the accomplishment of PAR objectives and tasks during the second phase (2016–2020).

It is noteworthy that institutional reform in Vietnam is always regarded as part of the PAR programs and plans, and it is defined as the most important aspect of most PAR programs and plans. However, Vietnam was less successful in completing in-depth reform tasks. Its most recent phase started in 2011 and will continue until 2020. In 2010, the government organized a Master program of administration reform that acted as a tool to identify a suitable legal system for accelerating administration reform in an attempt to industrialize and modernize the country. What the government attempted to build was an administrative system that was simple and clear to move freely from the bottom to the top, and free from the stiffness of bureaucracies and functional overlaps.

1.1. Public Administration Reform Master Program 2011–2020

The context in which the 2011–2020 PAR MP was developed was unlike that of the previous one, as were the approach to and focus of PAR. The 2011–2020 MP was clearly more comprehensive and its legal binding was stronger. Following the 2001–2010 PAR MP, this second PAR MP aims to carry out even stronger steps towards creating a more accountable, transparent, and participatory government system. The program aims to enhance the efficiency of state bodies and localities and lift the administrative burden from citizens and investors (both local and foreign) that are regarded as a big hindrance to domestic development, by further simplifying administrative procedures.

The 2011–2020 PAR MP was in line with the spirit of the country's 2011–2020 SEDS, one of whose strategic breakthroughs was "improving the socialist-oriented market economy institution, focusing on creation of an environment for equal competition, and administrative reforms"[1]. The 2011–2020 PAR MP was phased into two five-year stages, i.e. 2011–2015 and 2015–2020 with specific objectives as targets. During the 2011–2015 period, more than 11,700 legal documents that guided and managed the implementation of

1 The Socio-Economic Development Strategy 2011–2020 adopted at the XIth Nationwide Party's Congress of the Communist Party of Vietnam (http://vietnamlawmagazine.vn/development-objectives-set-for-next-decade-3241.html)

administration reform were issued by Vietnamese ministries, agencies, and provinces/cities.

A series of organization and operation principles were embodied to clarify the objectives of the administration reform for the 2016–2020 phase under Decree 123/2016-ND-CP dated 01-9-2016. The 2016–2020 Public Administration Reform Plan was approved in Decision 225/QD-TTg by the Government's Prime Minister on February 04, 2016 with the aim of concretizing and accelerating the implementation of the second phase (2016–2020) of the 2011–2020 PAR MP. The plan is being implemented with a focus on raising people's and enterprise's satisfaction levels for administrative procedures, education, and healthcare to over 80% by 2020; and applying ISO standards in public offices. The reform plan is composed of four major statements, the first of which is the purpose. The reform aims to specify the responsibilities, power, and duties of each ministry, and it particularly emphasizes the responsibilities imposed upon every activity of the ministries. The second is to change the management system to become interdisciplinary, multi-disciplinary, streamlined, effective, and efficient. New institutions will only be established if all legal conditions are met. The third one is to clarify the boundary between the duties and powers of each agency, bureaucracy, and unit of the ministries. In that manner, functional and task overlaps can be prevented. The last one is to operate the ministries in a public, transparent, and modernized manner.

Table 1-2 Summary of PAR MP Objectives and Targets for 2011-2015 and 2016-2020 Periods

2011-2015 PAR	2016-2020 PAR
• Removing overlaps, omission or repetition in the functions, tasks and powers of state administrative agencies • Renovating legal documents formulation and promulgation fundamentally • Improving existing institutions or establishing new ones to suit with socialist-oriented market economy mechanism • Reforming and simplifying administrative procedures related to citizens and organizations; introducing one stop service (OSS) and inter-OSS on a nation-wide scale • Improving public services and increasing citizen satisfaction (over 60% by 2015 in the education and health sectors) • Getting structure of cadres and civil servants in state administrative agencies based on job posts (50% by 2015) • Further renewing the salary regime for cadres • By 2015, 60% of official documents exchanged between state administrative agencies will be in electronic form • Having the websites and web portals of ministries, ministerial-level agencies, government-attached agencies and provincial-level People's Committees connected with the Government Web Portal (100% by 2015)	• Improving institutions of the socialist-oriented market economy • Shifting the system of state administrative agencies from central to grassroots levels smooth, clean, strong, effective and efficient • Fundamentally reforming administrative procedures, raising the satisfaction of the people and enterprises with administrative procedures to over 80% by 2020 • By 2020, the contingent of cadres, civil servants and public employees will be rationalized in terms of size and structure. They would be fully qualified and capable of performing public duties • Employing cadres and civil servants in state administrative agencies, based on job posts (100% by 2020) • Fundamentally reforming the salary system for cadres, civil servants and public employees. implementing new salary scales, tables and allowances • Increasing the satisfaction of citizens with services provided by public non-business units in the education and health sectors and that of the people and enterprises with the service of state administrative agencies to over 80% by 2020 • By 2020, 90% of official documents from state administrative agencies would be issued in electronic form

Source: compilation from Government Resolution No. 30c/NQ-CP dated November 08, 2011.

1.2. Major Achievements, Shortcomings, and Remaining Problems

The institutions of the country's administration have been reformed and gradually improved upon in accordance with the set target of the PAR programs and the requirements for rapid and sustainable development. The quality of administrative procedure handling has been greatly improved by OSS and inter-OSS mechanisms have been synchronously and efficiently enforced, resulting in a more enabling environment for the production and business activities of citizens and enterprises. The evaluation of citizens' and organizations' satisfaction with the services provided by administrative bodies has been enhanced, which serves as a measure of service quality.

The annual PAR INDEX announcement has become "an important criterion to judge the governance capacity of leaders of ministries, departments and localities."[2] The division of tasks and power among different organizations/agencies within the administrative apparatus from the central to local level has been clearly identified, and thus the overlapping or non-execution of functions and tasks and the problem of incomplete management coverage management has basically been removed. In other words, functions, tasks/duties, and the organizational structure of agencies in public administration systems have been modified to keep pace with the new situation. Building the contingent of cadre, civil servants, and public employees has been renewed, and the quality of this contingent has been improved as a result of reforms in civil and public service regimes. The application of information technology (IT) in the operations of administrative bodies has been concurrently conducted from central to local levels along the lines of "e-government" and "e-administration."

However, Vietnam has a shortage of knowledge and experience required for PAR. The professional level of the Vietnamese cadre and of civil servants and public employees in general does not meet actual requirements; they lag behind and are backward in both theory and thinking regarding PAR on one hand, and in execution methods on the other; and inertia in the apparatus

2 Noted by Prime Minister Nguyen Xuan Phuc (https://www.vietnambreakingnews.com/2016/10/deputy-pm-administrative-reform-remains-slow/)

remains strong. Bureaucracy (red tape) and corruption are still rooted in the country's administration, which requires stronger political determination to move forward and solid mechanisms to synchronously solve PAR-related problems.

1.3. Further Issues

In view of the past achievements and remaining problems with PAR in Vietnam, ensuring the accomplishment of the 2011–2020 PAR MP and 2016–2020 plan in particular, it is clear that PAR implementation methods require renewal and that Vietnam should learn more from international experience. The following are specific issues that should be addressed in the near future.

First, the stronger enforcement of the 2013 Constitution requires the institutionalization of the role, function, and organization of state bodies' activities at central and local levels on the basis of the clear identification of relationships between the state and the people, between the state and the market, and between the state and social organizations.

The reform of economic institutions should be in line with the principles of the market economy and global practices, and should clarify issues of ownership and property rights. Institutional reform regarding citizens and social organizations should ensure extensive democracy and the efficient mobilization of resources for the country's economic and social development.

The continued review of various types of administrative procedures, the removal of unnecessary ones, and the amendment and supplementing of incomplete ones to facilitate citizens' and businesses' operations will be required. Compliance with regulations that stipulate that administrative procedures and licensing procedures must be specified by laws and by-law documents and international conventions to which Vietnam is an active participant should be ensured on a broad scale. Methods to prevent variations in licenses that are not provided by law required being put in place. Openness and transparency need to be further strengthened and modern OSS and inter-OSS mechanisms should be effectively introduced.

The role, function, and tasks of state administrative apparatus and of each administrative body (both the central government and the ministries and local governments at all levels) should be improved in accordance with the spirit of the 2013 Constitution. The powers and responsibilities of the government, Prime Minister, government collectives, the chairmen of people's committees, and people's committee collectives should be clearly defined and increased. Regulations should be provided for the responsibility regimes for leaders in the system of administrative bodies. The decentralization and delegation of power between central and local levels should be further accelerated to meet the requirements for the management of a socialist-oriented market economy. The structure of multi-disciplinary and multi-area/field apparatus ought to be strengthened to bring the overall power into full play. The continued application of IT in the operation of state bodies should be promoted to enhance the efficiency and effectiveness of their operations. The online provision of public services at levels 3 and 4 (the highest levels) should be strengthened, and specialized sectoral databases should be complied and completed across the nation. The model and road map for the establishment of e-government can be defined along the line of a state administrative reform.

PAR has contributed to the implementation of other reforms and hence the realization of many development goals in Vietnam. Each PAR master program and plan was designed under different contexts, both international and domestic, and aimed to contribute to some common long-term development goals and objectives and the somewhat different specific development objectives that were set by the Party and Government of Vietnam for each development period. Clearly, despite great efforts towards carrying out those programs and plans, many reform tasks set by the 2011–2020 PAR Master Program and 2016–2020 PAR Plan remain incomplete, which threatens the overall success of the 2011–2020 master program and the success of many national development goals and reforms. A wide variety of tasks have to be tackled before 2020 if the goals and objectives of the 2011–2020 PAR MP and the 2016–2020 PAR Plan in particular, are fully accomplished. The following sections introduce the history of administrative reforms in Korea, which may provide helpful examples for the further success of the administration's reforms in Vietnam.

2. Korean administrative reforms: A historical review

South Korea achieved rapid economic growth under the leadership of a strong government during the 1960s and 1970s. The nation achieved quantitative economic growth based on the government's capacity to implement effective economic policies in a stable manner. Thus, it became the first and only country whose status has changed from an Official Development Assistance (ODA) beneficiary to a donor country, making it an exemplary case.

Although it is obvious that the emphasis on maximizing efficiency has driven the country to its current status, many have argued that the country needs reforms to ensure fairness in its political, economic, and social orders. Throughout its history, there have been many efforts to achieve fairer political, economic, and social order. Whenever a new administration started its term in office, they would set up independent "reform promotion organizations" in an attempt to reshuffle the administrative structure and tackle the most urgent reform issues. While early reform organizations involved in facilitating efficiency, a shift in their role has been found to place emphasis on balancing economic growth and social development in the latter stage. Specifically, reforms before the Kim Dae-jung administration mainly involved a top-down process and hardware changes such as governmental reorganization and statute revision, the approach of the Roh Moo-hyun administration changed to a bottom-up process and began focusing on revising software elements such as the old-fashioned culture, the poor work spirit, and policy content.

Table 1-3 Reform Promotion Units and their Goals

President	Reform Promotion Unit	Period	Goal
Park Chung -Hee	• Administrative Reform Investigation Committee	1964-1981	• Organizational Reshuffling and ensuring efficiency in the internal management
	• Prime Ministerial Office • Administrative Reform Committee	1972-1973 1974-1981	• predominance over the legislative branch • Improvement of government investment institutions
Chun Doo -Hwan	• the National Defense Emergency Policy Committee • Social Clean-up Committee	1980-1981 1980-1989	• Organizational Reshuffling • Personnel Administrative Reform • Establishment of a just society/Clean-up of the social evils Economic Regulatory Reform
RohTae -Woo	• the Administrative Reform Committee • Joint Deliberation Committee for the Transfer of Authority to the Local Governing Bodies	1988-1989 1991-1998	• Abolishing the legacy of authoritarian • Balanced Regional Development

President	Reform Promotion Unit	Period	Goal
Kim Young-Sam	• Administration Innovation Commission • Regulation on the Administrative Renovation Committee • Globalization Promotion Committee	1993-1998 1993-1997 1995-1998	• Administration reform • Abolishing the legacy of authoritarian culture • Regulation Reform • Launching the full-scale globalization drive
Kim Dae-Jung	• Presidential Transition Committee and the 2nd Nation Building Committee	1997-1998	• Organizational Reshuffling • Diagnosing Organizations • Balanced Regional Development • Public Sector Reform • Deliberation and Conciliation Regulation
	• Planning and Budget Committee (reshuffled into the Ministry of Planning and Budget)	1998-1999	
	• Administrative Reform Council (reshuffled into Government Innovation Promotion Committee)	2000-2003	
	• The Government Function Mediation Committee	2000-2003	
	• Transfer of Function to Local Governments Promotion Committee	1999-2003	
	• Government Innovation Promotion Committee	2000-2003	
	• Regulatory Reform Committee	1998-2003	
Roh Moo-Hyun	• Presidential Committee on Government Innovation &Decentralization	2003-2008	• Government Innovation & Decentralization
Lee Myung-Bak	• Presidential Transition Committee • Presidential Council on national Competitiveness	2007-2008 2008-2013	• Organizational Reshuffling • Enhancement of National Competitiveness
Park Geun-Hye	• Prime Minister's Government 3.0 Committee	2013-2017	• Enhanced public-private partnerships • Information disclosure & share

3. Lessons and implications

The gist of the administrative reforms lies in improving the organization management methods and work process. In this section, we suggest three stages of administrative reform—preparation, promotion, and sustaining—and propose major strategies for each step.

Stage 1	PLAN stage: Preparing for Public Administration Reform

Strategy 1. Building the legal foundation for sustainable reforms

The Government Organization Act, which was legislated in 2001 in Vietnam, still contains unresolved issues in various areas. The Act lacks stipulations regarding cooperation among agencies and clear distinctions between the different missions and tasks of ministerial and vice-ministerial positions. Although the Act was partly revised in 2015, the aforementioned issues remain unaddressed. Building the legal foundation should precede any other steps toward sustainable reform, as it determines the entire process of the establishment and implementation of reform policies. Thus, the role of organizations that support the legislative branch such as the National Assembly Research Studies (NARS) has become more crucial. The following section presents how the Korean government enacted and implemented fundamental acts for restructuring government organizations to manage the entire reform process.

• CASE 1. The Roh Moo-hyun Administration's "Promoting Government Innovation Act"

The "Promoting Government Innovation Act" was enacted in 2006 to support a comprehensive approach to government innovation with the following emphasis. First, the Act clarified the underlying spirit and principles, and specified a reform promotion unit. Second, by spelling out the duties of responsible agencies, the Act helped build support and trust among citizens. Third, the Act merged fragmented rules and legislation regarding government innovation into a comprehensive and unified form.

• CASE2. Strengthening the capacity of legislative units

The 2013 Constitution solidified the basic structure of Vietnam's government agencies, by introducing significant legal reforms. The responsibility of the National Assembly is stated clearly to prepare for the Constitution and to supplement, improve, and renovate the legal system. These operations were necessary to keep the rule-of-law regime going through the construction and development. Without the legal basis, there would be no consistent development or stability in the relevant laws for administrative reforms in Vietnam.

However, international and local experts still point to the lack of capacity in the National Assembly and its agencies. Of course, there have been some accomplishments in the implementation of Public Administration Reform. Despite all the efforts to strengthen the legal system, it has shown poor performance. Another challenge is the disproportion of the Ethnic Council and other committees of the National Assembly where most people are working temporarily. It obstructs consistent and collective decision making, which is based on majority vote rule. The series of legislative processes—development, planning, analysis, and policy verification—is incomplete. Thus, the intellectuality and broad participation of the National Assembly are not yet successful. This is a huge problem considering that maintaining Vietnam's position is important. Some note that the power of the National Assembly should be limited to a certain extent to prevent clashes between the rights and duties of deputies, which has resulted in conflicts of interest.

If the government and its agencies are to build a better and more reasonable legal framework, they must consider their own duties. One of the government's roles is to separate responsibilities between those of executive agencies in the legislative process and those of the legislature. Based on clearly defined responsibilities, the capacity of an innovative drafting agency must be specified by the government. It would consist of many experts and law makers of high professional experience and high quality. The process of law drafting is a combination of the following two processes: policy experts from ministries ensure issues are correctly translated into policies; legal experts at a drafting agency write out a complete and enforceable bill so that its implementation would create change. A theoretical and practical basis for developing and improving the legal framework for the PAR in 2016–2020 is provided by Vietnam's requirement to give a bigger role to the Institute of Legal Research at the National Assembly and the institutes of policy studies in the ministries and ministerial-level agencies.

Furthermore, it merits attention that the Vietnam Institute for Legislative Studies (VILS), which was established in 2008, is known for its competitiveness as a legislative research agency and is the third oldest legislative research agency in the world. In addition, the National Assembly Research Service (NARS) was founded in 2007 in Korea to address requests from the members of the national assembly's committees through research and analysis. The organization not only examines legislative and policy issues and informing the public of the results, they also oversee any violations that might have been made by the executive branch. These legislative research agencies such as NARS and VILS provide professional support to share advanced ideas and knowledge, leading to better quality laws. Building a strong legislative foundation for sustainable reform may be feasible when the supporting research units operate properly.

Strategy 2. Setting up networks among the independent "reform units" responsible for coherent and systematic reforms

Establishing feasible strategies and targets is fundamental to the implementation of sustainable and coherent reforms. An independent reform unit should be in charge of overseeing and managing the detailed elements of reforms and orchestrating the process. Despite several meaningful reforms in Vietnam over several decades, the outcomes have not quite met the expectations of citizens and officials, which is attributable to the absence of an independent coordinating organization. An agency should be established within the administrative branch to demand and perform stronger management of the reform networks and processes to increase the effectiveness of the reforms.

The Prime Minister of Vietnam issued Decision 74/2010/QD-TTg on the establishment of the Administrative Procedure Control Department under the Government Office on 22nd November, 2010, according to Decree 62/2012/ND-CP, issued for the management of administrative processes. The government and the Prime Minister assigned additional functions to the Ministry of Justice and its agencies to manage the administrative process and monitor how state administrative reforms are implemented nationwide under the Government's Resolution 30c/NQ-CP.

This process achieved much, but overlooked certain aspects. The duties and powers to control administrative procedures are too heavy for a single agency to manage. Arranging the controlling duties effectively requires that the country focuses on the networks of units. Furthermore, administrative procedures often feature hassles or contain loopholes in their implementation. Several ministries, sectors, and localities do not fully comply with the control procedures of administrative regulations when conducting projects and making draft legal documents. Along with the simplification process, the administrative procedure review unit needs to strengthen its role as an independent orchestration agency.

• CASE 1. Building a "comprehensive government network" for reform promotion

The Roh Moo-hyun Administration, "Participatory Government (2003–2008)," had driven its reform with a comprehensive government network and multilayered reform structures. The process started with the Presidential Transition Committee, which directed an initial reform stage. The main reform actors included the Office of the Senior Secretary, the Government Innovation Headquarters, and the Presidential Committee on Government Innovation & Decentralization, which was the major reform coordinator. The Presidential Committee on Government Innovation &Decentralization consisted of eight committees that were respectively responsible for administrative reform, personnel management reform, decentralization, fiscal reform, e-government, records management, policy evaluation, and policy public relations. Each committee put together the agenda and sub-agendas of its target. The implementation of specific sub-agendas aimed to promote the main overarching goal of reform initiatives. Each department at both central and regional levels had its own “reform” officials who were in charge of government innovation reforms, and these actors at different levels in the government were well networked to coordinate reform agendas.

• CASE2. Establishing independent and empowered “reform units”

The Steering Committee for the Administrative Reform of the Government was established by the Prime Minister in accordance with Decision 200/1998 / QD-TTg, dated October 14, 1998, and enhanced by the issuing of Decree 45/2003 / ND-CP of the Government on the functions, tasks, powers, and organizational structure of the Ministry of Home Affairs. The Decree also assigned the Ministry of Home Affairs the permanent mission of reforming the government administration. The Organization and Personnel Committee of the Government was renamed the Ministry of Home Affairs and was ratified by National Assembly IX (2002–2007).

The master program has been operated by the Ministry of Home Affairs and an independent committee unit. The program introduced seven systems of serial solutions with seven individual action programs and brought remarkable changes to the administration. The first significant program, called “the program on renewal of formulation, promulgation and improvement with the participation of the people,” played a crucial role in improving the quality of institutions. The favor of the Steering Committee’s significant devotion could help realize the master program for administrative reform for 2001–2010.

In 1999–2000, the Vietnamese government consisted of 26 ministries and 64 provinces. The Ministry of Home Affairs and the Steering Committee for Administrative Reform of the Government took control of the Secretariat with a number of ministries, scientific institutions to conduct research and assess the situation of Vietnam's administration on the basis of the requirements of the Resolution of the Party on the reform of the state. While the Steering Committee and the Secretariat collaborated with the heads of each ministry, the Standing Party Committees, People's Council, People's Committees of 64 provinces and cites, and central government agencies examined and analyzed how far the reforms had been made, checking the functions and tasks of the state management, and the organizational and personnel structure of each ministry, province, and city. The research results provided scientific and practical grounds for the promulgation of administrative reform program for 2001–2010.

Thus, legal frameworks were developed in the period, establishing the legal basis for implementing administrative reform programs. The Government of Vietnam focused on the establishment and development of institutions to prioritize the improvement of legal frameworks and the policy system. From early 2001 to July 2009, the government issued 133 laws, 337 resolutions, 46 ordinances, 1,141 decrees, and tens of thousands of legal documents. The government also instructed the review and improvement of legal document systems by sectors and fields, building a legal basis for operating its socialism-oriented market economy and having the capacity to mobilize resources for national industrialization and modernization (Tap ChìCộngSản, 2011). The government issued an average of 200 decrees each year, thereby establishing a solid foundation of institutional reform and of the implementation of legislative reforms coupled with administrative reforms.

Regarding South Korea, the Economic Planning Board (EPB) was created in 1961 and orchestrated the overall economic plans and projects of President Park Chung-hee as a means to promote economic development. This coordinating unit drafted and executed the Five-year Plans of Economic Development and led the national reform and economic growth. Over several decades, several reform bodies such as the Presidential Commission on Administrative Reform were established to manage national reform whenever a new president was elected. The names and major functions of each government's representative reform units are presented in the table below; these independent reform units were able to initiate and coordinate the critical reform agendas of the Korean central government.

Table 1-4 Representative Reform Units and their Functions

Government	Organization	Type	Functions
The Kim Young-Sam government (1993-1998)	The Administration Innovation Commission	The Presidential Council	The administrative reform implemented by the administration can be summed up as falling under the following major categories of government administration: (1) democratization: measures to suppress human rights infringements, simplification of the civil service, quality improvement of public services, deregulation, and liberalization of the private sector; (2) small government: organizational reshuffling; and (3) clean government: opening of property ownership, Act on Service Ethics, real-name financial transaction system, and more stringent audit and inspection.
The Kim Dae-Jung government. (1998-2003)	The Ministry of Planning and Budget (Administrative Reforms Unit) Administrative Reform council	The Presidential Council	The People's Government pushed for the comprehensive reform of the public sector in terms of both hardware and software. The hardware reform was largely implemented by the Planning and Budget Committee (reshuffled into the Ministry of Planning and Budget), the Administrative Reform Committee, the Government Innovation Promotion Committee, the Government Function Mediation Committee, the Regulatory Reform Committee, and the Transfer of Function to Local Governments Promotion Committee. On the other hand, the software reform was largely performed by the Central Personnel Committee. Below are the key characteristics of the public reform implementation system of the People's Government, as differentiated from those of the past governments.

Government	Organization	Type	Functions
The Roh Moo-Hyun government (2003-2008)	Presidential committee on government innovation	The Presidential Council	The Government Reform and Decentralization Committee, the key institution entrusted with the role of pushing for government reform, was formed and dismantled three times in accordance with the implementation phase of the reform policy. PCGID consists of expert advisory committees which has its own specialized role to play in reform
The Lee Myung-Bak government (2008-2013)	Presidential Council on National Competitiveness	The Presidential Council	Instead of establishing a powerful control tower, individual government ministries each took leadership in implementing their respective reform tasks. However, the Presidential Council on National Competitiveness was newly installed on the existing Regulatory Reform Committee to push for the regulatory reform and other reform tasks.
The Park Geun-Hye government (2014-2017)	Prime Minister's Government3.0 Committee	The Presidential Council	'Government 3.0 Promotion Committee' to design Government 3.0 anew from people's standpoint was officially launched in 2014. The Committee, as an affiliate of the Prime Minister's Office, was organized with eight civilian members including co-chairperson and six vice-minister level government officials. For efficient operation, an expert committee will also be operated. It has set out a plan to innovate Government 3.0 policy and service processes centering on the people through cooperation with experts from the private sector.

Stage 2 DO Stage: Promoting effective reforms

Strategy 1. Organizational restructuring built on vision and philosophy

Over the last 25 years, the Vietnamese government has put great efforts into meeting a variety of administrative demands, but it has made relatively modest progress. The government needs to modernize its administrative system to ensure sustained growth. The World Bank has emphasized that establishing a solid foundation for policy design governments will require reforms through qualitative and quantitative research and feedback, in addition to systematic evidence about the performance of administrative systems and their components. However, Vietnam has underdeveloped systems with regard to research and development (R&D), innovation, and information for policy decisions. Vietnam needs a more macro and long-term perspective.

Of course, there have been some accomplishments in the implementation of Public Administration Reform. However, the reforms could not fully handle the changes in managing the mechanisms and people's needs, and the implementation process has low efficiency and effectiveness. Here are some of its factors: First, the relatively unclearly defined tasks in coordinating mission between agencies and late guidance documents of ministries make reforms ineffective in the sense that there is a lack of fixed rules and comprehensive procedures throughout multiple sectors and levels of the Vietnamese government. Furthermore, the level of centralization is unclear, complicating the budgeting process of public service organizations. Moreover, contrary to what it planned, the government has not been downsizing effectively.

Vietnam can take a lesson from the case of South Korea. Simply reducing the number of ministries by merging several units is not a solution for excising low efficiency and effectiveness. Restructuring the organization requires that the Vietnamese government has a systemic design that is consistent with the founding principles of reform. In other words, organizational reshuffling in the government should avoid merging ministries to simply remove or add functions to the structure. A government's structure should implicitly illustrate the philosophy and vision of the administration in power. Thus, exhaustive analysis and investigation should precede administrative reform for organizational reshuffling. There have been a wide variety of attempts to reshuffle government organizational structures all over the world in the last few decades (Vogelsang-Commbs& Cummins, 1999; Park, 2011; Andrews & Boyne, 2012). Large-scale organizational reforms in a government require a huge budget and related resources, even when they have little substantive effect on the increase of a state's capacity (Palumbo & Maynard-Moody, 1991; Pollitt, 2009; Park, 2011; Andrews & Boyne, 2012). Therefore, management routines and practices, task characteristics, organizational culture and ministry mergers should be analyzed and evaluated in a more comprehensive and integrated manner.

• CASE 1. Avoiding the simple merger of ministries and encouraging efficient task reorganization

Efforts have been made since 2002 to the present to reshape the structure of the Vietnamese government. During the 2002-2007 governmental term, the Prime Minister provided instructions to the ministries, ministerial-level agencies, and government-affiliated agencies with regard to administrative reform principles that included outlines of decrees on reforms of said organizations. The reforms were intended to downsize the government so that the administrative management system could become as effective and efficient as possible. Among the 22 decrees that the government put out, seven were about regulations regarding ministries' functions, power, imperatives, and structures. During this term, the administration's structure became more organized and effective by distributing powers and functions and decentralizing the government. The government consisted of 26 ministries and ministerial-level agencies and 12 government-affiliated agencies. Then, it merged several ministries, resulting in 22 ministries and ministerial-level agencies for 2007-

2011. The following are examples of mergers; the Ministry of Fisheries joined the Ministry of Agriculture and Rural Development; the Committee on Population, and Ministry of Family and Children merged into the Ministry of Labors, Invalids and Social Affairs; the Committee on Sports and Directorate on Tourism were incorporated into the Ministry of Culture, Tourism and Sport; the Ministry of Industry and the Ministry of Trade merged into the Ministry of Industry and Trade; and the Ministry of Finance was restructured. The Customs Department, Securities Committee, and government Pricing Committee were merged into a single ministry. Along with these changes in central departments, local specialized agencies also reorganized to become more suitable to their region's specific situations and to better cooperate with the central departments. During the 2011-2016 government term in which the number of ministries and ministerial-level agencies remained the same, the number of government-affiliated agencies became eight; these numbers are expected to stay the same during the 2017-2021 term.

Most recently, Decree 123/2016-ND-CP dated 01-9-2016 was proclaimed, which regulated the functions, tasks, powers, and organizational structures of ministries and ministerial-level agencies. The following specify the organization and operation principles that ensure the administration reform objectives in the 2016-2020 phase of Article 5; (1) to clearly define the duties, powers and responsibilities of the ministries, the ministers and to highlight the responsibilities of ministers in all of the ministries' activities; (2) to reorganize the ministries to become multi-disciplinary, interdisciplinary, streamlined, effective and efficient, and to only establish new institutions if they meet all the conditions prescribed by law; (3) to clearly define the duties and powers of agencies, bureaucracies, and ministerial units to ensure no duplicated or repeated tasks; and (4) to enhance the publicity, transparency and modernization of the ministries' operations.

For instance, the Ministry of Industry and Trade is eager to put out proposals about organizational reforms during the 2016-2022 term, as it must implement Decree 39-NQ/TW by the Politburo, which is designed to reduce the size of its staff before 2022. The ministry reduced 35 departments and agencies to 28 by removing seven units to boost productivity. This movement aims to promote simpler procedures, effectiveness, less expenses, and a greater service spirit and responsibility of civil servants (Lao Động, 2016). The current restructuring process of the Vietnamese government is based on the comprehensive and multi-sector management model, which represents an important change from direct management by the central administration to indirect governance by law and policies. Thus, this model can improve the administrative system by organizing the functions of production and public service delivery.

However, the restructuring process could be overly intense and cause adverse effects. If the number of ministries falls too quickly, they may end up having more sub-units, which leads to more directorates and units and some ministries sharing the same functions and duties. Thus, reforms should have proper standards and solid principles. Sophisticated designs are required to build, reduce, or merge ministries. Meanwhile, ministries' administrative structures need simplification. The reform should include eliminating unnecessary processes, ineffective hierarchies, inaccurate duties and overlapping functions, and it must also boost the responsibility of each unit and individual.

South Korea set a good example for restructuring the government by considering policy objectives and founding principles. Regarding simplifying the administration, Vietnam may follow in South Korea's footsteps. However, a critical voice has also been raised that indiscreet modification might confuse work and cause unnecessary budget expenditure. For instance, the Park Geun-hye administration changed the Ministry of Public Administration and Security (MOPAS) to the Ministry of Safety and Public Administration (MOSPA), but MOSPA switched back to MOPAS after a few years.

After the 1980s, following the efficiency-oriented global trends based on the New Public Management Theory, the Korean government also strove to reduce its number of ministries and downsize the public sector. Although these downsizing efforts were believed effective, almost all administrations increased their number of ministries and employees at the end of their terms following the logic of politics rather than of efficiency (Moon, 2009). Despite continuous efforts to reduce the size of government, the number of the government ministries increased from 14 in the Chun Doo-hwan and Kim Young-sam administrations to 18 in the Roh Moo-hyun administration. The changes in the number of civil servants show a clearer trend; in every administration, the number increased in the last period. In particular, the number of civil servants was 471,438 in the early period of the Chun Doo-hwan administration, but it continued to grow and reached 600,000, recording a more than 30% growth rate (for details, see Appendix).

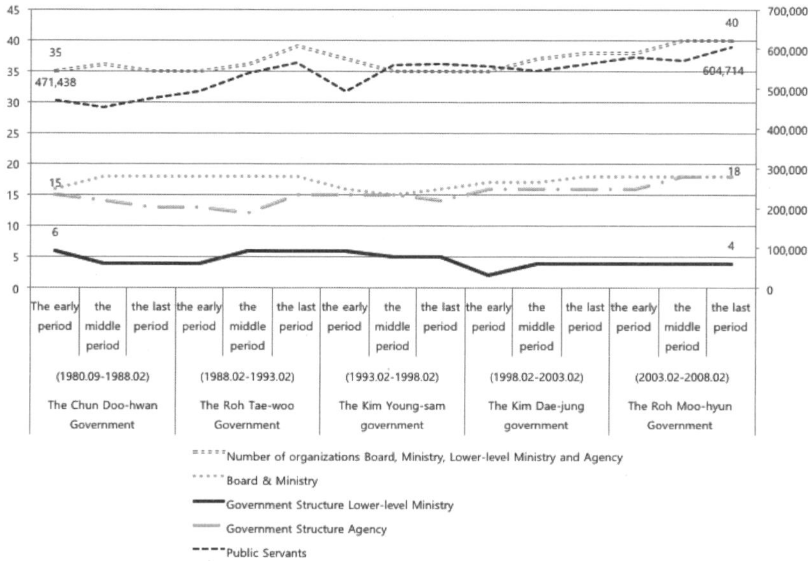

Source: Moon (2009), the office of 17th and 18th president websites (http://www.president.go.kr/ and http://17cwd.pa.go.kr/) and Statistics Korea website (http://www.kostat.go.kr/)

Figure 1-3 Government Organizations and public Servants in Korea, 1980 – 2008

Strategy 2.Effective functional re-alignments and collaborative policy management

In the process of the Public Administration Reform, Vietnam may enhance its administrative capacity and functions. For instance, if strict hierarchies are a major cause of ineffectiveness, the administration can solve this problem by implementing a more horizontal bureaucracy. It should flatten its pyramid-shaped structure and distribute functions and duties more effectively.

The Master Program of the Public Administration Reform that was implemented in 2001-2010 contained six fundamental reforms, one of which is the reform of the administration. Its goal is to establish an effective and efficient central system. Reorganizing the functions and responsibilities of the ministries is an important step to build such a state system; the reform needs a systemic plan and careful approach to reach its goal. Reshaping and systemizing the structure of the ministries, ministerial-level agencies, specialized districts, and provincial bureaucracies are the main purposes of Public Administration Reform, and this is the key to multi- disciplinary and multi-sector management.

However, Vietnam has enjoyed little benefit, as some ministries still share overlapping functions, which causes ineffectiveness and inefficiency. To address this inefficiency, functional re-alignments should be carefully designed when merging ministries to promote the capacity and performance of the government. Improper administrative reforms often have imbalanced or redundant functional relations and excessive control span, which undermines their effectiveness. The following two contrasting cases in Korea highlight the importance of careful functional alignment when a government changes its ministerial structure.

• CASE 1. Functional re-alignment in the Roh Moo-hyun administration: The Ministry of Gender Equality and Family (MOGEF)

The Ministry of Gender Equality and Family (MOGEF) of the Korean government is an exemplary case. Newly established in 2001, the Ministry of Gender Equality was assigned the duty of infant- and childcare, previously the remit of the Ministry of Health and Welfare, in 2004. This facilitated its transformation into a more comprehensive organization in 2005 by encompassing all women, family, and childcare duties (http://www.mogef.go.kr/). In the middle of rapid social changes and the dissolution of the traditional family structure, the functional re-alignment of the MOGEF was evaluated as an effective action.

• CASE 2. Mega-department reorganization: The Ministry of Education, Science, and Technology in the Lee Myung-bak Administration

Once divided into independent ministries, the Ministry of Education, Science and Technology (MEST) was established in 2008. The name changed to the present one after the Lee Myung-bak Administration annexed the former Ministry of Science and Technology (MST) and the Ministry of Education (ME). However, the Lee Myung-bak Administration's strong focus on educational polices meant that MEST was unable to effectively produce and manage science and technology policies. The merged ministries were not fully integrated into a single unit, thus they were less effective.

The aim of previous governments took on a simpler form with a single goal such as economic growth-oriented development. However, as sustainable and inclusive development has become a primary theme all around the world, the contemporary goals of governments are becoming more enriched and embracing various values. Thus, new governmental functions and policy management tools are necessary for solving the complex dilemmas between development and conservation, efficiency and responsibility, and growth and equality. Collaborative policy management among administrative units in the central and local government is indispensable to handle matters concerned with the conflicting values of reform goals and is essential to heighten the interconnectedness and coherence among seemingly incompatible reform units and tasks.

In 2016, the World Bank pointed out that the low capability of the Vietnam government meant that the state and local governments were unable to fully cooperate with each other, and the conflict deepened. The central government agencies have many subordinate units, which sometimes leads to overlapping directions between central and local governments. Since all of these are inefficient by causing unnecessary work in the process of policymaking and implementation, the functions of central and local governments should not be duplicated in order to establish a simple and clear administrative system. Therefore, cooperation is essential if a country wants to boost its integration plan across central and local governments, and transaction costs will decline when administrative units cooperate and divide their functions more clearly. In other words, administrative reform to reinforce cooperation requires various incentives and organizational efforts to sustain long-term public service reform and good governance. Clearly, all this aims to construct a simpler collaborative administrative system in which each unit operates and collaborates to accomplish national agendas. Below are exemplary cases of Korean administrative reforms that enhance the capacity of collaboration among governmental units.

- **CASE 3. Developing a reform roadmap for coherent innovation and consistent reform**

A reform roadmap that is systematically filled with specific directions and details of innovation, contains both a series of tasks to tackle and goals, timelines, and how to manage departments to facilitate actual performance. A roadmap secures the consistency and durability of innovation and becomes a tool for systematic administrative reform.

The Roh Moo-hyun administration, unlike its predecessors, constructed a comprehensive government innovation roadmap that was a blueprint of government reforms. The roadmap encouraged each department to reach consensus regarding the direction of innovation and to propel continuous changes in a step-by-step manner by helping the department recognize the consistency of reform activities and provide a yearly list of tasks.

• CASE 4. The executive prime ministerial and multiple vice-ministerial systems in the Roh Moo-hyun administration

The Roh Moo-hyun administration redesigned the government organization based on the principles of "an upward approach focused on key issues"and"inter-ministerial functional readjustment first, followed by ministerial integration design." When a new governmental function was required, the Roh administration attempted to address it by installing a specific committee rather than resorting to reshuffling the entire organization.

Key changes in the government organization include the upgrade of ministries' levels, the implementation of the executive prime ministerial and multiple vice-ministerial systems, and the introduction of the team system. Thus, the total number of ministerial- and vice-ministerial-level government officials increased to 125, and there were 81 ministers in total for Roh Moo-hyun's five-year presidency.

• CASE 5. The whole-of-government approach (the Lee Myung-bak administration)

The whole-of-government approach allowed government organizations to work across boundaries to achieve shared goals and integrate collaborative efforts (Christensen &Lægreid, 2007). The Lee Myung-bak administration understood that major regulations were associated with the affairs of multiple ministries; it was crucial that the Prime Minister's Office (PMO) and the Presidential Council on National Competitiveness (PCNC) coordinate their diverse stances across ministries. The PMO, PCNC, and other departments were encouraged to compete when pursuing regulatory reform through allocating duties according to their impact and importance to the agenda. Out of the tasks regarding the reformation of existing regulations, the PMO and PCNC were in charge of dealing with the core regulations and other regulations involving multiple ministries. The Regulatory Reform Task Force was supposed to tackle the challenges and monitor the effects of regulatory reform. In an effort to deal with new or intensified regulations, the PMO established a seamless regulatory reform system that reviewed the need and feasibility of regulations by examining citizens' stances, not those of the agencies in charge. This approach produced positive consequences in Korea. Comprehensive government reform programs showed that the government was committed to reform and could increase the confidence of both citizens and investors in the government's capacity to ensure a high quality regulatory environment (OECD, 2010). For Vietnam to overcome its new challenges in the new era, the governmental units at all levels must cooperate with one another and coordinate in their complicated tasks. The whole-of-government approach will be useful in making a greater potential impact on building an inclusive nation (OECD, 2015).

Strategy 3.Building partnerships for co-prosperity

The imbalance between regions is a serious challenge for growth.

Sustainable development is possible when the state decentralizes its power to the citizens. The power and responsibility of the local Vietnamese governments has surged significantly in recent decades. Hanoi and Ho Chi Minh have received special decrees from the central government; these two cities were granted more independence and authority than other cities in Vietnam, which led to an imbalance between regions. Solving this requires that the Vietnamese government implement both decentralization policies and policies that intend to bring balance among local administrations. Therefore, it must push its strategies for the social integration of poor and minority races ahead and balance development between urban and rural areas.

The 2016 Vietnam country report by the Korea Eximbank overseas economy research institute pointed out that during the country's economic reform and opening process, foreign investments were going only to the rich in big cities such as Ho Chi Minh, Hanoi, and Hai Phong city, and the gap between regions and economic groups was increasing. In particular, Vietnam's Gini coefficient rose from 0.39 in 1999 to 0.43 in 2010. In 1999, the income of the top quintile was 7.6 times higher than that of the bottom quintile, but that increased to 9.2 times in 2010. Although the national poverty rate was 13.5% and that in urban areas was 4.8%, 23.8% of people in rural areas and 62.8% of minority races were below the poverty line.

According to the 2014 OECD report, the Vietnamese government was trying its best to handle the complaints of people in rural areas and minorities by implementing rural development and antipoverty policies. However, the disparities between urban and rural areas cannot be solved by just developing rural areas.

In addition, Vietnam suffers from imbalance in the business field. Only 2% of Vietnamese businesses are large corporations, and midsize businesses also account for just 2%. All other businesses in Vietnam are small. Furthermore, it should diversify its export industry, considering that most businesses in the export industry are in clothing and fishery product areas. The state should play an important role in supporting small businesses by reforming policies, establishing institutions, increasing its capabilities and building infrastructure. Below are examples of how Korean governments have attempted to improve the national capacity for balanced co-prosperity among different sizes of firms and different regions.

• CASE 1. The Small and Medium Business Administration (SMBA)

In South Korea, the Small and Medium Business Administration (SMBA) is in charge of creating environmental conditions for fair competition between small businesses so that all businesses can grow together. SMBA plays two roles; the administration promotes shared growth by mitigating the polarization between small and large businesses. It takes control of the procurement process between large and small businesses, carries out new product development projects, provides technical cooperation, and expands the market for small businesses.

Additionally, it tries to strengthen the competitiveness of small businesses by improving both product and service quality. It protects small businesses from the unreasonable demands of large corporations and to monitor the fairness of trades. Unfair trades and price-fixing are prevented by the SMBA's imperative to report any violation of four laws to the Fair Trade Commission, and the administration is working on enacting standard working guidelines that state as such.

• CASE 2. Presidential Commissions on sustainable and balanced co-prosperity

While managing sets of conflicting social values and complicated problems, Korean governments have established a wide variety of presidential commissions such as the Presidential Commission on Sustainable Development, Presidential Committee on Balanced National Development, and Korea Commission for Corporate Partnership. Since the Roh Moo-hyun administration, Korea's Small and Medium-sized Enterprise (SME) policies have shifted from protecting and selectively promoting SMEs to focusing on coexistence and cooperation between major conglomerates and SMEs, following the global trend of balance and co-development. For example, the Korea Commission for Corporate Partnership (KCCP), which was founded in 2010, is now making major contributions to the diffusion of the idea of mutual growth by encouraging cooperation among large, small, and medium-sized enterprises.

A series of business policies from successive governments, such as the policy on mutual growth from Park Geun-hye's government, shared the same context. "Mutual Growth" among large, small, and medium-sized enterprises has aimed for continuous development by forming and maintaining stronger reciprocal relationships. On July 2011, master plans and implementation strategies had been established for 2011-2013, that were targeted at mutual growth in business areas. Since 2011, KCCP have released an annual "Win-Win Index" that details two types of assessment: a performance evaluation of large corporations' compliance with the agreement on fair competition and mutual growth, and the satisfaction estimation by small and medium-sized enterprises about the actual implementation of mutual growth policies.

Besides, the Korean government has enforced various policies through which to build relationships for a fair deal by combining more efforts for co-development, accelerating scientific and technological cooperation between large, small, and medium enterprises, which is of benefit in the sharing and planning of mutual growth in major industries. Besides, a wide range of affirmative actions have been introduced that improve equal employment opportunities for the disadvantaged, including various employment quota systems for female employees, local citizens, the disabled, and high school graduates, to name a few.

Stage 3	CHECK AND ACT Stage: Evolving toward a sustainable reform

Strategy 1. Reform evaluation and feedback loop

Policy evaluation is the process of assessing value, production, and results, in which the evaluation results lead to a decision making and feedback loop. When the reform process and outcomes are systematically evaluated, the resulted information can be appropriately used in the next step of decision making process, assisting to set the direction, improve the quality and secure responsibility for public reform. Also the feedback loop enables administrations to manage outcomes, improve tasks, secure responsibility, and provide information. Therefore, the whole reform process should not only include planning, decision making, and execution, but also evaluation and a feedback loop to secure its success and continue public reforms.

Although the evaluation system plays an important role in the sense that it increases the effectiveness and sustainability of reforms in the public sector, governments often find it difficult to construct a high-quality evaluation and feedback-loop system in the early stages of public reform. While participating in a global society and transforming itself into a socialistic market economy, Vietnam has focused relatively more on the execution of reforms than on the reform of evaluation and feedback (KIPA, 2013). However, Vietnam has made changes to secure the efficacy of public reforms and state administration in line with changes in international societies, emphasizing evaluation and feedback loop systems. Various indexes have been developed, including the PAR Index, and the Provincial Competitiveness Index (PCI).

The PAR index is a tool for monitoring administrative reform activities such as administration management and system enforcement, and determines the ranking of public administrative reforms in ministries and provinces. Starting as an aspect of the 2011–2020 Public Administration Reform Program, the PAR Index was developed by the Ministry of Home Affairs to improve public reforms in all areas of ministries and has been updated annually since 2012. Various efforts have been put into improving the contents and methodology of the index to secure its sustainability and increase the effectiveness of public reforms (Vietnam Business Forum Magazine, 2015).

The criteria of the elaborate evaluation and feedback loop system are now continuously revised and modified in many areas such as personnel management and performance information. The focus is placed upon developing indexes that include input, process, output, and effects while also building a strong systematic basis for the feedback loop such as the application of evaluation information.

Evaluating complex administrative demands and the reactions of government organizations is not easy. However, evaluation and feedback must be insured to achieve sustainable and effective reform. Its current focus on the development of various indexes for performance evaluations means that the Vietnamese government may now consider the establishment of a more comprehensive formal evaluation system and feedback process. When information derived through indexes is used in the next decision-making process, the chances of successfully solving the problem can be increased. The evaluation system should also include information about the feedback, since a mere focus on evaluation itself would lead to erroneously sticking to rankings or quantitative measurements themselves rather than improving performance quality. Furthermore, connecting evaluation with incentives will lead to increased interest and responsibilities for government officials.

• CASE 1. Performance evaluation and feedback

Government performance evaluation is the assessment of policies carried out by a designated central administrative unit to increase the efficiency, effectiveness, and responsibility of the central government and agencies. The Vietnamese government used a different approach to various indicators to measure different perspectives of the administration when it introduced the PAR index to correctly measure the effects of reforms and evaluate their outcomes. The implementation of the PAR index demonstrates the determination of the government and the Prime Minister to renovate monitoring and assessment practices to ensure the advanced performance and effectiveness of public administration reform. The PAR Index is defined by a system of criteria with detailed rating scales for each criterion. The criteria-based evaluation of administration reform can be achieved via two ways: First, administrative agencies conduct a self-assessment of their administrative reform outcomes. Second, they can apply social survey methods to assess the outcomes of the administration reforms of ministries, ministerial-level agencies, provinces, and national-level cities. The surveys require the active, enthusiastic, objective, and equal participation of organizations in the evaluation of the administrative reform outcomes produced by ministries, ministerial-level agencies, provinces, and national-level cities.

The new public administrative reform instrument has a number of far-reaching implications. First, the PAR Index provides a comprehensive, substantive, and objective assessment of administrative reform outcomes in ministries, ministerial-level agencies, provinces, and national-level cities. The self-assessment of administrative agencies and third-party assessment on reform practices are emphasized, especially with regard to enterprises, entrepreneurs, and citizens who are the direct recipients of public services delivered by administrative agencies. Second, the PAR index could serve as important instrument with which to evaluate the advantages and disadvantages of the public administration reform process, thereby enabling ministries, ministerial-level agencies, provinces and national-level cities to consider and adjust the objectives of administrative reform annually. Moreover, it also indicates proper measures to ensure the advanced outcomes of the public administrative reform of ministries, agencies, and localities. Third, the PAR index is supposedly defined upon specific quantitative indicators, on which ministries, ministerial-level agencies, provinces, and national-level cities could compare, evaluate, and rank their annual PAR outcomes.

Maintaining an evaluation index for administrative reforms would surely promote improved PAR outcomes. However, the feedback loop established within the evaluation system would further ensure that the results are reflected in the reform process cycle. Korea has designed a more comprehensive performance evaluation system that includes effective feedback loops. The Framework Act on Government Performance Evaluation (FAGPE) was enacted in Korea in 2006. In affiliation with the prime minister's office, the Government Performance Evaluation Committee was established to effectively evaluate central administrative agencies, local governments, and public institutions. The FAPGE was legislated and systematically operated to improve public efficiency and effectiveness by overcoming the limitations of the regulatory administration system centered on the input and process. In this manner, it can secure public responsibility and improve work efficiency. Similar to Vietnam, there are two types of government evaluation based on the evaluator: self-evaluation whose evaluators and evaluatees are the central administrations and local governments themselves and specific-evaluation by which the prime minister evaluates central governments to manage the government synthetically. If needed, re-evaluation (a second evaluation of the results, methods, and process of the original evaluation by other administrations) is conducted to secure objectivity and credibility. The principal agents of the evaluation system include the prime minister, the Minister for the Cabinet Office, the Ministry of Strategy and Finance, the Ministry of Home Affairs, and the Ministry of Personnel Management. Government performance evaluation improves policies and organizational management. When a problem is inspected by self-evaluation or in an assessment process, the head of a central department or agency can directly command corrective measures, or order an inspection and require submission to the Government Performance Evaluation Committee for further action. According to the evaluation results, an organization can have a different amount of managerial autonomy when adjusting personnel and position.

• CASE 2. Government Innovation Index (GII)

Korea's Government Innovation Index (GII) was selected as one of the best practices of public administration and renovation by the UN in 2006. The GII is an objective assessment tool of the Roh Moo-hyun administration that reduced assessment burdens, resolved evaluation inefficiencies, and checked the implementation of government innovation.

The current status of public officials' reform capacity was determined and public officials were induced to participate voluntarily and put effort into administrative reform, by the Roh administration's performance of a Readiness-Ability-Willingness (RAW) survey in the early period of the innovation (2003). As the GII, the first unbiased diagnosis, replaced the RAW survey, it overcame the shortcomings and enhanced the objectivity of the survey tool. GII-based diagnosis can efficiently help drive innovation with strategic change management. The results of the survey enabled the government to establish innovation strategies according to which stage of innovation the government was in, organizational size, and intrinsic characteristics, which led to comprehensive innovation management.

Strategy 2. Reform maintenance and transformation

Administrative reform brings higher effectiveness when sustainably maintained in the long term. Rather than enforcing new reform programs each time, adjusting and expanding current reform initiatives can contribute to the success of reforms and cut down on wasted resources.

• CASE 1. Evolving from the five-year Economic Development Plans to the Economic and Social Development Plans (1962–1996)

The early success of economic reform in Korea is attributable to the establishment of a strategic planning unit in the central government and its coordinated efforts towards changes. Under strong leadership, the coordinating unit, the Economic Planning Board, and the Five-year Planning of Economic Development (PED) could accomplish economic expansion and sizable growth for employment rates and income. Key objectives changed from the first to the seventh development plan to accommodate the most urgent issues in each period. Economic growth was the most significant goal in the early development periods from the first to the fourth plans, and inclusive growth for balanced and efficient development became a concern afterwards. Furthermore, the plans expanded to include issues of regional balance and social policies for the disadvantaged.

There were three sequential planning steps from 1962 to 1996; the first was state-led planning (1962–76). The first, second, and third Five-year Economic Development Plans were suitable for an under-developed, small-sized economy with a relatively simple structure. These plans focused on setting up sectoral investment plans as well as mobilizing and allocating resources to support their implementation. This was supplemented by annual Economic Management Plans. The second planning step was Indicative Planning (1977–1991); the fourth, fifth, and sixth Five-year Economic Development Plans were designed to cope with the economy's growing size and complexity. A Medium-term Fiscal Plan was introduced in the early 1980s to bridge the gap between EDPs and annual budgeting. The last planning step was Strategic Planning (1992–96); the seventh Five-year Economic and Social Development Plan addressed strategic issues that were tackled by the concerted efforts of the government and the private sector under the plan. High-technology facilities were built in seven different provincial cities to balance the industry's geographic distribution across the country. Following the global trend, a new approach began integrating social values into the goals of economic development and the development plan's title gained the adjective "social."

The Five-year Economic Development Plans were implemented over 30 years, and they evolved and were modified appropriately to take reality into account. The groundwork was to first expand policy target areas from economic growth to social growth under long-term development, and to consistently continue it according to the changing plans from the state-led plans to the indicative and strategic plans.

• CASE 2. The transformation of a reform, strengthening coordination among agencies: Government 3.0

E-government is a type of government reform that has been conducted worldwide, and is regarded as an effective tool with which to improve the government's competitiveness. E-government can strengthen the ties of functions by improving the quality of national services and making processes efficient and more accessible to citizens. Establishing e-government is a major challenge in Vietnam, because it is difficult to focus on the improvement of the work structure between central and local governments by utilizing information technology. In addition to direct support from the Korean government for implementing effective e-government, the opportunity to share Korea's experiences would contribute to the success of Vietnam's reform and empowerment.

Korea has started building its foundation for first-class e-government systems by developing its infrastructure in the 90s. The first E-government Act was enacted and the E-Government Special Committee was established in 2001. By sharing experiences and information among departments via e-government systems, the Korean government was able to increase the level of its functional alignments among independent units from a holistic governmental perspective. The initiation of e-government's 11th project in 2002, "egov.go.kr," the E-Government Road Map, which is composed of 31 main subjects, was built in 2003. In 2001, the government legislated the "Act to Promote the Digitalization of Administrative Work etc. for the Upgraded E-Government." Although this act initiated the early stage of the computerization of administrative documents, the government's major tasks and decision processes were still paper-based. Later in 2010, the E-Government Act was amended to significantly upgrade the level of digital services for citizens. Based on these legal mandates, the Korean government accumulated its efforts in a step-by-step manner towards creating high quality e-government services. It started by constructing databases of administrative information and building an information super-highway during the early 2000s. The government further developed legislation with a series of steps in which it disseminated globally accepted open standards and built a database of national knowledge information resources. It also gave information literacy lectures to citizens, constructed information model villages, and promoted a one person–one computer policy.

Keeping up with the transition into a knowledge-based society, required simultaneously improving the law, the system, and the environment, and promoting the growth of tech industries. All the information computerized by each department and sub-unit was released to the public, which contributed to the increase in transparency and accountability in managing administrative processes. The government put more effort into establishing the comprehensive government-wide foundation of digitalization and finally launched "Government 3.0."

Government 3.0 is defined as a "people centered government reform" that seeks to promote communication between departments, make people's lives easier, and create jobs. The idea stresses openness, publicity, communication, cooperation, and participation, so it provides administrative services that focus on the needs of individual citizens. Government 3.0 officially started in 2013 with the announcement of the visions and master plan, won first prize at the UN E-Government evaluation in 2010, and was ranked first at the 2015 OECD data openness evaluation.

In Vietnam, the construction of e-government is one of the main tasks of the Ministry of Home Affairs, particularly with its focus on the improvement of the work system between the central and local government. Its acute awareness of the meaning and role of administrative modernization has meant that Vietnam can expect that the application of science and technology to public administration operations will both increase productivity and contribute significantly to changing the working methods of the cadres and civil servants towards a modern administrative environment. Thus, the implementation of the scheme to renew the executive mode and modernize the work offices of the public administration system for 2003–2005 (Project 169) and the project of computerization of public administration management in 2001–2005 (Project 112) have contributed to achieving the objective of modernizing public administration with the following results: First, the working principles and operational coordination in the administrative apparatus have been defined more clearly. The government issued Decree 144/2005 / ND-CP on coordination among public administration agencies in the construction and inspection of the implementation of policies, strategies, planning, and plans. Second, the implementation of Scheme 112 initially formed the Government's electronic information system, including the data integration centers of the ministries and provinces, the local area networks (LAN) of each internal organization of the ministries and provinces, and the wide area network that links the provinces' computer systems. Electronic information systems have started deploying basic services such as e-mail, and the software application computerization of state management. The government portal was built and started operating. Representative examples include: the ongoing testing of the computerization process of issuing land use rights certificates such as the ownership of housing certificates in Hai Phong and Da Nang; the computerization process of issuing developing permits in Hai Duong, Da Nang, and Ho Chi Minh City; and the computerization process of issuing business registrations in ThuaThien Hue, Ha Tay, and Can Tho.

Despite these results, there remain many limitations in terms of professionalization and the skills of administration and public sector staff. The level of knowledge and skills among staff and officials with scientific qualifications to handle micro- and macro-management issues are remain low and do not meet the requirements of a modern administration. The implementation of action programs is slower than expected, which leaves the stage of completion of Scheme 169 or big computerization projects under Scheme 112 being slowly implemented.

Enduring efforts by the Vietnamese government are required to improve level of e-government. In particular, the enhancement of e-government will impact public administration agencies' organization and operation at all levels in preparation for the next stage of modernization. A wide variety of information should be shared among central governments, local authorities, and private organizations. This process will help increase transparency and make policies more effective. In addition, providing the private sector with adequate information will create added value, ultimately leading to increased national competitiveness.

Strategy 3. Cultural and behavioral changes

The government works on changing the attitudes of government officials to improve the quality of government services. Higher consumer expectations, continual fiscal pressure, and the growing conviction that public services should continually justify their outputs in terms of price and quality have proven valuable (Kim, Pindur& Reynolds, 1995). Accordingly, governments have paid more attention to benefitting their customers. For example, they have endeavored to form a customer-oriented administrative culture that breaks from the convention that they regard citizens as mere service subjects. Thus, in creating a "public value" approach, it is argued that public services can add value to society in the same manner that private (for profit) organizations create value for shareholders and other stakeholders (Moore, 1995). Consequently, public intervention only makes sense when meeting the requisite needs for citizens' positive social and economic outcomes. In other words, the participation of citizens and businesses in the policy process through the synchronization of mechanisms including direct participation and representativeness (which is very often challenging) has been regarded as an institutional condition for the generation of legitimacy and the social ownership of government interventions or public management in general while enhancing trust and confidence in government (Fung, 2006). In the processes of a public service delivery system, governments are not only required to examine citizens' priorities, needs, and satisfaction level with public services, but also to re-coordinate their institutions based on their customers' opinions. This report suggests customer satisfaction surveys and low performer management as representative examples of this trend.

• **CASE 1. Customer satisfaction survey**

Considering the disparity in the quality of public service delivery among localities and regions, there have been calls for public administrations to further improve public service delivery and meet the increasing demands of citizens given people's increased living standards and educational backgrounds. Thus, the Vietnamese government has been monitoring the performance of the administrative reforms by surveying citizens' level of satisfaction. According to a report by the Government Steering Committee for Administrative Reform (2016–2020), the reform will focus on improving people's and enterprises' satisfaction with administrative procedures, education, and healthcare (Vietnam Business Forum Magazine, 2016). Resolution 30c / NQ-CP dated November 8, 2011 in which the Government promulgated the Master Program of State Administrative Reform for 2010–2020 set an ambitious target that the satisfaction of citizens and organizations with services provided by state administrative agencies will reach over 80% by 2020, and that people and businesses can be served through various means at any time and any location. Ensuring participation has also been further confirmed in other more recent important regulations such as the Law on Issuing regulation documents 2015, in which it was emphasized that "authorized bodies have to organize to collect the opinions from the subjects directly impacted by regulatory documents."

One major achievement to addressing this initiative is reflected in the Satisfaction Index of Public Administration Services (SIPAS). A rationale has been established for measuring and determining the level of satisfaction of individuals and organizations for the service of state administrative agencies in a specific and quantitative measurement, as set out in Resolution 30c / NQ- CP. The Minister of Home Affairs issued Decision 1383 / QD-BNV approving the Scheme for the development of satisfaction measuring for citizens and organizations with respect to the services of state administrative agencies. Starting in 2015, the scheme is designed to objectively assess the quality of public administrative service delivery. Through this effort, state administrative agencies have captured the requirements and desires of citizens and organizations to take measures to improve the quality of services and increase the satisfaction and benefits of citizens and organizations. The index was calculated based on the percentage of organizations and citizens who provided satisfactory or very satisfactory assessments for the question of overall assessment with regard to whole services based on the following four dimensions: access to services, administrative procedures and protocol, serving behavior of civil servants, and the results of public service request handling.

The Government assigned the Ministry of Home Affairs to direct and implement the scheme, and the Vietnam Fatherland Front (specifically, the Vietnam Veterans Association, a member of the organization of the Fatherland Front was selected) to supervise the scheme. The survey's objectivity was ensured by the local government authorization of an independent organization to conduct the survey, and the department of home affairs took responsibility to manage and supervise it. For instance, Ho Chi Minh City assigned the Ho Chi Minh Institute for Development Studies, an independent organization, to conduct the survey with citizens and organizations via telephone and questionnaires.

This was the first time that Vietnam's government had employed an objective and quality assessment tool from the perspective of users, and it was also the first time that the government had provided citizens and organizations with a tool with which to capture their demands for better public services, particularly in terms of services for the poor, ethnic minorities and people with disabilities. Measuring the satisfaction of citizens and organizations has partially contributed to changing the mindset and working practices of state administrative agencies toward listening and receiving feedback from citizens and organizations. However, the reliability of the surveys, which accurately reflected the satisfaction of citizens and organizations with regard to public services, depended on a sizable quantity of the citizens and organizations' users of public services (those who use such services 100 times or more per year). Thus, it is not advisable to conduct surveys on specialized public services that do not serve large numbers of citizens or organizations

Until now, the Vietnamese government has striven to establish institutions for interactions between the government and its citizens. Despite its great achievements, much evidence is found that more attention should be paid to further civil engagement. For the next step, more active participation is required to create a customer-oriented culture. The Customer Satisfaction Survey in Korea showed the efforts towards forming a customer-oriented administrative environment. The Customer Satisfaction Survey digitalized the satisfaction level of individuals or corporations through using the goods or services of public organizations. As the administrative reform shifted from the supply side to the consumer side, customer satisfaction surveys in the public sector expanded and grew in importance. Customer satisfaction is used as a performance indicator for public organizations because it is regarded as an outcome measure with which to evaluate the final project's expected effects (Lee, 2016). The first customer satisfaction survey in South Korea was introduced for the Framework Act on the Management of Government-Invested Institutions in 1999, and this expanded to government-affiliated organizations in 2004. As the "Act of Management of Public Organization" was declared in 2007, the Customer Satisfaction Survey was reorganized as all-encompassing survey tool and the survey results were reflected in the management performance assessment of public organizations. After implementing the Management Evaluation System for public organizations including public enterprises, the measurement of customer satisfaction became more important as a main indicator of their performance (Han & Shin, 2006: 107; Kim, 2012).

Thus, the Customer Satisfaction Survey for public organizations in South Korea contributed to strengthening the customer-oriented management culture through service users' evaluation (MOSF, 2009). Hence, the Customer Satisfaction Survey took a large share of the evaluation of public organizations' performance and ended up settling Customer Satisfaction Management in South Korea. The National Pension Service (NPS) showed the best example of this; first, the NPS defined a recognition loophole that citizens knew little about the (pension) service, and intensively raised citizens' awareness to improve their satisfaction level. This scheme was derived from focus group interviews, and the respondents marked their lower satisfaction. In the process, researchers realized that the lower satisfaction was not caused by the quality of the service, but by service users' insufficient information about the NPS service. Therefore, the Customer Satisfaction Survey provided an opportunity for public organizations to determine their problems and solutions while also checking the level of satisfaction with policy targets. Thus, the process itself contributed to greater citizen participation and discussion.

• CASE 2. Low performer management

Balancing the performance and motivation of employees is one of the biggest challenges in managing an organization. Dismissing employees by strict rules would impede employees' motivation, whereas no performance management for low performers may ruin employee' morale. Therefore, enhancing the performance of an organization requires the proper management of low-performing employees. The policy of dismissing low-performing officials was first introduced in 2006 along with the Senior Civil Service (SCS) System that recognized where more qualified individuals outperformed senior officials. Although the evaluation committee had the right to recommend that ministers and the presidential office lay off some poorer performers, no civil servant has been dismissed over the last 10 years since the policy was adopted (The Korea Herald, 2015).

The effectiveness of the policy was enhanced when the Ministry of Personnel Management of the Park Geun-hye administration decided to provide reeducation opportunities and to take measures to improve low-performing employees. The goal of performance management in Korea did not aim to fire low-performing employees, but to improve their productivity and give them the opportunity to be trained and repositioned. In this manner, performance management in the Korean public sector includes both higher performance and lower performance categories (Axelrod et al., 2002; Seong et al., 2013; Hwang et al., 2014).

• CASE 3. Be cautious of reform fatigue

The Korean governments' reforms were often initiated without a comprehensive evaluation of the preceding governments' reform efforts, leading to failures. Reform fatigue refers to the public's unwillingness towards excessive reforms. Korea has experienced numerous reforms since the 1998 financial crisis; it clearly contributed to the rapid growth in the short term, yet also spread the epidemic of reform fatigue. In 2006, the Ministry of

Government Administration and Home Affairs conducted a survey of 2,548 civil servants to evaluate the current status of the Participatory Government innovation. The results showed signs of ever-accumulating reform fatigue while the public had experienced fully fledged government innovation since 2003. In the early years of the reform, referred to as No Action, Talk Only (NATO), fatigue was caused by the agonizing direction. In addition, fatigue was accumulated in the middle period due to the increases of reform evaluation and task aggravation. The merit-based system, internal competition, and work overloading lowered job satisfaction. Reform fatigue was blamed for various reasons, mainly due to the rapid and excessive reforms, especially for those that had little effectiveness (OECD, 2000). Reformers should bear in mind that these risks can severely undermine the outcomes of public reforms.

IV. Conclusion

Sustainability should be the most important quality of Vietnamese socio-economic development to move on to the next stage of national success. Stable long-term socio-economic growth is only possible when economic growth accompanies social integration, which can be achieved by solving various social problems such as income inequality, regional disparity, corruption, and social conflicts. National reform should be based on a long-term, balanced approach and driven according to careful, systemic plans. First, Vietnam should enact laws to implement reforms and establish or overhaul relevant institutions. The reform plans will require cooperative management, monitoring, and modification to be effective. We analyzed successful and unsuccessful cases of the reforms that South Korea has taken over the last five decades to suggest the guiding principles, goals, and strategies that Vietnam's reforms will require to be effective. The results can be summarized as follows.

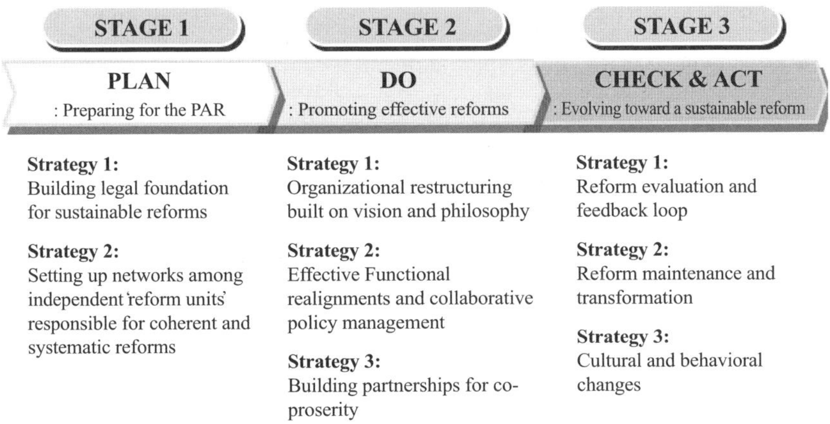

Figure 1-4 Three Stages of Administration Reforms

The guiding principles of Vietnam's institutional reforms should include three key components: (1) building an inclusive political system, (2) forming a stable and predictable government, and (3) enhancing fair economic and social orders. When setting the goals of reforms, the government should encourage citizens to participate in economic and social activities, form a stable and predictable government by establishing and implementing credible rules and systems, and secure fair political, economic, and social rules. The government should set up guidelines for policy implementations and abide by them to reduce unpredictability.

The goal of Vietnam's institutional reforms is the pursuit of responsible and market-friendly reform. Aiming at quantitative growth, social integration, and stable, predictable social order will allow the nation to build a new public management paradigm that can help achieve sustainable growth. Two strategies are required to realize this goal: (1) designing institutions for inclusive growth and (2) establishing a discipline for moderate and balanced institutional reform. Simply pursuing quantitative growth or greater efficiency is insufficient for redesigning fair political, economic, and social order. Vietnam ought to focus on reaching the three sub-goals: fair distribution, provision of equal opportunities, and quality and stable employment. In addition, the state and government should encourage citizens' participation, establish executable and predictable rules of the game, and enhance the government's capacity to secure the consistent implementation of policies when establishing disciplines.

Along with the aforementioned principles, goals and strategies, we further suggest what lessens could be drawn from Korea. Over the last 25 years, the Vietnamese government has put great efforts on meeting a variety of administrative demands, but it has made relatively modest progress. The government needs to modernize its administrative system to ensure sustained growth. Thus, as noted in Figure 1-4, we suggest strategies in three stages for Vietnam's administrative reform: (1) Plan, (2) Do, and (3) Check & Act. In the Plan stage, Vietnam needs to groundwork for Public Administration Reform (PAR), and the legal and institutional foundations for PAR should be established at this stage. The country may build a legal foundation for sustainable reform and set up networks among independent reform units. The networks are responsible for coherent and systematic reforms. Building the legal foundation should precede any other steps toward sustainable reform, as it determines the entire process of the establishment and implementation of reform policies. We suggest The Roh Moo-hyun Administration's "Promoting

Government Innovation Act" and the case of "Strengthening the capacity of legislative units" to refer to.

The Do stage is the step in which effective reforms are implemented. Effective implementation requires preparing organizations, cooperative management, and partnerships with the following three specific strategies. First, the government should restructure organizations based on vision and philosophy. Organizational reshuffling in the government should avoid merging ministries to simply remove or add functions. A government's structure should implicitly illustrate the philosophy and vision of the administration in allocating authority between ministries. Therefore, exhaustive analysis and investigation should precede administrative reform for organizational reshuffling. South Korea set a good example for restructuring the government by considering policy objectives and founding principles. Simply reducing the number of ministries by merging several units shouldn't be regarded as panacea to resolve organizational ineffectiveness. Second, it should realign functions and build collaborative policy management for efficiency. Reorganizing the functions and responsibilities of the ministries is an important step to build an effective and efficient central system; Reshaping and systemizing the structure of the ministries, ministerial-level agencies, specialized districts, and provincial bureaucracies are the main purposes of Public Administration Reform, and this is the key to multi-disciplinary and multi-sector management. However, Vietnam has enjoyed little benefit, as some ministries still share overlapping functions, which causes ineffectiveness and inefficiency. Combining several ministries and organizing their functions would allow the administrative system to have organized management. Functional re-alignments should be carefully designed when merging ministries to promote the capacity and performance of the government. Improper administrative reforms often have imbalanced or redundant functional relations and excessive control span which undermines their effectiveness. Five cases in Korea are discussed to highlight the importance of careful functional alignment when a government changes its ministerial structure. Third, it should build partnerships for co-prosperity. The imbalance between regions is a serious challenge for growth. Sustainable development is possible when the state decentralizes its power to the citizens. Still, the Vietnamese government must push its strategies for the social integration of poor and minority races ahead and balance development between urban and rural areas. In addition, Vietnam suffers from imbalance in the business field. The state should play an important role in supporting small businesses by reforming policies, establishing institutions, increasing its capabilities and building infrastructure. Examples of how Korean governments have attempted to improve the national capacity for balanced co-prosperity among different sizes of firms and different regions utilized by The Small and Medium Business Administration (SMBA) and Presidential Commissions on sustainable and balanced co-prosperity.

The final stage is the Check & Act stage, in which reforms in progress are monitored and modified so that the reforms in the next round are more sustainable. Evolving reforms and increasing reforms' sustainability and effectiveness require the following three strategies: (1) reform evaluation and feedback loop, (2) reform maintenance and transformation, and (3) cultural and behavioral changes. The whole reform process should not only include planning, decision making, and execution, but also evaluation and a feedback loop to secure its success and continue public reforms. Vietnam has developed various indexes including the PAR Index, the Vietnam Provincial Governance and the Provincial Competitiveness Index (PCI) to secure the efficacy of public reforms and state administration emphasizing evaluation and feedback loop systems. Korea has designed a more comprehensive performance evaluation system that includes effective feedback loops, like the Framework Act on Government Performance Evaluation (FAGPE) and Government Innovation Index (GII). Administrative reform brings higher effectiveness when sustainably maintained in the long term. Rather than enforcing new reform programs each time, adjusting and expanding current reform initiatives can contribute to the success of reforms and cut down on wasted resources. The early success of economic reform in Korea is attributable to the establishment of a strategic planning unit in the central government and its coordinated efforts towards changes. The plans expanded to include issues of regional balance and social policies for the disadvantaged. As the transformation of a reform, strengthening coordination among agencies by Government 3.0 is an exemplary case. Establishing e-government is a major challenge in Vietnam, because it is difficult to focus on the improvement of the work structure between central and local governments by utilizing information technology. The opportunity to share Korea's experiences would contribute to the success of Vietnam's reform and empowerment.

The participation of citizens and businesses in the policy process through the synchronization of mechanisms including direct participation and representativeness (which is very often challenging) has been regarded as an institutional condition for the generation of legitimacy and the social ownership of government interventions or public management in general while enhancing trust and confidence in government. Vietnam should also be especially cautious about causing fatigue among civil servants through rapid and excessive reforms. An active and vital officialdom can achieve substantive and effective reforms.

Along with institutional and administrative reform, the following four subjects may be emphasized to realize Vietnam's successful administrative reforms and further reflect the Vietnam Vision of 2035. First, administrative reform should be built upon legal and institutional foundations; checking the relevant laws is the most urgent requirement of stable reforms. In addition, there should be specific systems such as Line that assist communication between central and local governments in the reform process.

Second, the Communist Party of Vietnam (CPV) must greatly improve its leadership capacity and the Government must execute effective and efficient administrative reform in realizing leadership vision and facing with increasingly complicated challenges from the changing world. The CPV should enhance the nuclear role of unified leadership from the grassroots to central levels to enforce the reform's effectiveness and efficiency while also improving and enhancing network and cooperative management systems with the government as a stable reform driver with which to readily solve complex problems. Furthermore, the CPV and government must improve their expertise and objectivity by hiring experts in the administrative reform field, while partly interacting with open public. The party should continue to reform its leadership mode, and the government's performance capacity should be enhanced to promote stable, effective administrative reform through close connections to businesses and mass and social organizations.

Third, the officialdom will be required to make cultural and behavioral changes. The government may put much effort into breaking away from traditional practices and shifting into a new culture and behavior. In addition, it is greatly important that the evaluation system and incentive programs are developed and improved to use the civil servants who drive the reforms at their full potential and contribute to national development in a creative manner. The government should be cautious of fatigue among civil servants and urge them to participate in reforms more actively and creatively.

Lastly, there should be evaluation and feedback systems that can monitor the process of national reforms. The existing evaluation indexes are insufficiently effective; they can be improved by linking internal and external evaluations, revising the evaluation methods of the heads of organizations, and strengthening the role of audit committees. The evaluation system can also be improved by including both qualitative and quantitative indicators.

Vietnam may only be able to accomplish successful reforms and socio-economic development when it checks and improves its relevant laws based on the guiding principles, goals, and strategies of administrative reforms, establishes organizations that are responsible for constantly pursuing reforms, strengthens cooperation and partnerships, evaluates reforms both scientifically and systemically, boosts reforms via feedback, and promotes cultural and behavioral change.

V. Policy Suggestions

When devising future courses of action, the Vietnamese Government will need to address the issue of how to sequence several actions as both the order in which actions are developed and the timing of each must be set in a specific manner; we suggest three policy recommendations for the aforementioned stages of reform with which to realize Vietnam's successful administrative reforms and further the Vietnam Vision of 2035.

In the PLAN stage, establishing empowered "reform units" would be necessary to render networks effective among units. Only when empowered units exist can networks exist among independent "reform units" that are responsible for making coherent and systematic reforms. Regarding South Korea, the Economic Planning Board (EPB) was created in 1961 and orchestrated the overall economic reforms of President Park Chung-hee as a means of promoting economic development. This coordinating unit drafted and executed the Five-year Plans of Economic Development and led both national reform and economic growth. Moreover, several other effective reform bodies were established with which to manage national reforms over several decades. For instance, the Government Reform and Decentralization Committee was one of the key units entrusted with the role of pushing government reform forwards in the Roh Moo-Hyun administration. The committee was highly significant for addressing and resolving regional disparities as one of the main initiatives during his term. Given the complexity of values that Vietnam must pursue, creating fully empowered, well networked reform units is markedly significant. Those units will support the ongoing execution in Vietnam to ensure the achievement of sustainable development.

In the DO stage, Vietnam needs sound umbrella organizations that coordinate think tanks to enhance the coherence and systematics of reform strategies, initiatives, and actions. The benefits of having multiple policy research institutes and think tanks lie in the fact that each institute can focus on producing relevant policy recommendations on subjects related to their own expertise while others pay attention to policy issues in their own arenas. Thus, it is critical to facilitate a research environment in which each think tank can work proactively with a proper degree of autonomy and responsibility. However, given that many think tanks exist that support the Vietnamese government, building orchestrating organizations that can formally coordinate the dispersal of policy support for think tanks at the ministry level is necessary. In Korea, the National Research Council for Economics, Humanities and Social Sciences (NRC) and the National Research Council of Science & Technology (NST) are known national umbrella organizations that support and promote government-funded research institutes in corresponding sectors. Established in 1999, the NRC aims to innovate in the policy research ecosystem of the National Policy Research Institutes and upgrade the Research Council's core values in the Economics, Humanities, and Social Sciences sectors.

In 2017, NRC supported and promoted 26 government-funded research institutes including the Korea Development Institute (KDI), the Korean Educational Development Institute (KEDI), and the Korea Institute for Industrial Economics & Trade (KIET). Similarly, NST was built in 1999 with the aspiration of providing policy support for national research projects and driving the development of knowledge industries in science and technology sectors. There are 25 affiliated research institutes, including the Korea Institute of Science and Technology (KIST), the Korea Research Institute of Standards and Science (KRISS), and the Korea Institute of Science and Technology Information (KISTI). The Vietnam Chamber of Commerce and Industry (VCCI) has been noted for its great influence as a leading policy think tank for the Vietnamese government, emerging as a medium with which to identify policy problems and put pressure on changes in governance. Settling and reinforcing institutes with a coordinating organization would contribute to creating a sustainable foundation of national governance under such a vision and philosophy.

In the CHECK&ACT stage, there should be evaluation and feedback systems that can monitor national reform processes. Vietnam does have highly utilized government performance and reform indices with which it can enhance organizational effectiveness; for example, SIPAS and the PAR Index bring in policy implications that asks the government at all levels to open up for greater information access and transparency, simplify of administrative processes, increase the use of ICT when organizing public service works, reduce fees, and improve public ethics and behavior. However, these tools are not fully utilized, in that their results are merely considered when designing future incentives or goals. To take the example of Korea, performance evaluation in Korea aims to evaluate performance in three dimensions: individual, organizational, and project, the results of which are routed back to the inputs used to redirect the organizational structure. Gathering evaluation results from all levels allows Vietnam to create a comprehensive evaluation system in which information is properly reflected when designing budgets and organizing personnel and incentives. Furthermore, Vietnam's numerous tools need to be further developed and refined to accurately measure objectives. Tools constantly evolve to meet the system's current policy demands and these efforts can be expected to preserve their objectivity and credibility. These steps in the feedback system will ultimately be reflected to enhance the organization's performance. Adapting knowledge to local context requires complicated but constant efforts. Vietnam needs to take a long-term perspective to adopt the full-fledged feedback loop system. Officials need to develop the policy agenda with exhaustive efforts built on well-supported research and studies. If required, launching a more complete performance management program is highly viable with the collaboration of international organizations such as Korea International Cooperation Agency (KOICA). Based on the cooperation with expert organizations, Vietnam would be able to further enhance its extant instruments to manage performance.

Reform has reached a critical point in Vietnam and the three aforementioned suggestions at each stage can help reflect concrete actions in the near future. Materializing the Vietnam Vision for 2035 will require considering these suggestions as high-priority when designing the Vietnam Socio-economic Development Strategy for 2021–2030.

CHAPTER TWO:

GOVERNANCE REFORM

Hyun Joon Kim

Professor, Department of Public Administration, Korea University

CHAPTER TWO:

GOVERNANCE REFORM

I. Introduction

Good governance is a necessary condition for economic and social development. For developing countries pursuing sustainable progress, establishing principles for good governance and reforming existing governance forms is an urgent task for removing the barriers to development. This chapter outlines the important governance reform agendas for Vietnam by reviewing the past and present governance reform initiatives in Vietnam. Korean governance reform experiences relevant to Vietnamese governance reform are selectively introduced to develop policy recommendations for Vietnam.

II. Setting the Scope of Governance Reform

Reforming governance is ultimately aimed at establishing a sustainable governing system that will enable Vietnam to achieve the goals of Vietnam 2035. One of the critical factors for successful governance reform is specifying the scope of reform clearly, because the term "governance" may refer to a variety of political, social, and economic interactions between public, private, and nonprofit sectors. Even more, the term may refer to various kinds of relationships, such as public–private partnerships, citizen participation, intergovernmental collaboration, and even international organizations' involvement in domestic policy issues. Drawing the boundaries of governance properly, therefore, should be a first step toward the successful development of a governance reform road map.

Traditionally, state government's role in a market economy includes:

- Provide a legal system to make and enforce laws and protect private property;
- Provide/invest in public goods that individuals and the private sector would not/cannot provide;
- Correct market failure (externalities and economic slowdown-unemployment)
- Maintain competition by regulating monopoly;
- Redistribute income by taxing those with high income and helping those in need;
- Stabilize the economy by controlling inflation, keeping unemployment low, and promoting economic growth.

This report looks at the State of Vietnam based on this theory of the state's functions in the market economy. It will not, however, capture all functions of the state governance in Vietnam; rather, it will look at factors hampering its effectiveness as described in the following scope of the report.

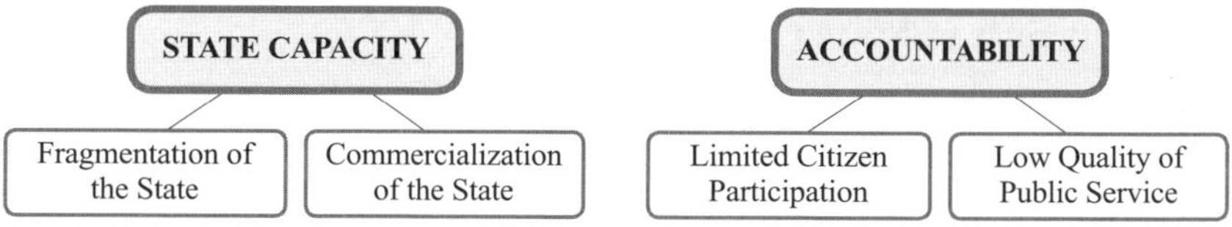

Figure 2-1 Governance reform agendas adapted from the Vietnam 2035 report

The scope of governance reform adopted for the Vietnam DEEP Project is drawn by analyzing the "Vietnam 2035" report. Pillar III, "a Capable and Accountable State", introduced in the report addresses two critical constraints to the progress of Vietnamese governance system: the constraints to state capacity and the constraints to state accountability. We believe that the two types of governance constraints have become major barriers against fully utilizing the potentials of Vietnamese human resources as well as against maximizing the effects of fiscal and institutional reforms.

The governance section of our report is primarily focused on addressing these two major constraints. These two key bottlenecks will be further elaborated in this report based on the framework indicated in Figure 2-1 and the role of the state as mentioned above. In order to develop policy recommendations for strengthening state capacity and accountability for better governance, we first diagnose major governance challenges in the Vietnamese context. We subsequently select best practices from the Korean governance reform experiences applicable for enhancing Vietnamese governance.

III. Addressing Key Governance Issues in Vietnam

1. Constraints to State Capacity

1.1. Fragmentation of the State

One key issue constraining the development of state capacity is the fragmentation of government authorities. Striking a balance between centralization and decentralization of governing authorities and responsibilities is particularly important in a state pursuing economic development: regional and local authorities need to be empowered to effectively manage policy issues related to local issues, while central authorities control excessive competition across jurisdictions and set standards for common policy agendas. However, the Vietnam 2035 Report shows that administrative authorities are not effectively distributed within the central government as well as between central and local authorities.

The unbalanced distribution of governing power has caused many problems. For instance, capital investments made heavily at the provincial level create serious redundancy across jurisdictions. Yet, central authorities have not been effective in checking the self-interest seeking behavior of local entities. Meanwhile, a large number of less affluent local governments are heavily dependent upon support from the central government which has very limited revenue sources. Under the circumstance, reforming fragmented governance in Vietnam is an important task in pursuit of balanced socio-economic development of Vietnam.

1.1.1. Blurred lines of responsibility within central government

It is very common for a government agency desiring to maintain and even expand its power. Such a tendency has been strengthened in Vietnam during the recent economic development period. Currently, the role and mandates of each central government agency (i.e., line ministry) are stated in decrees approved by the government. These decrees are often formulated by the line ministry itself and then reviewed by the Ministry of Home Affairs (MOHA) and Ministry of Justice (MOJ). Such autonomy given to each government agency has led to the overlapping and fragmentation in state governance functions. Here are some examples exemplifying this problem: i) The food safety authority belongs to three ministries – the Ministry of Agriculture and Rural Development (MARD), Ministry of Industry and Commerce (MOIT), and Ministry of Health (MOH)[3]; ii) The Ministry of Natural Resource and Environment (MONRE) is responsible for state management of water source pollution in general and river basin water pollution, the Ministry of Construction (MOC) for state management of urban sewage water pollution, and MARD for state management of rural and agriculture water pollution.

The Vietnamese government has too limited coordination capacity to overcome the problems caused by the blurred lines of responsibility. When a complex problem occurs, identifying a responsible government entity becomes an annoyingly difficult job due to the unnecessary fragmentation and overlaps in the governing system.[4] Blurred lines of responsibility promote the culture of irresponsible behavior by passing the buck to other agencies.

1.1.2. Unbalanced relationships between central and local governments

The Doimoi reform and the transformation of the economy from a centrally managed to a marketized mechanism necessitate a change in the old state governance style. Decentralization in Vietnam is defined as the clear

3 For instance, the MARD takes the state management role of food safety in the process of growing vegetable by farmers, while the MOIT takes the same role in process of vegetable transportation and distribution in the market, but MOH takes the same role in food safety at consumption.

4 This issue can be seen in Fumosa's sea environmental pollution tragedy in April, 2016. When the pollution happened in Central Vietnam's sea, the MONRE said it was the responsibility of local government, and vice versa. Both organizations said it was partly the responsibility of MOST, the MPI, etc. Ultimately, the Prime Minister had to direct MONRE to establish an inter-ministerial team to come to the site to investigate the causes of the tragedy.

identification of role, responsibilities, and mandates of the governments at different levels to achieve effectiveness and efficiency in state administration. In theory, the central government should focus on macroeconomic management and delegate other state governance functions to local authorities. Such changes are aimed at motivating local governments to be innovative, proactive and autonomous in dealing with their local socio-economic issues by fulling utilizing their local knowledge. In spites of arduous reform efforts made over the last two decades, there still remain several areas where decentralization have not been fully incorporated in the governing process.

First, some line ministries still maintain state mandates suitable for implementing at the local level. For example, function of deciding the school's education curriculum is still under the control of MOET, although provincial governments are believed to the function better to meet the local educational needs.

Second, too much governance burden has been imposed on small and weak provinces that do not have their own governing capacities. Apart from the five centrally managed cities,[5] which received the most comprehensive decentralized state governance power, there are many local authorities differing greatly from the five major cities in terms of demographic characteristics and economic, fiscal, administrative capacities. Uniformed decentralization arrangements ignoring the differences at the local level will limit the outcomes and effects of the decentralization initiatives.

Third, inconsistency in the development master plans between the central and the local governments should be resolved. The central government drafts national, regional, and provincial level plans as well as sectoral master plans

5 Including Hanoi, Ho Chi Minh City, Danang, Can Tho and Hai Phong.

and requires local governments and line ministries to formulate the sectoral/ local master plans. In their own planning process, local governments and line ministries prioritize their own interests without fully considering the impacts on broader national interests. Overarching laws, government's decrees, and other forms of development plans formulated at central level are not immediately implementable at the local level because these documents should be detailed into the form of circulars by the line ministries.

Fourth, the current decentralization is not sufficiently comprehensive because it ignores financial capacities differing across local governments. While local provinces have full autonomy in formulating and implementing their local socio-economic development plans, all of them do not enjoy full autonomy in mobilizing and spending financial resources needed for implementing the plans. One of the reasons was that only 13 of the 63 provinces/central managed cities in Vietnam can self-finance their development plans with their local revenue; the others depend on financial supports from the central state budget. This implies that they cannot independently formulate their annual development plan (particularly, development investment plan) without considering how much they would get in financial support from the central budget.

1.2. Commercialization of the State

One of the constraints often found in developing countries is that state-owned enterprises (SOEs) play the key roles in the economy. On one hand, such state commercialization might facilitate rapid economic progress by maximizing the efficiency of resource allocation. In the long run, however, excessive dependence on SOEs hampers the further development of the economy by shrinking the business opportunities for private entities.

Such phenomena are also found in Vietnam. The Vietnam 2035 report addresses that the state participates in the market directly through SOEs and the knit and close links between the state and some segments of the private sector have been strengthened. One of the biggest problems caused by excessive state commercialization is that the economy becomes inefficient by lowering the performance and productivity of economic actors and causing the concentration of capital.

The government of Vietnam gets involved in businesses through various channels. First, it does so directly through SOEs. As of 2015, there are more than 650 SOEs organized in the form of 100% state-owned companies, accounting for only 0.1% of existing businesses.[6] The number of SOEs has been declining in recent years as a result of accelerated state-owned companies' equitization process in recent years. In fact, the SOEs reform process was carried out very slowly, and the result failed to meet the expectations. The equitization process was seen as significant in terms of the number of equitized SOEs, but they were targeted mainly on small one and the share of state capital in extant SOEs is still very large;[7] SOEs still operate in the areas that are profitable and are best left to the private sector (like trading, beverages, hotels, etc.).

Second, the government controls the allocation of key resources, such as natural resources, land, and capital, and it also plays a key role in allocating these resources. According to the Constitution, natural resources are under so-called "all people's ownership" and the right to exercise the ownership is awarded to the state (government). When the government owns SOEs, and

6 According to current enterprise Law (2015), SOEs is defined as those with 100% of state owned chatter capital. However, there are a large number of companies, formerly were SOEs but equitized in recent years. The share of state capital in these companies are large (many of them are more than 50%). This means that state's role is still dominant in these companies.

7 Many equitized companies have more than 50% state capital.

also allocates the nation's natural resources, it distorts the markets of these resources; the SOEs will enjoy preferable conditions to access to the economic resources, while pure private enterprises undergo relatively constrained access.

Third, master plans for economic development at various levels of government are seen as barriers as they were not properly formulated and not adapting very well to the changing market conditions. As of 2015, there are almost 19,000 master plans for the periods up to 2020, developed and approved by the government authorities both at central and local levels. Pursuing harmonized development under such complexity is becoming a huge challenge. Unavoidable rigidity commonly present in government master plans makes it difficult promptly adjusting themselves in response to the market changes. In addition, even when funding is secured for new investment, no actual project can start until the authorities approve the adjustment of the relevant master plans.

Fourth, conflicts of interests in the market are prevalent due to the excessive involvements of line ministries in policy making in particular business domains as well as the operation of SOEs. Line ministries' power to govern policies in a particular domain tend to favor their own SOEs. Such a practice distorts market mechanisms and violates the legal principle of providing an equal playing field.

2. Constraints to State Accountability

2.1. Limited citizen participation

Economic growth increases not only the wealth of the society but also its complexity. With the citizens' ever growing demands for more and better services, the government should expand its capacity to satisfy diverse expectations and ease the tensions among social groups advocating their own interests. Complex social issues cannot be managed by one single state authority. Checks and balances should be a governing principle in policy decision-making and resource allocation in a balanced and accountable manner. A functioning accountability mechanism defines the roles and responsibilities of key actors and provides a set of procedures for policy making and implementation. In order to support the accountability system's operation, robust open communication and information sharing channels should be established to make the governing process transparent and responsive.

For democratic governance, the public is given with easy access to the information about legislation, government operation, performance and any other critical government functions. The state must ensure the provision of participatory channels for citizens to give feedback on policy implementation and public service provision. Unfortunately, it would be difficult to say that citizens are becoming more vocal in Vietnam and committed to advancing the ideals of democratic governance to make the government be more accountable.

One critical accountability problem examined in the Vietnam 2035 report is the limited voice and participation of citizens. Even though Vietnamese civic organizations are burgeoning, only the state-sanctioned organizations are allowed to participate in the policy process. Citizen participation is mandated by many grassroots decrees, yet the People's Committee still holds the decision-making authority. Even worse, access to policy information is still restricted.

Limited citizen participation is observed in various forms. First, participation of citizen/stakeholders in the policy-making process is limited. Although the existing regulation requires government authorities/policy formulators to involve the public and stakeholders in the policy formulation, this requirement is either neglected or followed in form only. In many cases, the stakeholders are not notified about the process, not being properly consulted or provided opportunities to comment on the new regulations before they are promulgated. This issue was partly solved in recent years through media and internet channels when new regulation drafts are made public on the internet for getting comments and are also publicly discussed on TV for getting public consensus/understanding before the regulation is approved.

Second, citizens do not have sufficient and timely information about government performance/activities to exercise their rights of monitoring and evaluating government performance. The volume of publicly available government performance data is very limited, and they are not made public on time.

Third, participatory channels are too few to allow the public to provide their opinions government policies and public services. While traditional channels for participation, such as consultation workshops and posting written opinions on the state authority's web site, are available, these channels do not attract broad public attention or facilitate interactive dialogues between policy makers and the public. In recent years, other more effective channels were used, such as TV, internet, policy dialogues in newspapers, and so on. Yet, the use of these channels is limited to special cases.

Fourth, the role of civil society organizations has increased in recent years, but they are not equally treated. There are currently thousands of civil society organizations operating in Vietnam. They include government-affiliated institutions, semi-governmental organizations, and NGOs (including INGOs). The first two groups are very close to the government; they are totally or partly financed by the state budget and play like "extended hands" of the state in the society. Meanwhile, other NGOs face difficulties in accessing the state information and play limited roles in policy dialogues.

2.2. Low Quality of Administrative Services

For many years, the state of Vietnam was solely responsible for providing all kinds of public services in the society, and private sector and non-government organizations were not allowed to participate in this area. In the last 15 years, the private sector has gradually stepped in and took over some portions of works in public service provision, particularly in public utilities (public transport, clean water supply, solid-waste collection, etc.) and social and human service areas (education, healthcare, etc.). However, because of the financial constraints and the poor state management in the public sector, the services provided by the state generally fail to satisfy citizens' expectations.

What are the causes of such problems? First, state servants do not consider citizen as their "customers"; they show negatively bureaucratic behavior when interacting with citizens. There have been some improvements in recent years due to administrative reform efforts, more transparency in administrative procedures and the installation of one stop services" for business procedures. However, its impacts are only effective in limited areas.

Second, social and human service providers[8] operate like administrative agencies. They are fully financed by the state budget and provide services based on the plans approved by the state authorities. Due to the historically authoritarian attitudes prevalent in these organizations, they do not pay proper attention to improving public service quality.

Third, the interaction between public service providers and users/customers is very weak. The customers' voice in providing feedback on the public services is not properly considered. Recently, some progress has been made as

8 For example, state schools, universities, hospitals, clinics etc.

a result of reforms implemented in administrative and healthcare organizations.

Fourth, the state budget allocated to public service organizations is too limited to improve service quality. In order to overcome the constraints, the government adopted the policy to attract private investment through PPP mechanisms, but it is premature to see significant changes in improving public service quality.

Fifth, the use of IT in public service provision is still limited. IT would enable public service providers to create faster and easier administrative procedures and to reduce transaction costs for businesses and citizens when interacting with state authorities. In addition, the intensive use of IT would avoid the public servants' corruption and abuse of bureaucratic power.

These four issues identify the key areas that the Vietnamese government should focus on to improve the quality of public services and to enhance administrative accountability. In order to overcome the inefficiency caused by needlessly complicated administrative procedures the Vietnamese government may pursue two directions simultaneously. First, it is necessary to utilize information technologies to improve the overall efficiency of government works. Adoption of advanced e-government services for G2G is also necessary to increase the information capacity of local governments. Second, efforts should be made for developing integrated online civil service systems for citizens. The Vietnamese government has already recognized the importance of providing integrated public services for greater citizen satisfaction. Adopting alternative solutions for public service provision empowered by electronic media should be seriously considered to address the issues undermining the government accountability.

IV. Major Governance Reform Initiatives in Vietnam

Reforms on state governance were introduced over the last decade. During 2006–2010, the reform was targeted on administrative procedures. In 2011, the government introduced a new program for administrative reform for the period of 2011–2020. The new program was aimed at: i) building and improving market institutions; ii) creating an equal, transparent, favorable business playing field for all kinds of businesses operating in the economy; iii) building effective, productive, and "clean" (i.e., corruption-free) administrative agencies at both central and local levels; iv) ensuring the democratic base for citizen and protecting human rights; and v) developing the capable, accountable administrative staff who have good skills and competency to provide satisfactory public services to citizens.[9] For 2011–2020, this program focuses on specific reform areas: institutional reform, administrative procedure reform, reform of state organizational apparatus, enhancing capability and quality of government staff, public finance reform, and administration modernization.

In 2016, after the new government was elected in June 2016, its reform agenda for 2016–2020 was announced by the new Prime Minister, who committed to building the "un-corrupted, development-enabling, accountable, and "service" government". This phrase implies that:

First, the government should be corruption-free, responsible, accountable and transparent. This would require all government authorities and their staff to take responsible for implementing law/regulations as the first priority. The government and its staff should do whatever the law allows them to do while it has

---

9 See in details the government's Resolution No 30c/NQ-CP dated 8/11/2011 on a comprehensive program on administrative reforms for 2011–2020.

to ensure that people can do whatever the law does not prohibit. In addition, the government's regulations, programs, decisions, and policies should be transparent and accountable to citizen and ensure that the public can check this principle.

Second, the government should enable development. This means that the government and its apparatus should be effectively organized and execute their functions professionally. As the key mission of the government is to establish a foundation for the national sustainable development, the government should create opportunities for all citizens to enhance and express their capacity and innovativeness in order to participate in, and to gain from, development processes. The development-enabling government should create the institutional framework necessary to provide favorable conditions for business opening-up and operating.

Third, the government should not only formulate good programs and policies; it is required to be able to implement them effectively in practice.

To realize the above new government slogan, the government has introduced several state governance reform regulations and reform programs for 2016–2020 and beyond, including:

- *Government's Resolution No 36a/NQ-CP dated 14/10/2015 on the development of an e-government*

  The objective of this policy is to promote the development of e-government, improve the quality and effectiveness of state agencies to better serve people and enterprises, improve Vietnam's position on e-government in the UN ratings, and ensure openness and transparency in state agencies. The resolution set specific targets to be achieved, as illustrated in Box 1 below.

- *Prime Minister's Decision No 225/QD-TTg dated 4/2/2016 on approval of state administrative reform in the period 2016–2020*

During this five-year period, the government will focus on institutional reform, enhancing the government staff quality in order to provide good and effective public services, upgrading quality of administrative services and public services. The policy framework of this decision to be implemented in 2016–2020 is presented in Box 2.

- *Government Resolution No 19/NQ-CP dated 28/4/2016 on improving national business environment and enhancing national competitiveness in the period 2016–2017*

This document set the main tasks and measures for ministries, agencies, and local governments in the two-year period; these focus on improving the market economy mechanism for comprehensiveness and modernity based on the market economy and wide and deep integration in the world economy. The strategic breakthroughs were to i) step up the restructuring of the economy concurrently with the innovation of a growth model, improving productivity, quality, effectiveness, and competitiveness of products, enterprises, and the economy; smoothly and effectively operating markets; and ensuring that resource allocation for production and price management are in accordance with market mechanisms. ii) Concentrate on steering the intensification of administrative procedures restructuring and reinforcing the public service ethos of official and civil servant; iii) Reinforce the effect of administrative disciplines and rules, the cooperation, inspection, and examination; iv) Speed up the innovation, increasing the intensification of applying information technology in state management, especially in the administrative procedure process.

- *Government Resolution No. 35/NQ-CP dated 16/5/2016 on supporting enterprise development policy until 2020*

This document aimed at building up and improving economic institutions, creating a business investment environment favorable to business growth and enabling it to become a driving force of the economy. The resolution set a target to reach at least 1 million enterprises operating in Vietnam by 2020, including potential large-scale ones. The private sector is expected to contribute to approximately 48–49 % of GDP, and about 49% of the total social investment. The enterprise development agenda of this document is based on the key principles summarized in Box 3 below. On the basis of these principles, the resolution set government policy measures to promote business development for 2016–2020, which include: i) administrative reforms; ii) creating favorable business environment for startups and innovative enterprises; iii) ensuring the freedom in business and award enterprises equal business and resources opportunities; iv) reduction of business costs; and v) protection of enterprises' lawful rights and interests.[10]

It is obvious that reform policies over the past few years indicate the commitments of the Vietnam government in trying to build up favorable conditions for development and enabling good governance. The content of policies as mentioned above clearly aimed at addressing and solving state governance challenges already discussed. While the results of these reforms require time to be implemented and it is too early to assess their impact, at least these reform commitments would help to get the business community's and society's trust and hopes about the positive changes in state governance in the near future. The most important current challenge now is how to implement effectively the policy measures as stated above in practice.

---

10 See more in details at: http://www.dalat-info.vn/en/procedures--favorable-policies/resolution-no.35-nq-cp-dated-16-5-2016-issued-by-the-governmenton-enterprise-development-policy-to-2020-34938.phtml

V. Korean Governance Reform Experiences Relevant for Vietnam

1. Governance Reform Initiatives to Improve State Capacity

1.1. Restructuring of Local Government Organizations

During its development era, Korea's local governments expanded dramatically. In 1980, for example, the total number of local government employees was 109,362 and the ever-increasing demand for local government services doubled within 10 years. Economic development also provoked the emergence of large metropolitan governments to support the rapid industrialization in Korea.

Korean local governments, however, have experienced several administrative problems as byproducts of economic development. The Kim Dae-jung administration identified three major challenges in local government organizations: 1) there are both inter- and intra-organizational functional overlaps; 2) excessive investment in managerial support incurs administrative inefficiencies; and 3) local governments lack customer-centered service systems.

The restructuring of local governments during the Kim Dae-jung administration was aimed at transforming them into efficient, flexible, and productive organizations. The reform initiatives stressed the importance of acquiring capabilities to respond to the changing environment quickly and effectively. To achieve the goals, the central government drove the local governments to integrate similar or duplications functions, to reform operation systems, to actively utilize outsourcing administrative works, and to invigorate grassroots organizations to promote citizen participation.

The Kim Dae-jung administration started formal restructuring in 1998. The first step was reducing the number of government employees and administrative agencies. In one year, 174 bureaus disappeared in Korean local governments and 35,149 local government employees left the public service. The reduction was widely supported by the public since it was considered a necessary step to resolve a prevalent distrust against the government in the financial crisis (Kim, 1998: 133).

The Kim administration achieved the unprecedented massive reduction in the public sector in the following ways. First, it adjusted the retirement age of public employees. The retirement age was shortened for public employees in the general administration by 1 year and for those in the educational administration by 3years. Next, targets for honorary retirement in the public sector were extended. Though the National Civil Servant Act was enacted in the 1980s to stipulate the honorary retirement of public employees, the Kim administration attempted to extend its target much more widely. It provided financial incentives for those who choose early retirement. Third, it set a maximum limit of the total number of public employees working for the central ministries and agencies and managed the limit carefully (Kim, 2002: 13). After the downsizing, the Kim administration started management consulting for the local governments to identify the areas where further downsizing was urgently needed.

It was the first local government restructuring in Korean history. After the two rounds of local government reform, 178 bureaus and 1,249 sections had been abolished and total local government employees reduced by 56,633 (i.e. 19.4%). The restructuring created an institutional basis for advancing the local governments' capacities in Korea (The Korean Institute of Public Administration [KIPA], 2015).

1.2. Special Account for Balanced National Development

For rapid economic development, Korea has adopted the so-called selection and concentration strategy. The central government selects the industries and regions where the state concentrates all the available resources for strategic purposes. Seoul and its surrounding metropolitan areas attracted a largest proportion of investment, infrastructures, and population. Even now, the capitol region accounts for 46% of the national population, and 55% of manufacturers were in the region as of 2016. Such concentration of economic, human, and social resources in the Seoul metropolitan areas has resulted in numerous social problems, including high housing costs, traffic congestions, environmental issues, and so on. Furthermore, the strategy of selection and concentration created inequalities in economic opportunities, education qualities, access to basic human services, and many other aspects of quality of life outside of Seoul metropolitan areas. Other regions, especially those regions relatively isolated from industrialization, have experienced the problems of decreasing population and stagnant economies (Lee, 2004).

In 2004, the Roh Moo-hyun administration enacted the Special Act for Balanced National Development aiming at reducing the concentration of economic power in Seoul metropolitan areas. The bill enabled the government to provide financial and administrative support or support for decreasing the disparities between the developed and the underdeveloped. To do so, it allowed for creating a special account designated solely for balanced national development and placed 80 percent of liquor tax revenues and overpopulation costs as the annual revenue source for the move, while designating 20 percent of liquor taxes as the revenue source for a special account for regional innovation projects (Korea Development Institute, 2016).

The volume of the special account was estimated at about 5.5 trillion won in 2005. With the special account, the government was able to implement its regional projects systemically. According to the Act, the budget management procedure runs as follows. Before the end of March, the central ministries provide budget preparation guidelines to local governments in advance. Then by the end of April, local governments apply for budgets. They submit a budget request form to the ministries and the Presidential Committee on Balanced National Development after prioritizing investment plans in their respective region by themselves. After submission of the requests, the ministries and the committee review the budget plans from the local governments based on the performance evaluation of the local governments in the previous year. In the process, the original plan that the local governments submitted can be adjusted by the central government. After the execution of the budget, the ex post facto evaluation is implemented (The Presidential Committee on Balanced National Development, 2005).

Implementing the special account has significantly changed the dynamics between the central and local governments. Firstly, local governments can choose how to use the budget according to their own priorities. In the past, the local governments had to visit relevant central ministries to secure the budget for their preferred regional projects. However, under the special account system, the opposite is now happening. That is, it is the central government that has to persuade relevant local governments to apply for its planned development projects. Furthermore, each central ministry must create better policies to attract local governments' participation to secure a greater budget for itself. Thus, the local governments have a significant influence on the central government budget process, unlike in the past. Also, within the total amount of budget, it is allowed to redirect to other purposes or transfer to the next month more freely in the special account so that the relevant government agencies can enjoy greater autonomy in execution as well as in planning for budget (Ministry of Strategy and Finance Republic of Korea, n.d.).

1.3. Executive Agency System

Another governance reform initiative adopted by the Kim Dae-jung administration was the Executive Agency System. Public agencies, which are semi-autonomous public organizations supervised by the government, were known to be inefficient and effective. Reforming public agencies was one of the most important governance reform issues in Korea. Hence, the government started seeking an alternative policy tool to change inefficient and low performing SOEs and public corporations (i.e., public agencies).

In 1999, the Kim Dae-jung administration adopted the ideas of an executive agency system from the British experiences. The bottom line of the reform was incorporating the principles of competition and autonomy into the management of public agencies. This initiative has been also referred to as "agencification." The Korean government reformers expected that the agencification of public institutions would promote a performance-oriented culture and more customer-oriented business practices in public agencies due to liberation from the government sponsor's control. Shortly speaking, agencification was aimed at transforming government-owned or government-controlled public agencies to become more business-like organizations (Kim, 2000: 84).

The Act on the Installation and Operation of an Executive Agency in 1999 defines the key characteristics of executive agencies in this way. The government transferred its executive power to the agencies to give them autonomy and independence. The agencies' chief executive positions, which had been filled by the officials appointed by the government, are now filled by the candidates selected from an open competition. The agencies' chief executives hold full authority over personnel, budgetary, and any other managerial issues within the agency. Yet, they are held accountable for the performance of the agency. Chief executives' employment contracts are renewed every three years. If they fail to meet performance standards specified in the agency's business plans, they will lose their jobs.

The Roh Moo-hyun administration made some improvements to the executive agency system. In order to promote innovation, the Roh administration improved the job security of chief executives by extending the term of chief executives to a minimum of two years. Another important addition to the executive agency system is the total personnel expense ceiling system. The government only sets the total amount of budget, with full discretion given to the executive agency on how to allocate the budget (KIPA, 2015).

2. Reforming Governance for Greater Government Accountability

2.1. Citizen Participatory Budgeting System

The Citizen Participatory Budgeting System is originated from Porto Alegre's trial in Brazil in 1989. Guaranteeing citizens' participation in the budgeting system is pointed out as one of the effective ways to improve the democratic responsiveness to citizens and transparency of the government.

The success in Porto Alegre attracted much attention from the world, and its budgeting system has been considered a faithful reflection of the ideal of direct democracy (Kim, 2015: 25).

In 2004, the Roh Moo-Hyun administration recommended its local autonomous governments adopt a new system that guarantees the transparency of the local budgeting process and allows local people to participate in the process actively as guided by the Decentralization Road Map of the Presidential Committee on Government Innovation and Decentralization (2003.7.4). In response to the effort of the central government, in spite of political ebbs and flows, the reform initiative diffused rapidly among local governments. In 2011, the National Assembly revised the Local Financial Act requiring all local governments to adopt the Citizen Participatory Budgeting System (Kim, 2015: 26). Although it was not the forerunner for implementing the system, Seoul Metropolitan Government is evaluated as one of the best cases of the Citizen Participatory Budgeting System (Participedia, n.d.). Thus, in this section, we exemplify the case of Seoul Metropolitan Government to analyze the detailed process of the Citizen Participatory Budgeting System.

The Citizen Participatory Budgeting System in Seoul Metropolitan Government mainly consists of the General Committee, including 250 citizen members, and eight subcommittees according to policy fields. Two-hundred seats are assigned for citizen members selected by public invitation via the Internet, and the rest are filled by recommendations from NGOs, the Metropolitan Council, and Participatory Budgeting Committees in each affiliated autonomous district or the Mayor. The overall composition of the General Committee is settled under deliberate consideration of gender, age, or even social minority issues to guarantee citizens' participation as much as possible (Participedia, n.d.-a).

As the phase for gathering opinions, any ordinary citizens who reside in Seoul can propose their opinion for participatory budgeting by passing from district-level Participatory Budgeting Committees or suggesting the Metropolitan-level Committee directly through the Internet or mail if the ordinary citizen thinks his or her issue is beyond the district-level.

If a suggestion is related with a district-level issue, it will be reviewed by the district-level committee initially. By institutionalizing the dual process from the district to the metropolitan level, opportunities of participation are guaranteed for the locals to understand and discuss their own issues actively (Kim, 2014). Considering the budget allowance for each district, the district-level committee reviews the suggestions from the locals and chooses some of them to submit to the metropolitan-level committee.

The metropolitan-level committee then classifies the suggestions by the above eight policy fields, and each respective subcommittee deliberates on them. The core of the Citizen Participatory Budgeting System in Seoul Metropolitan Government lies in the role for the eight subcommittees. Before assigning members to each subcommittee, the city government provides a program for educating all citizen members to enhance their understanding of the system. After the program is over, the citizen members are affiliated with each subcommittee according to individual preferences. In each subcommittee, the members can participate in the budgeting process quite actively to choose the suggested plans to submit the General Committee, such as hearing from the proposer, on-the-spot investigating, and modifying the detailed budget items autonomously. Finally, in the General Committee, all 250 members participate in deciding the final business plans of the participatory budget by majority vote (Jeong, 2014).

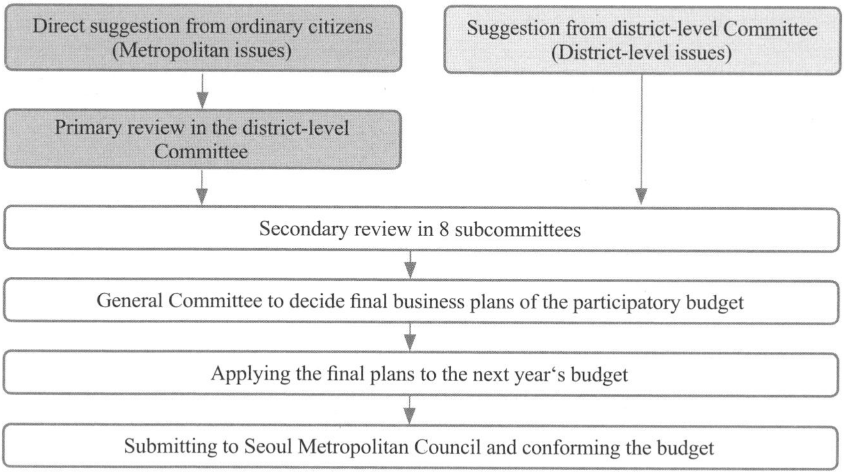

(source: Participatory Budgeting in Seoul Metropolitan City [PBSMC], n.d.-a)

Figure 2-2 Process of the Citizen Participatory Budgeting System in Seoul Metropolitan City

2.2. Minwon 24: integrated online civil service

Korea has been well known for its continuing efforts for pursuing e-Government as a crucial means to make its government more competitive (Ministry of Public Administration and Security & National Information Society Agency, 2014: 4). The Kim Dae-jung administration made the implementation of e-Government a major national priority in the 2000s. It concentrated on 11 major tasks for e-Government (2001–2002), and the Roh Moo-hyun administration initiated 31 major tasks for the e-Government roadmap (2003–2007).

The integrated online channel for processing civil services, Minwon 24, is well-known as an example of public sector innovation. Although Minwon 24 was established in 2002 as one of the core initiatives to promote e-government in Korea, it is still one of the most widely used online civil service systems in

Korea. In its inception, the portfolio of services available online were limited. Now, through Minwon 24, citizens can access 51% of public services online. Minwon 24 undoubtedly contributes to reducing the costs of traveling for civil service applications on the side of citizens and the costs of providing offline services on the government side (OECD, n.d.-a).

Minwon 24, however, was not created quickly or easily. There were years of ongoing investments made by the Korean government. From 2002 to 2008, 300 most requested services were put online based upon the suggestions and comments from government agencies and citizens. As a part of the civil services advancement project in 2009, 5,000 civil services were reviewed as candidates for their online compatibility. Ministries in charge of those services also provided their opinions about the potential benefits of putting those services online. After all these efforts, an online portal named Minwon 24 was launched offering 3,020 public services.

Collaboration of multiple agencies across organizational boundaries is essential for Minwon 24. It was a huge challenge to motivate all the related parties to join the Minwon 24 initiative. Coordinating the conflicting demands from the participating organizations was a daunting task. Difficulties experienced include how to resolve the concerns raised by the citizens regarding data security, digital divide, and data ownership, among many others. To overcome all the setbacks, the Korean government organized numerous conferences and workshops at which all the authorities concerned developed shared visions for the online civil service system (OECD, n.d.-b).

2.3. e-People (Shinmungo): Electronic Participation System

The Korean government launched a web portal for online petition and discussion, named "Shinmungo," which provides an integrated one-stop channel for electronic participation. The name "Shinmungo" (Big Drum) originates from a historical record where people could strike a drum when they wanted to have a say in government affairs during the Joseon Dynasty (e-People, n.d.-a). The Korean government initiated the e-People in 2005, and it connected more than 900 central and local government organizations and other public institutions in 2015. e-People connects all branches of government at every level to the citizens. The use of e-People has become quite popular, with 2.9 million petitions filled in 2015 alone (KOREA.net, n.d.).

This service was needed because it was difficult for citizens to figure out where and how to express their opinions and make petitions. Citizens did not always know which ministries or agencies were responsible. Through e-People, citizens can report unfair administrative handling and infringements of their rights and interests, and make suggestions for improving policies, as shown in Figure 2-3

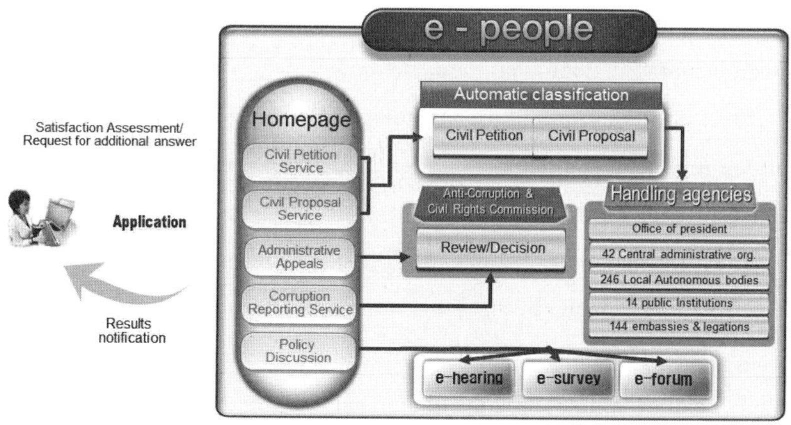

(Source: Participedia, n.d.-b)

Figure 2-3 e-People Operation Procedure

Shortly after a petition is received, it is transferred to the relevant government agency. Then the agency will review the content and take appropriate action to resolve the problem within a certain period of time as promptly as possible. In this procedure, a petitioner can be informed of the overall procedures and the result of his or her petition. Thanks to a rapid development of Information and Communication Technologies, the average speed with which the petitions are resolved through e-People has been accelerating, and thus the level of satisfaction of its users has also increased significantly. Furthermore, access to e-People is not limited only to Koreans. It enables foreigners access the website and make petitions. e-People services are provided in 14 languages other than Korean (KOREA.net, n.d.).

2.4. Public Service Charter for Improving Public Service

The Public Service Charter was introduced to promote ideals of customer-centered public service provision. The main goal of the charter is to improve the quality of public services and thereby enhance citizens' confidence in the government (Kim, 2006).

The Public Service Charter stipulates the service quality standards that service recipients can expect. Under the charter, clear standards of service delivery should be published and well displayed at service points; the citizens should be enabled to file complaints if the service received is substandard; there should be transparency in the delivery processes; information about available services should be explained in plain and understandable language; citizens should be allowed to choose the kind of services they want and their inputs on services offered be sought where necessary (Moon, 2004).

The United Kingdom pioneered the use of the citizen's charter in the early

1990s. A large number of other countries benchmarked the UK in embracing the charter initiative. The Public Service Charter was introduced in South Korea by the 70th Presidential Order and Guidelines on the Enactment of the Public Service Charter during the Kim Dae-Jung administration in 1998. The Public Service Charter was first applied to 10 organizations in 1998, and in 2004, there were 7,582 different Public Service Charters in the central and the local governments. The Public Service Charter spread so quickly in Korea because the global trend towards enhanced customer satisfaction in the public sector was firmly embraced by the Korean government and the implementation of local autonomy policies created the incentives for local governments to improve the interaction with citizens.

Key elements comprising the Public Service Charter are as follow. First, it has to inform its clients of the detailed service performance criteria. This allows its clients to predict in advance what service they will receive. Next, the Public Service Charter has to specify the detailed procedures for its clients to suggest how they are satisfied with the service. For this purpose, the corresponding organization should provide specific information so that clients can contact them at any time. Lastly, criteria on correction or compensation for erroneous service have to be specified in the Public Service Charters. That is, if there are some defects in a provided service, the corresponding organization should correct them promptly, and then provide appropriate compensation for them to resolve the client's complaint. It should be noted that the organization decides the correction or compensation by the autonomous service performance criteria, not by relevant acts (Song, 2005).

In the Roh Moo-hyun administration, however, the Public Service Charter was criticized for being too focused on formalities and because performance improvement did not meet the expectations. To solve this problem, the Roh

Moo-hyun administration tried to introduce a "Customer Service Standard" system as an alternative.

The Customer Service Standard was presented in the Public Administration Reform Roadmap of the Presidential Committee on Government Innovation and Decentralization, which supervises the administrative reforms in the Roh administration (Kim, 2006). Under the Road map, the Roh administration set to the goal of improving customer's satisfaction on quality of public service of the overall central government by more than 10% during his incumbency. In order to achieve the goal, a certification system for the Public Service Charter was implemented. By the certification system, each organization is evaluated in terms of whether it includes substantial contents related with "core" service that they can provide in the Public Service Charter. They expected this system to serve as an incentive for each organization to create a better Public Service Charter (Presidential Committee on Government Innovation & Decentralization [PCGID], n.d.).

VI. Lessons Gained from Korean Governance Reform Experiences

The government of Vietnam is heavily committed to necessary reforms to ensure good and accountable state governance. A set of comprehensive state governance reform agendas for the period 2016–2020 and the years beyond are indicated in the Prime Minister's Decision No 225/QD-TTg dated 4/2/2016. The Vietnamese reformers expected that this reform initiative would help to improve the state governance performance in coming years. However, from the Korean experiences, the most important factor for the successful implementation of reforms measures is to ensure that Decision No 225 is enforced and enacted by all related stakeholders at all levels of government administration. Any recommendation for further advancement of Vietnamese government should be focused on the following directions:

- Enhance the government's responsibility, autonomy, and accountability in implementing its functions and mandates. This principle should be undertaken at all levels of administration, both central and local. At the same time, they should be responsible for their decisions by law;
- Expand the role of civil society and citizen participation in policy formulation, raising awareness of public issues and monitoring the reform agenda implementation process. In fact, the role of civil society is always granted by the law; however, in practice, participation of civil society in policy development is still limited. In this regard, civil society should play a proactive role in all steps of the policy formulation process and consider this as its right rather than remaining passive; and
- Improve the public service reform/quality through enhancing the performance management system. Especially, the government should consider public satisfaction as a crucial factor determining the quality of public service performance. The government should use modern and independent tools in assessing quality of public services and utilize the information for improving the public service provision.

These three points can be utilized as filters to sort useful implications from the Korean experiences.

1. Implications of Korean Experiences for Improving the State Capacity of Vietnam

1.1. Restructuring of Local Government Organizations

Governments at all levels, including People's Councils and People's Committees, take full responsibility for socio-economic development as well as security and order in the areas under their authority. This requirement leads to the organizational structure of the government at all levels being built in line with the central government. This means the local government structure is almost replicating that of the central government. This situation leads to cumbersome machinery, uncontrollable payroll increase, and low efficiency of the apparatus. Therefore, as in the case of Korea's local government restructuring, the Vietnamese government has been seeking alternative ways of balancing the authorities and responsibilities between the central and local governments. Issues of restructuring local government organizations together with downsizing both the central and local-level agencies were discussed at the 14th National Assembly meeting.

The experiences of restructuring local governments in Korea may provide useful considerations for crafting Vietnamese reform. Similar to the current situation in Vietnam, Korean local governments had mirror images of central government structures and did not have capabilities of implementing policies and conducting administrative works effectively. Korean local governments were excessively dependent upon the control and support from the central government. Therefore, there is one big difference between Korea and Vietnam in that Vietnam is experiencing the problems of centralization and decentralization simultaneously while the major local government restructuring issue in Korea was how to reduce the control from the central government. In terms of advancing economic development, Vietnamese local governments hold too much freedom to make decisions for investments and business development at the provincial level. On the other hand, local governments lack capabilities and incentives to restructure themselves without proper guidelines and supports from the central authority.

Although institutional contexts for local government restructuring are so different between two countries, the Korean experience of restructuring local government organizations may provide some important implications for Vietnam. Most of all, the Vietnamese government needs to specify the areas in which the central government can provide administrative guidelines and mandates with which local governments can develop their restructuring plans. The central government's roles should be focused on providing core principles that local governments must follow, such as setting the scope of changes within which local governments can choose the scale of changes for their own, and fixing the time frame in which restructuring should be accomplished. However, the central government's role is not limited to developing the plan itself. There should be champions in the central government to lead, advise, monitor, and evaluate the progress and results of local government reforms. These leadership roles should be executed by the public bureaucracy together with think-tank institutions providing technical assistance for restructuring. In the case of Korea, the Korea Institute of Public Administration and the Korea Research Institute for Local Administration conducted a full-scale investigation to identify the administrative tasks to be transferred from the central to the local governments. This does not mean that local governments should be passive followers. In the Korean case, representatives from the local governments participated in the planning process to improve the feasibility of restructuring. Likewise, it is highly recommended for Vietnamese local governments to participate and voice their priorities and concerns from the very beginning of developing restructuring plans.

1.2. Special Account for Balanced National Development

Recently, the Vietnamese government has devised programs to support balanced developments of local communities. Beginning from 2016, Vietnam continues to implement two National Targeted Programs. One is the Sustainable Poverty Reduction program designed for poor districts and communes, which are often located in mountainous provinces and populated by many ethnic minorities. The other is the New Rural Development Program aimed at bringing up rural communes through the achievement of 19 socio-economic criteria. However, the budget for these two programs comes from the central and local budgets rather than forming a separate mechanism, such as in Korea (Prime Minister, 2016a, 2016b).

The key motivation of crating the Special Account for Balanced National Development was clear in Korea. Korea reached the point at which further socio-economic development would not be possible without balanced development throughout the country. Likewise, Vietnam is rapidly approaching the point at which the benefits of economic developments concentrate on major cities and provinces. Therefore, this is the proper time to think about adopting aggressive measures to promote balanced national development. Considering the fragmentation of the state as depicted above, pursuing balanced national development in Vietnam might be far more challenging than in Korea where the central government was maintaining relatively strong political and administrative influences over local governments. Two major issues need to be customized for the Vietnamese context. First, the Vietnamese government should identify the proper revenue sources of account. Second, a proper division of labor between local and central governments should be established.

1.3. Executive Agency System

Among the issues of weakening the state capacity of Vietnam, excessive commercialization of SOEs has been considered as a serious barrier to the advancement of marketization and the promotion of administrative effectiveness. The Executive Agency System was chosen by the Korean government after experiencing many failures in the previous attempts of vitalizing various forms of SOEs and corporations. Vietnam is also carrying out similar activities – namely, the Socialization of Public Services. On February 14, 2015, the Government issued Decree No. 16/2015/ ND-CP regulating autonomy mechanism of Public Service Delivery Agencies (PSDAs). The decree identifies the basic public services in the fields of education, health care, sports, culture, science and technology, and media. Then, these public services are divided into two main categories: public services funded by the state budget, and public services are funded by the market. According to this provision, PSDAs would have three autonomy rights: autonomy in performance of tasks, autonomy in organizational structure, and autonomy in human resources. For a successful implementation of PSDAs, the managerial arrangements of the Executive Agency System need to be seriously considered for Vietnam. One of the limitations of Korean SOE reform was that the central government was trying to maintain its control over the SOEs business management too closely. Since SOEs are located in both public and private spheres, government bureaucracy cannot effectively monitor the business processes of SOEs as they do within the government organizations. A better way of holding the SOEs accountable while not impeding the market mechanism is governing the SOEs through managing the chief executives responsible for the results. Specific steps for developing a Vietnamese version of the Executive Agency System should be developed through cautious review of the details of Korea case.

2. Implications of Korean Experiences for Improving the Accountability of Vietnamese Government

2.1. Citizen Participatory Budgeting System

Active citizen participation is considered as one of the critical conditions determining the development level of a society. Vietnam recognizes the necessity of increasing citizen participation in terms of providing citizens more access to government information and more opportunities of participating in policy making and evaluation. Facing the societal demands for more citizen participation and pursing balanced development throughout the country, the Vietnamese government may consider adopting the citizen participatory budgeting system as a stepping-stone toward the full-fledged development of citizen participation.

Yet, Vietnam has no equivalent experience at the centrally-run city's level. According to the National Assembly's Ordinance No. 34 in 2007 on *the exercise of democracy in communes, wards and towns*, at the commune level, ordinary people have been granted the rights to discuss and directly make decisions including those on finance, infrastructure, and public welfare facilities within the commune. More specifically, the Ordinance requires that any decision being voted for by more than fifty percent of the commune residential voters will come in effect and be enforceable for the local governments. A fair expectation is that some large and developed cities and provinces, which have been adopting other administrative reform measures aggressively, may initiate the adoption of the citizen participatory budgeting system. The specific lessons to be gained from such pilot experiments would produce useful policy implications to develop best practices applicable for other Vietnamese local governments.

2.2. Minwon 24: Integrated Online Civil Service

Providing government information and public services online has been an important policy agenda in Vietnam. The main shortcoming in Vietnam's efforts for putting civil services online is that there is no focal point of implementation at the central government level. However, some provinces have enacted the one-stop-shop Public Administrative Center (PAC) where citizens can enjoy the benefits of integrated procedures. The leading provinces include Quang Ninh, Da Nang, Binh Duong, and Hanoi. Quang Ninh province alone has established both Provincial Public administrative center and 14 district-level PACs in all districts in its jurisdiction. According to the Quang Ninh province's latest reports, 100% of administrative procedures are included in the provincial PAC. The on-time processing rate is usually over 95%. The public satisfaction index for public administrative procedures is also at over 80%. In Vietnam, the average number of administrative procedures at the provincial level is over 1000, at the district level about 200, and at the commune level about 100. The example of Quang Ninh indicates that Vietnam has a potential to develop a Vietnamese version of Minwon 24. When Korea was starting E-government in the mid-1990s and early 2000s, several local governments led the development of E-government transformation. Experiences gained from leading local governments were shared with other local governments and acquired by the central government. Such initiatives also played an important role in promoting the system integration industry of Korea by creating a huge public sector market.

From a strategic point of view, developing a fully integrated online civil service portal may be suitable for a long-term goal. What is urgent for Vietnam is probably creating an IT governance model identifying the actors to participate the national E-government initiatives as described in *Government's Resolution No 36a/NQ-CP dated 14/10/2015*. The strong leadership awarded to the steering committee of E-government is considered as one of the most important factors for the success of E-government in Korea. More than any other reform initiatives, E-government-oriented transformation should be well supported by highly capable think-tanks. In Korea, multiple research institutes specialized in ICT development and policy provided professional technical supports for policy making, system development, and even for training public employees. On top of that, integrating online services is possible only when the government has the capacity to analyze the entire business processes and streamline and adapt them to fully utilize the technical potentials of ICT.

2.3. e-People (Shinmungo): electronic participation system

E-participation is considered the most advanced stage of E-government in the E-government development stage models. Vietnam was ranked 89th out of 193 countries and territories in the E-government Development Index (EGDI) in 2016 according to the e-government survey 2016 conducted by the United Nations. Vietnam has issued Resolution 36a/NQ-CP on E-government with the aim of boosting the development of E-government, improving the quality and efficiency of state agencies, and better serving the people and business.

A meaningful step toward making an electronic participation system similar to e-People has been made in Vietnam. According to a report on the implementing of Decree 36a in 2016, 29 out of 30 ministries and government agencies and 59 out of 63 provinces and cities have adopted plan of action to establish E-government. The central government has developed some websites to provide better service for people's participation, such as e.gov.vn, nguoidan.chinhphu.vn (meaning Citizens to Government) and doanhnghiep.chinhphu.vn (meaning Business to Government). Both websites provide businesses and citizens with a system of receiving, answering, and responding to people's requests. This is an interactive channel between the government and the people led by the Minister, Head of the Government Office. People can easily access the system from computers and internet-connected mobile devices to send, track, and receive feedback answers for their requests on delay behavior, causing troubles, or improper implementation of regulations of cadres, civil servants, or public employees in handling administrative procedures, or on wrongful or illegal mechanisms, policies or administrative procedures Through this system, state administrative agencies at all levels are able to receive and respond to feedback and suggestions of people in each field, each handling agency; All feedback, request and recommendations of the people are received to by the Government. The Office of Government has the responsibility to guide, monitor, synthesize, encourage, and inspect ministries, sectors, and localities to respond to the feedback and recommendations of the people. Again, what is needed for Vietnam is identifying the barriers against implementing the E-government initiatives.

2.4. Public Service Charter for Improving Public Service

Quality of public services is a function of various managerial factors.

Adequate inputs including financial and human resources supported by proper management capacities and institutional arrangements are all required for improving public service quality. From this perspective, Vietnam's recent initiatives titled as Provincial Competitiveness Index (PCI), Provincial Governance and Public Administration Performance Index (PAPI), Public Administration Reform Index (PAR Index), and Satisfaction Index of Public Administrative Services (SIPAS) are important efforts for improving government accountability. PCI is implemented by Vietnam Chamber of Commerce and Industry (VCCI), PAPI is by the UN Development Program (UNDP), PAR Index is by Ministry of Home Affairs, and SIPAS is jointly implemented by the Ministry of Home Affairs, Central Committee of the Vietnam Fatherland Front (VFF) and the Central Office of the Veterans Association of Vietnam (VAVN). Measuring satisfaction is an important managerial method to improve public service quality, because measuring satisfaction itself can pressure public employees to improve service quality, the information on service satisfaction can be utilized for learning, and incentive systems based on satisfaction can be developed as a new motivation tool.

The Public Service Charter can complement the current efforts aimed at improving citizens' satisfaction with public service. Public employees' voluntary efforts will make a huge difference in the results of service quality improvement. Additional efforts should be made to change the norms about the proper relationship between the public employees as service providers and the citizens as customers receiving public services. Vietnam should review whether the SIPAS initiative is well targeted on citizens' expectation or too focused on administrative purposes by applying the principal notions of the public service charter.

VII. Policy Recommendations

1. Prioritizing Korean Models Adopted for Vietnamese Governance Reform

The analyses of the seven Korean cases and the institutional, political, social, and economical contexts of Vietnamese governance reform agendas show that the Korean cases suggest relevant and potentially useful implications for Vietnamese governance reform. Nevertheless, their applicability varies because of the issues uniquely related to each reform agenda. After a series of discussions, we reached a consensus that four Korean examples are readily applicable to the Vietnamese governance reform: the Special Account for Balanced National Development, Citizen Participatory Budgeting System, e-People (Shinmungo), and Public Service Charter.

A Special Account for Balanced National Development may provide Vietnam with a new mechanism to mobilize financial resources for a nation-wide rural area development program. According to the PM's decision dated June 8, 2016, on the approval of the nationally targeted program of New Rural Development until 2020, Vietnam needs to allocate around 193,000 billion VND (or 9 billion USD). Most of the budget is supposed to come from the central and local government budget on an annual basis, yet it would be very challenging to secure the budget for this program under the existing budget constraints. A specially designated fund for the rural development program can be an alternative way of mobilizing and overseeing the resources for the targeted program.

Citizen Participatory Budgeting may draw significant attention from the government as well as from the general public as something unprecedented in Vietnam. It would promote the people's voice in making decisions for governmental activities that traditionally have been considered solely as the state's responsibility. Under Ordinance 34 on the exercise of democracy in communes, wards, and towns, the decision-making power of the people on budget is limited to communes and wards. Citizen Participatory Budgeting will enable citizens to get involved in major issues of municipal budgeting to a larger extent and at a higher level. Thus, the Citizen Participatory Budgeting system could be regarded as a novel mechanism of direct democracy to complement the existing representative democracy.

e-People (Shinmungo) is also a good example of increasing direct interactions between the people and the governmental authorities. Through such a system, the government would be able to respond to and serve the needs of the people better and faster. Moreover, Shinmungo can be a convenient channel for the people to make policy suggestions to the government. We expect that Shinmungo may be a benchmarking example for the websites such as nguoidan.chinhphu.vn and doanhnghiep.chinhphu.vn in Vietnam which are currently in the early stage of development.

Issuance and application of a Public Service Charter would be a driver for the citizen satisfaction-oriented public service improvement. The Public Administration Reform Master Program of Vietnam has already set the requirements for improving the quality of administrative services. To enhance the convenience of processing administrative procedures, One-Stop-Shop sections have been set up in all communes, wards, and districts, and many provinces have established Centers for Public Administration. However, the process of administrative services still lacks transparency, the quality of service is low, and the risk of bribery is still high. The application of a Public

Service Charter, first to the Centers for Public Administration and later to the commune-level OSS sections, will contribute to increasing transparency in the administrative procedures, reducing bribery, and improving the quality of public administrative services.

We categorized these four model cases from the Vietnamese government perspective by using two dimensions. First, we assessed the speed of reform required for each initiative if it is ever adopted by Vietnam. It ranges drastic or gradual. Second, we determined what scale of change would be appropriate for each reform. This dimension ranges from small- and moderate-scale to large- and full-scale changes. Three HCMA experts conducted a brainstorming session and suggested that the four selected models could be categorized as illustrated in Figure 2-4 A Special Account for Balanced Development should be implemented rather promptly at full scale. This is because the agenda of balanced development has already been initiated by the PM and the problems of fragmentation are becoming more serious as Vietnamese economic development continues. e-People (Shinmungo) is also considered a model that needs to be adopted and implemented quickly. Yet, this model would be more appropriate for implementing on a relatively small scale. The conceptual model, system structure, and applications developed for Shinmungo can be applied to Vietnam's own projects, such as nguoidan.chinhphu.vn and doanhnghiep.chinhphu.com, through some customization. Shinmungo's experience would be very useful for Vietnam to reduce the cost to be incurred from trial and error development. A Public Service Charter is relatively easy to adopt, because it is focused more on proclaiming and spreading the notion of citizen satisfaction as an important public service value. In comparison, it could be relatively challenging to adopt Citizen Participatory Budgeting because it requires significant changes in the existing budgeting and policy making procedures. Considering the growing importance of expanding the channels of citizen participation, Citizen Participatory Budgeting could be an important juncture for Vietnam in its ongoing efforts for strengthening accountability to citizens.

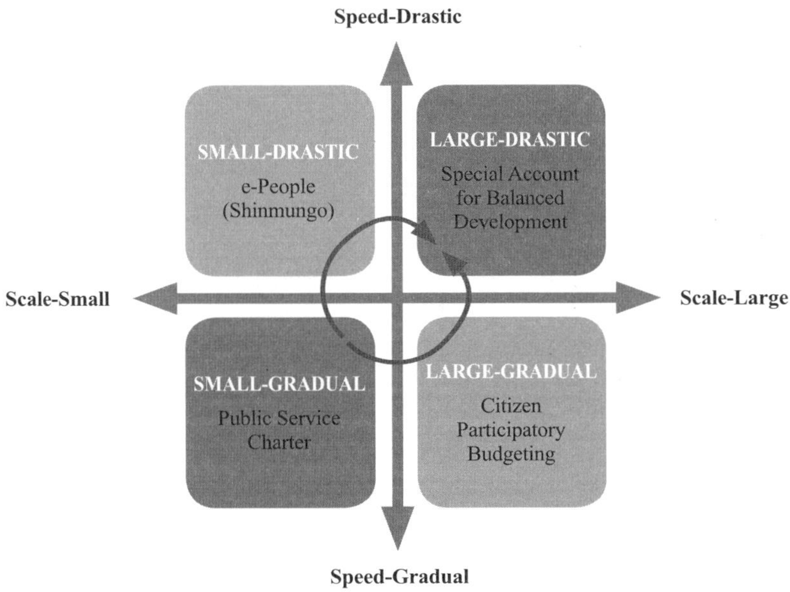

Figure 2-4 Categorizing Korean Cases from the Vietnamese Perspective

Besides the categorization of the models, we further assessed the expected duration of each reform agenda, if they are ever adopted by the Vietnamese government. Figure 2-5 shows that a Public Service Charter is considered as a project that would show results in a short term. Citizen Participatory Budgeting and e-People would take longer to implement than a Public Service Charter, yet the duration of these two reform agendas could be shorter than a Special Account for Balanced Development. The curved arrows in Figure 2-4 indicate that government reforms would be effectively implemented from the small-scale gradual reform agenda first to the large-scale drastic reform agenda later because of the differences in duration expected from the agendas.

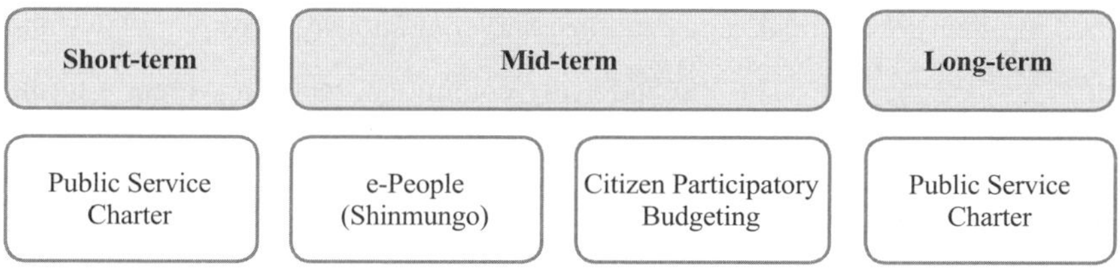

Figure 2-5 Expected Duration of Reform Agendas

2. Policy Recommendations for Four Selected Models

It is beyond the purpose of this report to outline the detailed action plans for all four selected models. Probably useful for Vietnam is developing policy guidelines that the Vietnamese government needs to consider to avoid the problems that Korea has experienced and to customize the Korean models to the Vietnamese context. For that purpose, this section discusses governing mechanisms and implementation strategies adopted by the Korean government for the four governance reform initiatives and then suggests recommendations for Vietnam.

2.1. Public Service Charter

Governing mechanism: Multiple organizations joined the governing process to implement the Public Service Charter (PSC) in Korea when it was in full-scale operation in 2003. Figure 2-6 describes the key actors and their roles and relationships. The Ministry of Government Administration and Home Affairs (currently, Ministry of the Interior) led the deployment of the PSC by developing the master plan for PSC, monitoring and evaluating the status of the PSC in other government organizations, and continuously improving laws and rules applied the PSC. The PSC advisory committee, reporting directly to the Minister, was composed of experts. Meanwhile, the PSC supporting unit was staffed and managed by the Korea Institute of Public Administration.

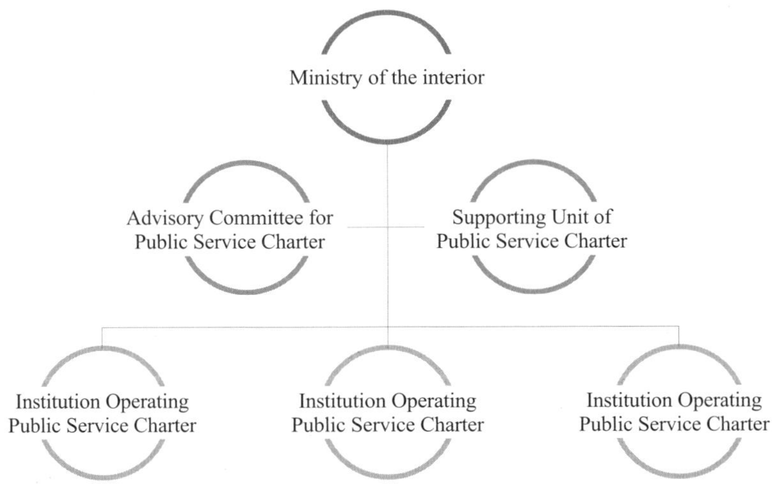

(Source: Geum, 2003, p.46)

Figure 2-6 Public Service Charter Governing Structure

Implementation: The PSC initiative in Korea encountered numerous problems in implementation. In the early stage, the PSC was not widely recognized by the citizens, who were supposed to be immediate beneficiaries of PSC. Many public organizations implementing PSC did not have internal organizational units designated for PSC; hence the implementation of PSC tended to be either slow or incomplete. Monitoring and evaluation of PSC was weak at the agency level and the Ministry of the Interior's monitoring and evaluation system was not effective in the field organizations. Other frequently cited problems of PSC implementation include the lack of proper incentives to promote public officials' commitment to the PSC and the absence of feedback loop to improve the PSC practices.

Recommendation for Vietnam: For successful adoption of a PSC in Vietnam, the earlier difficulties experienced by the Korean government should be avoided. It should be noted that a PSC is not aimed at introducing new governance tools which can immediately produce tangible results. Rather, a PSC sets the principles for how to increase the quality of public services and how to enhance the citizens' satisfaction with public services. Roles to be played by each participating organization should be carefully defined to make the PSC sustainable. Proper monitoring and evaluation is another critical condition for success. Otherwise, the PSC may become another source of red tape.

2.2. e-People (Shinmungo)

Governing mechanism: Shinmungo was developed and run by the Anti-Corruption and Civil Rights Commission, which was established in 2008 at the ministerial level. It upholds the mission of building a transparent and fair society and protects people's right and interests. It is important to note that one of the key success factors we identified in the history of Korean e-Government is the presence of leading organization. The Commission has been championing Shinmungo since its inception in 2004. The Commission's role was not limited to simply putting the off-line participation venues onto the online platform. It continuously provided all the participating ministries, agencies, and local government with consulting and education services to enhance their capacities of processing citizens' appeals, petitions, suggestions, or any other requests channeled through Shinmungo.

Implementation: This project has been implemented following three stages: pilot operation, integration of 49 central ministries and agencies, and expansion to 246 local governments and 14 major public agencies, as shown in Figure 2-7 Even after the initial development period, the Commission has continued to make investment for the service infrastructure and expanded the e-government services interlinked with Shinmungo. As the service matured, needs for collaboration between organizations also increased. In 2016, for example, the Commission collaborated with the Ministry of the Interior to conduct a comprehensive evaluation of civil applications that used to be conducted by the Commission and the Ministry separately. Efforts of collaboration were even extended beyond the sectoral boundaries. The Commission provides the Q&A services about civil applications and policies through private web portals such as Naver and Daum, which are the main search engines of Korea (Anti-Corruption & Civil Rights Commission [ACRC], 2017).

Pilot Operation ('03. 08. ~ '05. 08.)	**Integrating Central Government Services** ('05. 11. ~ '06. 07.)	**Integrating Public Organizations at all levels** ('06. 10. ~ '08. 02.)
• Confirmed as e-Government road map project • Pilot operation in seven central government organizations.	• Integration of 49 central ministries and agencies' systems	• Expansion to 246 local governments and 14 major public agencies

(Source: ACRC, 2017, p.65)

Figure 2-7 e-People Development Stages

Recommendations for Vietnam: Shinmungo is considered as a successful governance reform case in Korea because it removed many of the chronic administrative inefficiencies. It reduced the civil application service time and improved the quality of services, transparency, and accountability. It is also important to note that Shinmungo has been adopted or is being considered for adoption by numerous other countries, such as Tunisia, Indonesia, and Uzbekistan. Therefore, we would recommend the Vietnamese government to appoint a ministerial-level government unit to lead the citizen participation reform including the development of the e-People system. This unit should be empowered to develop plans, lead the development process, coordinate participating public organizations, and attract the financial and technical supports for Korean agencies or any other capable organizations (ACRC, 2017).

2.3. Citizen Participatory Budgeting

Governing mechanism: Citizen Participatory Budgeting (CPB) in Korea was first introduced by a couple of local governments in early 2000. The nation-wide adoption of CPB was made possible in 2003 by the Roh Moo-hyun administration, which stressed the importance of balanced development in all areas in Korea (Park & Nam, 2012; Kwon, 2015). In order to adopt the CPB, the government had to establish a legal basis to do so. For example, in 2005, the Local Finance Act was revised to allow CPB, and the 2004 Guidelines for Local Government Budget included the clauses to recommend the local governments to adopt CPB. In 2010, the Ministry of Public Administration and Security (currently, Ministry of the Interior) distributed three different types of CPB Municipal Ordinances samples. Each local government can choose one form of ordinance most suitable for its jurisdiction. Therefore, there are some variations across local governments in terms of the volume of budget to be determined by CPB and the scope of public affairs to be funded by CPB (Kwon, 2015). From experience, we find that there should be a balanced distribution of responsibilities between the central and local governments. The central government should be responsible for establishing a legal basis of CPB and also provide policy guidelines with which local governments can develop their own CPB principles customized for their own needs.

Implementation: A typical procedure of operating CPB is illustrated in Figure 2-8 In general, CPB-funded government programs or projects are initiated by residents. Residents can propose agendas via website, mailing, faxing, or visiting the government office. Public hearings, surveys, and debates are often utilized for collecting public and professional opinions.

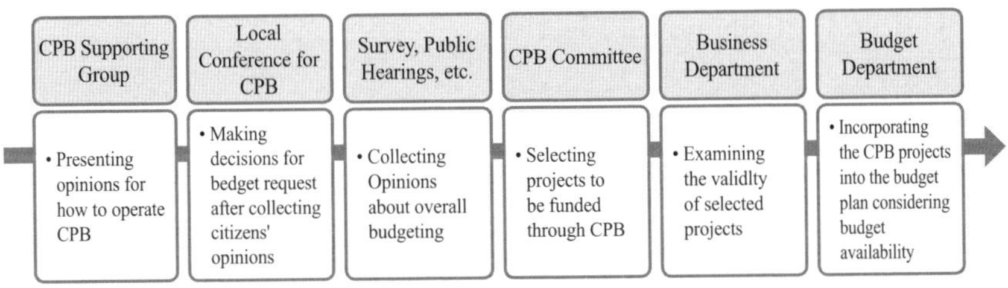

(Source: Lim, Lee, & Seo, 2013, p. 93)

Figure 2-8 Citizen Participatory Budge Operation Procedure

Recommendations for Vietnam: Exemplary practices of CPB can be easily drawn from Korea as well as from other countries that have already adopted CPB. Vietnam needs to scan and test the feasibility of different models by carefully considering the constraints and opportunities of the Vietnamese situation. Vietnam has already recognized and stressed the importance of democracy at the commune level. For small jurisdictions, Vietnam may consider adopting best practices from leading Korean municipalities that have a long history of CPB. These municipalities include the Dong district in Ulsan metropolitan city and the Buk district in Gwangju metropolitan city. For provincial or metropolitan governments such as Quang Ninh Province and Da Nang city, Seoul Metropolitan Government could be a useful benchmark. In 2014, Seoul selected 223 projects approved through CPB. The total budget request for the projects amounted to 50.3billion KRW (PBSMC, n.d.-b). Probably the biggest challenge for Vietnam will be how to motivate citizens to join the CPB and how to maintain their continuous interests in community affairs. It is, therefore, /recommended to initiate pilot projects in some large metropolitan municipalities where citizens are more active and vocal regarding local policy issues.

2.4. Special Account for Balanced Development

Governing mechanism: The Special Account for Balanced Development (hereinafter, the Account) was one of the presidential agendas in the Roh Moo-hyun administration. Although there were serious disputes about the Account, the National Committee on Balanced National Development, which was one of the key presidential committees, continued to develop the plan for the Account with strong support from President Roh. The Committee played the role of coordinating key ministries: Ministry of Industry and Energy (currently, Ministry of Trade, Industry and Energy), Ministry of Planning and Budgeting (currently, Ministry of Strategy and Finance), and Ministry of Government Administration and Home Affairs (currently, Ministry of the Interior). The

Special Act of Balanced Development was drafted by the Committee and legislated in 2005 to provide legal guidance for the Account. One of the critical contributions of the Committee was that local governments' opinions were extensively collected and applied to the Act as well as the implementation plan (PCGID, 2008).

Implementation: A critical problem was encountered once the Account was put into practice: how to determine the total amount budget to be distributed to each local government rationally and fairly. Since there was only limited time available for developing the rules of distribution in the first year, the Ministry of Planning and Budgeting improvised a formula based upon the previous three years' total budget sizes of provincial governments. To avoid the confusion and dissatisfaction, the Korea Institute of Public Finance (KIPF) developed a regression model to estimate the amount of budget to be allocated for each province the next year (PCGID, 2008).

Recommendations for Vietnam: Considering the complexity of the Account model, Vietnam should plan ahead and start the program when important arrangements are in place. As the Korean case shows, the Account involves multiple central ministries as well as all levels of local governments. Adoption of this model also requires changing and legislating laws and recalibrating the existing budgetary system. A very careful study should be conducted in advance by cooperating with the Korean government organizations involved in operating the Account. Especially, collaboration between the KIPF and an equivalent Vietnamese think tank is a necessary condition to implement the model in Vietnam.

3. Overcoming Barriers against Governance Reform

Developing strategies to overcome barriers is very important for successful governance reform. We believe that three issues should be carefully addressed. These issues are not limited to specific subjects of governance reform; rather they are associated with the characteristics of Vietnamese bureaucratic culture and political leadership.

First of all, the Vietnamese government needs to be well prepared for dealing with the resistance from the people with vested interests in maintaining the status quo. Those people who benefit the most from existing management system tend to hold strong political influence. A high-ranking official of the Communist Party of Vietnam states, "the threat from vested interests is the biggest threat among all threats"(translated from Vu Ngoc Hoang, "Nguy cơ “lợi ích nhóm” bao trùm lên mọi nguy cơ khác", Nhân dân Newspaper, 28/07/2016). Since governance reform pays attention to how to change the existing mechanism and remove policy loopholes, as vested interests will use all their resources to resist the changes. Such resistance is further strengthened by Vietnam’s collective political leadership principle in decision making: a decision will be adopted only with clear majority or even must be unanimously agreed. If there are still different opinions, the status quo will be preserved until an absolute majority is achieved. Hence, blocking governance reform efforts is easier than promoting them.

The next issue is to eliminate the public administration inertia accumulated in the Vietnamese bureaucratic culture as well as in the fragmented Vietnamese administrative system. The inertia of public administration is a phenomenon embedded in the administrative system. Most people tend to feel comfortable with the old administrative routines and procedures. Moreover, public bureaucrats are the ones who will implement reform, but they are also the targets of the reform. As analyzed above, the fragmentation of government authority also contributes to the administrative inertia as coordination in the implementation process is very difficult to achieve. Thus, strengthening the mechanisms of controlling and monitoring public bureaucrats is important. It is noteworthy that the current prime minister established a special task force (*Tổ công tác của thủ tướng*, the decision No 1642/QĐ-Ttg, 8/2016) to inspect the implementation of PM orders and instructions in many branches and provinces to overcome administrative inertia.

The last (but not least) challenge is to overcome the lack of strong and cohesive leadership originating from the Vietnamese political system. This has been an ongoing dilemma making successful reform hard to achieve. The Communist Party of Vietnam and the government have both expressed clear will to reform in many important documents, but reform remains very slow. Furthermore, cohesion among leaderships at various government levels is also weak, especially between the two most important leadership positions: head of party and head of People committee.

We can think of a couple of conditions that may help the Vietnamese government rise above the barriers and minimize the negative effects from the challenges. First, significant efforts should be made to promote the development of civil society. If the success of governance reform only depends on the good will of political leadership and government bureaucrats, Vietnamese governance reform initiatives might not reach the desired goals. Organized citizens' pressure on reform will mobilize political support for the reform and also provide reform ideas that cannot be thought of by the government bureaucracy. Second, Vietnam needs to drastically improve the capacities of national think-tanks specialized in the key governance areas.

Think-tanks staffed with top-notch experts have been one of the key success factors of Korea's development. Making investments for policy-oriented research agencies with a certain degree of independence from the executive power to investigate and publish governance reports is a precondition for harnessing accountability of the central and local government agencies. Think-tanks should be considered as a critical asset comprising the state capacity to set up development priorities. Besides, the presence of such institutions providing objective professional policy recommendations and guidelines is an important political instrument to secure political justification for governance reform.

CHAPTER THREE:

Human Resource Management (HRM) Reform

Yoon Jik Cho

Professor, Department of Public Administration, Yonsei University

CHAPTER THREE:

HUMAN RESOURCE MANAGEMENT (HRM) REFORM

I. Introduction

1. Vietnam 2035 and Administrative Reform

The World Bank and Ministry of Planning and Investment of Vietnam government worked together to establish a worthy vision for the Vietnam government. The report provides three pillars to achieve the suggested vision: 1) economic prosperity with environmental sustainability, 2) equity and social inclusion, and 3) a capable and accountable state. The report also emphasizes that to achieve the vision, "the institutions of governance will need to become modern, transparent, and fully rooted in the rule of law." (World Bank & Ministry of Planning and Investment of Vietnam, 2016, p.7). Those values are directly related to transparency and accountability, which are considered important in the reform initiatives of this research.

Among the three pillars suggested, the third pillar, "bolstering the state's capacity and accountability," is closely related to the government reform. The report argues that the following three conditions should be met to achieve the desired outcome from the third pillar: "1) a well-organized government, with a disciplined, meritocratic bureaucracy, 2) and adherence to market rationality in economic policy making, and 3) mechanisms to ensure checks and balances in the government and broad public participation" (World Bank & Ministry of Planning and Investment of Vietnam. 2016, p.11). Out of the three conditions, human resource management (HRM) reform is required to address the first condition.

2. TAP (Transparent, Accountable, and Performing) Government

If one accepts Vietnam 2035 as a critical vision statement for Vietnam, then the direction of reforms should focus on strengthening those three pillars. As noted, the administrative reform efforts should focus on the third pillar. Considering the fundamental concepts to achieve the third pillar, the second year research team provides a concept called "TAP (Transparent, Accountable, and Performing) government" that helps to achieve Vietnam 2035. The three values included in the acronym are quite familiar and have been discussed as critical factors to make high-quality government. Although those values are not very new, that does not mean that most countries have been successful in fully internalizing those values in their governance and seeing those values fully nurtured. Both developed and developing countries have room for improvement in actualizing those three values. Thus, by establishing TAP government, the Vietnam government will have sufficient capacity to successfully and sustainably achieve Vietnam 2035.

II. Global Trend of HRM reform

1. Human Resource Management Trend in Worldwide

Before discussing specified initiatives of HRM, it will be helpful to review the global trend of HRM. From the experiences of other developed countries, such as OECD countries, we will understand the advantages as well as challenges of employing new reform initiatives. According to a recent OECD report (2015), the past experience of OECD countries teaches that normative and structural conditions are critical in designing and implementing HRM initiatives. That is, like other reform initiatives, the HRM reform should consider specific contexts of a country and needs to consider what kind of incentives will be effective in the given context.

In spite of the necessity of considering contextual differences, one can also find common features about the overall change of HRM system. Representatively, in many countries, the main structure of employment in the public sector is the career civil service system. That is, the traditional idea was that working in the public sector differs from working in the private sector. For the successful conduct of public service, governments need to attract competent young people by offering a high level of job security, so that those job candidates can consider government work as their permanent job (OECD, 2003). However, during recent decades, the distinctiveness of public service has been blurred, and one may not find clear differences between government work and private sector work (Bourgon, 2008). Reform initiatives based on New Public Management (NPM) are based on the idea that private sector reform initiatives can be successfully transferred to the private sector.

By considering the overall reform trend of OECD countries, Bourgon (2008) identifies five common features: 1) hybridization of a career-based system and a position-based system, 2) emphasis on performance, 3) special attention to senior management,4) reduction of protection, immunity, and privilege, 5) decentralization of HRM policies. Lah and Perry (2008) argue that the basic ideas of the Civil Service Reform Act of 1978 in the U.S. were widely spread across countries. By reviewing HR institutions of 30 countries, they found that four elements, including performance appraisal, merit pay, senior executive service (SES), separating positive and regulatory personnel functions, are commonly adopted. Those elements overlap with the common features that Bourgon (2008) suggests. By using the typology of Bourgon (2008), the following sections will review each feature of global HRM trends.

A. Hybridization of Public Human Resources Models

First, what Bourgon (2008) found is that no civil service system in any country is a pure form of the career-based or position-based system. Rather, although the basis of the system is different, most countries have a hybrid HRM system. That is, if one country has a HRM system based on the career-based system, then that country seeks to introduce some elements of the position-based system. In the opposite case, the country tries to employ some elements of the career-based system. Moreover, the tendency to decrease the weaknesses of their own system becomes more active whether it is position-based or career-based system (Nigro & Nigro, 1986; Choi, 2015, reprise). For countries adopting the career-based system, the main challenges include how to make their civil servants responsible to a rapidly changing society and how to make them more specialized. On the other hand, for countries using the position-based system, the concern is how to develop generalists who have a comprehensive view and how to nurture common values among civil servants (Yoo & Park, 2013). For example, although Canada adopts a position-based model as their basic system, it also seeks to use a career-based approach for their senior managers and economists (Bourgon, 2008). Vietnam also seeks to mixture the career-based and the position-based systems. The issue will be how to integrate those two systems and at what levels.

B. Emphasis on Performance

Since the introduction of New Public Management, performance has been a core concern of the administrative reform. In the HRM reform, most governments have emphasized improving individual performance for better quality of public service. From this aspect, performance management became a core part of HRM (Kim & Hong, 2006). The government began to prepare a system that links individual task goal to the organizational goal and reflects the performance evaluation for important personnel decisions. The efforts nurtured a result-oriented culture that places performance at the core of HRM (Lah & Perry, 2008). Now, many countries produce the objective performance information to differentiate high performers from low performers, and reward top performers. According to an OECD report (2005), all OECD countries except Greece, Iceland, Japan, Luxemburg, and Spain have a performance management and appraisal system.

C. Attention to Senior Management

Another common feature is the attention to senior management. According to the OECD report (2005), numerous countries have established a senior civil service group and differentiated its management from that of other civil servants. Attention to senior civil servants is related to the performance-based HRM in two ways. First, the role of senior civil servants is critical in designing and improving the system. They are the part of the top management that has the authority to make the system better. Secondly, considering their influence and authority, their own performance itself in managing agencies and relevant policies is critical for enhancing the overall performance of agencies (Ketelaar, Manning & Turkisch, 2007). Senior civil servants act as the stewards of the professional public service as well as being responsive servants of elected government. Accordingly, finding a proper balance between the two roles is critical and challenging (Bourgon, 2008). To address the relevant challenges, establishing rules of administrative ethics and facilitating ethical culture are important.

D. Reduction of Protection, Immunity and Privilege

Countries adopting the career civil service system assume that public service jobs need to be permanent employment positions, which gives a high level of job security. Permanent employment is expected to attract competent young people and assure the consistency of public service. Although such a system remained effective for decades, the situation was substantially changed in the late 1980s (OECD, 2003). One of the reasons is that the distinction between public and private sectors lessened. By the increased demand that government should run like a business, many governments focus on assuring flexibility to adapt to changing environments and increasing performance. As a result, contracting out government services becomes common practice, and countries such as Belgium, Canada, New Zealand, and Sweden, which guaranteed a lifelong employment, tend to change their laws by abandoning the privilege of public officials who enjoyed permanent employment (OECD, 2005). However, the abolition of permanent positions also has disadvantages and side-effects. One of them is the possibility that public officials may not have a long-term perspective in pursuing a policy and have a short-sighted view by focusing on maximization of their own interests. In addition, job security has been a prominent advantage of public sector jobs. If government jobs do not have it any more, it might be more challenging to attract competent people to the public sector, and the relative competence of the public sector might be lower than that of the private sector. Thus, caution is required concerning the abolition of job security.

E. Decentralization of Human Resource Management Policies

Another common feature of HRM in OECD countries is that they tend to decentralize HRM policies in its implementation, while the scope varies across the countries (OECD, 2005). The trend of decentralization is also related to the New Public Management reform. The basic idea is that each government department or agency has the best knowledge of what practices are appropriate when considering its specific contexts. In addition, by providing more flexibility and discretion, the decentralization is expected to lead to better performance. As a result, many OECD countries initiated the delegation of HRM policies, where the specific strategies can be classified into three areas: "1) transferring responsibility for human resource management from central bodies to line departments, 2) simplifying rules and procedures, and 3) developing more flexible policies" (OECD, 2005, pp.111–112). The efforts for decentralization are also related to the economic hardship of many countries.

According to Kicker and Randma-Liiv (2015), the world financial crisis in 2008 led to substantial economic hardships for many countries. OECD countries and many EU countries, including but not confined to Belgium, Denmark, Estonia, Germany, and the UK, sought employment freeze, salary cut, downsizing, and reorganization to assure financial soundness. That is, besides enhancement of performance by providing more flexibility and discretion, a part of the rationale for decentralization is to save costs of the central government, which is related to the reduction of privilege of public officials.

F. Summary

In summary, the global trend of HRM reform can be summarized by the above five elements. There has been an influence of New Public Management, and OECD countries emphasized the adoption of private-sector practices and enhancing performance. Recently, experiencing economic crisis, many countries have employed the decentralization strategy to resolve financial burden and increase performance by assuring flexibility. In doing so, some countries abolished some privileges that public officials have enjoyed. Under the global context, countries seek to harmonize the career-based and position-based system, and make efforts to reduce corruption while emphasizing innovation and openness. Now, many countries, including Korea and Vietnam, recognize this global trend of HRM reform. However, knowing is one thing and practicing is another. As Moon and Hwang (2013) indicate, one can observe a variation across countries in terms of the extent to which the core values and reform initiatives are internalized and achieve their main purposes. No country is perfect, and one needs to continuously evaluate the status quo and identify areas for future improvement.

III. Administrative Reform in Vietnam

1. Brief Public Administration Reform History in Vietnam

1.1. Public Administration in Vietnam before 2000

According to Moon and Hwang (2013, p127), it was not long ago that the socialist transitional countries established the formal legal framework for the civil service. In case of Vietnam, as soon as it had just gained independence, President Ho Chi Minh issued Decree 18-SL/1945 on 18/8/1945 to convert the French Colonial public service regime into a capacity and ethic-based public service regime. The Decree 18-SL/1945 and the Constitution was enacted in 1946 were the foundation of modern and democratic public service regime in Vietnam. In 1950, Vietnam enacted Decree No.76 on issuing the Statute of Civil servants, which stipulates the obligations and rights of civil servants; the organization, governance, and utilization of civil servants throughout the country. The full-scale, fundamental administrative reform was conducted with the launch of Doi Moi. The constitutional amendment of 1992 placed the congress and the government as the core axis with the Communist Party (Seo & Im, 2013).

In 1995, Resolution No.08-NQ/HNTW of the Central Party of Vietnam (hereafter, CPV) sought to further strengthen the State of Vietnam, with a focus on one-step administrative reform. The Resolution indicated the orientation and duties in the coming years as follows: (i) Continuing to renovate organization and operation of the National Assembly; (ii) One-step administrative reform, including institutional reform; reform to the organizational machinery and operation of the administrative system; and building the contingent of civil servants; (iii) Innovating the organization and operation of agencies in the Justice branch; (iv) Bringing into full play the role of the citizens; and (v) Strengthening the leadership role of the CPV to the State. This Resolution served as a foundation for the public administration reform in Vietnam, and in 2001 the Public Administration Reform (PAR) Master Program was officially launched.

Regarding the HRM, the enactment of Ordinance 25/CP of 1993 became the basic framework for the civil service system with a series of decisions by the Government Committee for Organization and Personnel (Moon & Hwang, 2013). In 1998, the Ordinance of Cadres and Civil Servants was issued, and the Vietnam government revised rules of the whole HRM process, including recruitment, disciplines, retirement, leave of absence, training, etc (Seo & Im, 2013).

1.2. The Public Administration Reform (PAR) Master Program (2001–2010)

Since the *Doi Moi* demonstrated its fruitful outcomes, another major government reform effort was shaped in 2001. The Vietnam government launched 10-year long term plan for its reform, which was called Public Administration Reform (PAR) Master Program. The main purposes of the program include "successfully building a democratic, strong, clean, professionalized, modernized, effective and efficient public administration system which operates in line with the principles of the socialist ruled-by-law State under the leadership of the Party." (Can, 2013, p.111)

The PAR Master program provides nine specified objectives, four content areas, seven action plans, and five solutions. The nine objectives are as follows: "1) Improving administrative institutional system, regime, and policy; 2) Erasing and cutting off administrative procedures with red tape, complicatedness; 3) Identifying clearly function, task, and responsibility for organizations in the PA system; 4) Structure of the government will be appropriated in an orderly manner; 5) Up to 2005, identification of decentralization for PA; 6) Up to 2010, civil servants will be professionals and modernized with rational structure and size; 7) Up to 2005, civil servants' salary will be reformed; 8) Up to 2005, financial mechanism will be reformed in the line with PA organizations and public service; 9) Civil service will be modernized" (Can, 2013, p.111). Among the nine objectives, the 6th and 7thare directly related to the HRM reform.

Regarding the four content areas, the PAR Master Program 2001–2010 identified four key reform areas: including 1) institutional reform, 2) organizational reform, 3) reform of the cadre and civil servants, and 4) public finance reform (In the second phase of the program, 2006-2010, one more key reform area was added, which is the modern ization of public administration system).

The seven action plans include 1) Program to renovate the development, issuance, and quality improvement of legal normative documents, 2) Program on roles, functions, and organizational structures of the agencies in the administrative system, 3) Staff downsizing program, 4) Program on quality improvement of the contingent of cadres and civil servants, 5) Program on salary reform, 6) Program on innovation of financial management mechanisms for administrative and public service delivery agencies, and 7) Program on modernization of administrative system. Out of the seven national action plans, number three, four, and five are closely related to the HRM.

In fact, the attention of the Vietnam government on HRM was not new. Before the PAR Master Program, the Vietnam government sought to reform the

HRM in the public sector. The major changes in civil service can be explained by three milestones with several reform elements. (See Figure 3-1).

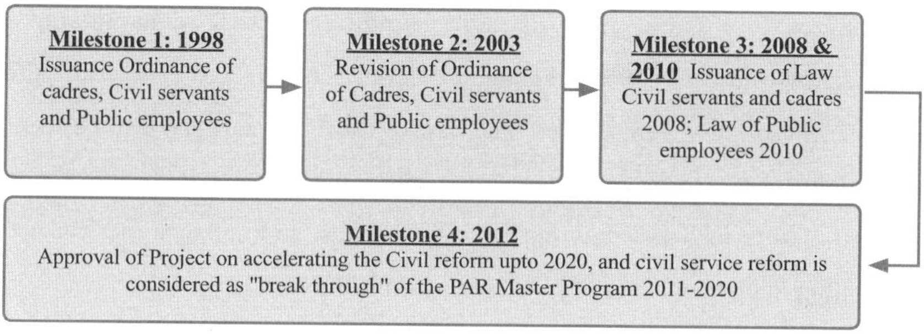

Source: Ngoi (2016)

Figure 3-1 The process of civil service reform within the framework of PAR

Milestone1. In 1998 'Issuance Ordinance of Cadres, Civil servants and Public employees': By the Ordinance, the personnel working in the State-owned enterprises (SOEs) are clearly separated from the personnel working in the bureaucracy. That is, the people working in the SOEs are not regulated by the Ordinance. The Ordinance newly introduced competitive examinations for recruitment of new civil servants and public employees as well as examinations for grade promotion.

Milestone2. In the 2003 'Revision of Ordinance of Cadres, Civil Servants and Public Employees' separated the management of public employees working in the public service delivery agencies from the management of civil servants and cadres working in the administrative agencies. As a result, two different laws were founded: the Law of Cadres and Civil Servants and, later, the Law of Public Employees. Another critical content of the revised Ordinance is the increased level of delegation. The revised Ordinance delegated the right to recruit public employees to the leaders/heads of public service delivery agencies based on work contracts. It reflects the global trend of decentralization of personnel management and recruitment.

Milestone3. In 2008 and 2010, the "Issuance of Law of Civil Servants and Cadres 2008," and "Law of Public Employees 2010" consolidated a clear distinction between management of civil servants and cadres and the management of public employees. The Law of Civil Servants and Cadres seeks to combine the career system (closed system) and positioned system (open system), assure leaders' individual responsibilities, and enhance merit-based promotion. Such new features are summarized in Table 3-1.

Table 3-1 The new features in the Law of Cadres and Civil servants 2008

Reform Features	New Implications
Civil service scope	Reduced, as the Law excludes most of those who work for public service delivery agencies – for instance, in hospitals, schools, universities, research institutes. Only the top leaders of those agencies are considered as civil servants.
Civil service structure	The Law differentiates cadres, civil servants and commune civil servants.
Obligation of cadres and civil servants	Obligations are emphasized and articulated in greater details. Additional obligations are clarified for civil servants who have managerial and leadership positions.
Recruitment	Compared with the Ordinance of Civil servants, Cadres and Public employees, the new Law provides principles of recruitment such as transparency, subjectivity, effectiveness, and equality (i.e., selecting qualified candidates by competitive selection methods).
Salary and compensation	Link compensation to performance (e.g. the best performers receive a pay raise).
Promotion	Promotion is based on competitive examination in a career system.
Performance management and assessment	More attention to performance appraisal and accountability. Look for better ways for performance appraisal.
Competence and merit	Promotion to leadership and managerial positions is based on merit and competence.

Source: Extracted from Law No. 22/2008/QH12 on Cadres and Civil Servants; Ngoi (2016).

The main areas of reform differ depending on the priorities of the CPV and the government. For instance, reforming the administrative procedures was considered as a "breakthrough" of the PAR in the period 2001–2010. On the other hand, during the 2010–2020 period, civil service reform is mainly emphasized.

1.3. Public Administration Reform (PAR) Master Program (2011–2020)

Since 2011, the 2nd phase of the PAR Master Program was initiated. In the 1st phase of the PAR Master Program between 2001 and 2010, the basic structures to modernize the HRM system were established. Many related laws and regulations were enacted for specified fields of HRM. Beginning in 2011, the Vietnam government has sought to conduct those newly enacted laws. Simultaneously, the Vietnam government tries to reflect the global trend that emphasizes the responsiveness to citizens (Seo & Im, 2013).

The current HRM reform in Vietnam also emphasizes performance management. Especially for performance evaluation, the evaluation result serves as a basis for placement, training, rewards, etc. Low performers are often relocated to other tasks and they might even be dismissed. Based on such a powerful drive for reform, the Vietnam government seeks to enhance the quality of public service. It also stresses the importance of administrative ethics (Seo & Im, 2013).

The recent HRM reform especially emphasized several elements. In 18/10/2012, The Prime Minister issued the Decision No. 1557/QD-CP on approving the Civil Service Reform Plan, which includes accelerating decentralization on HRM; Position-based system (job description); improving the quality of recruitment examination and promotion examination; innovating the performance appraisal; talent attraction and retention policies; innovating regarding the method of leadership and managerial promotion (pilot competitive examinations); and down-sizing policy. Related to the downsizing policy, in 2014, the Government enacted the Decree No. 108/2014/ND-CP on the staff reduction policy, and the Central Executive Committee of CPV enacted the Resolution No. 39-NQ/TW in 2015. The Resolution includes staff reduction, restructure of cadres, public servants, and public employee system, cutting down public expenditure, reforming salary policy, etc. These reform efforts are not much different from the global trend of HRM reforms.

1.4. Outcomes of the PAR Master Program from 2001 to 2010

There are several outcomes from the PAR Master Program. This section reviews the existing outcomes from the reform focusing on HRM aspects as well as discussing future challenges. By 2009, the Ministry of Home Affairs had conducted several major reforms in HRM. It standardized recruitment and promotion exams to line ministries and provinces. It also doubled civil service wages while giving agencies autonomy to raise wages further (Hausman, 2010). Another achievement of the PAR program is the enactment of the Corruption Prevention Act in 2007 (55/2005/QH11). The law regulates the obligation of public officials in detail and provides proper practice guidelines. However, better achievements are desired (Seo & Im, 2013). According to the scholars, one of the reasons of the corruption by public officials in Vietnam is related to the low level of salary (Acuña-Alfaro, 2013). Figure 3-2 shows that over 30% of civil servants do not focus on their jobs during their working hours to make extra money, and that 30% of them used their positions to receive extra benefits. The key reason of remaining in the position is the opportunities for extra income. Gainsborough et al. (2009) argue that corruptions of public officials in Vietnam should be seen as the normal status rather than an aberration. However, to break the chain of corruption, one may need to consider a substantial change, including strict application of regulations, strengthening administrative ethics, and guaranteeing higher salaries for civil servants.

Some issues regarding incentives and salaries in Viet Nam (i)

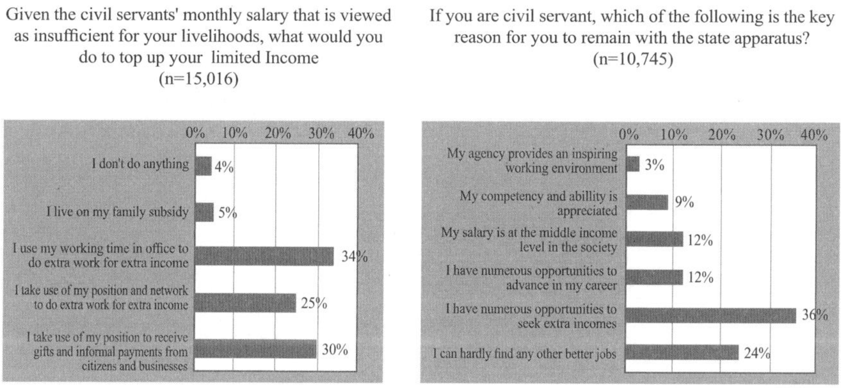

Source: Acuña-Alfaro (2012) Based on online survey on Vietnam.net; Acuña-Alfaro (2013) reprise

Figure 3-2 Incentives and Salaries in Vietnam's– opportunities to seek extra incomes

In spite of the substantial achievements of the PAR Master Program, some scholars note that further improvement can be made. For example, Can (2013) argues that the reform programs need to be more detailed and sophisticated, which will make it possible to assure accountability and conduct performance management. Improving openness and transparency is also required to fully eradicate red-tape and corruption (Seo & Im, 2013). In addition, enhancing competence of public officials also has room for improvement (Can, 2013).

2. HRM System in Vietnam

2.1. Main Features of Civil Service System in Vietnam

Basically, the civil service system in Vietnam is based on the rank-in-person system. Civil servants are selected by a competitive recruitment process, and they are required to complete a probationary period once they are enrolled in the civil service (Poon, Hùng & Trường, 2009). As civil servants move into higher grades, they generally have greater influence on management and policy making (Poon, Hùng & Trường, 2009). According to the Law on Cadres and Civil Servants, people working in the public sector are categorized into four groups: 1) Public Officials (cadres) (can bo), 2) civil servants (congchuc), 3) commune officials and servants (can bo, congchuc cap xa) and 4) public employees. The explanation of each group is as follows.

First, public officials (can bo) have a fixed term. They can work for various entities including the party, socio-political organizations, and administrative agencies (Poon, Hùng & Trường, 2009). Second, like public officials, civil servants (congchuc) work for the party, socio-political organizations, and administrative agencies. The number of civil servants and public officials is about 300,000. One can classify civil servants into four groups: "senior experts (Group A), principle experts (Group B), experts (Group C), and below expert (Group D)" (Poon et al., 2009, p.3). As a general practice, it takes five years to move from expert to principal expert level and five years to move from principal expert to senior expert grade (No.11/2014/TT-BNV dated 09/10/2014). Third, commune officials and servants (can bo, congchuc cap xa) work at the commune level, and number about 200,000. One can classify those employees into two groups: elected officers (e.g. chair and vice chair of the

People's Committee) and appointed officers (professional staffs) (Poon, Hùng & Trường, 2009). Finally, public employees (vienchuc) are people who work in public service delivery agencies. The estimated number of those employees is 2,102,477 people in 2016.

2.2. Grade-based Civil Service Structure in Vietnam

The overall grade system of civil servants in administrative agencies is composed of five categories: 1) Staff and equivalent grade, 2) Clerical and equivalent grade, 3) Expert and equivalent grade, 4) Principal expert and equivalent grade, and 5) Senior expert and equivalent grade. The grade system applies to both central level as well as provinces and centrally manages cities.

The civil servant grade structures have been formed by the restructuring of the organizations, with allocation of the civil servants for the jobs in the agencies. Therefore, there are differences in the ratios of senior expert grade, principal expert grade, expert grade, clerical grade, and staff grade among the ministries, agencies, and sub-national governments. The changes and addition of civil servants in the State agencies and organizations are in response to the specific mandates, but the grade balance has not been considered sufficiently. For example, for the past 10 years, the civil servant recruitment by personnel quotas has focused too much on the qualification standards or criterion. Therefore, the number of civil servants at expert grade has increased, whereas the number of those at other grades or lower grades has not been supplemented enough.

Regarding title-based civil servant structure, the formation of the career-based civil servant structures are linked to the grade structures. That is, civil servants being appointed to leadership and management positions are also appointed to the corresponding grades. According to the laws, every state agency or organization is established with a head title and two deputy heads. In reality, some ministries or sub-national agencies have more than three deputy heads as authorized in special cases. For example, in the annexation of Ha Tay and Ha Noi, the number of deputy heads in organizations is often six–eight. In some other cases, if there are leaders approaching the retirement age, the agency is able to appoint more (with the agreement from the relevant authorities) for replacement. However, in state administration agencies, the rule is that there is only one head and two deputy heads in each agency.

3. Major Reform Outcomes and Remaining Challenges for Vietnam HRM

One can summarize the key changes of the Vietnam civil service reform as follows. First, there was a fundamental change in civil servant recruitment. In the past, the recruitment regime was that university graduates had to be nominated to get jobs in the agencies or localities. The regime was changed into the regime in which the university graduates have right to take competitive recruitment examinations to the agencies where they desire to work. The recruitment was also decentralized, so that each ministry or province can conduct its own recruitment examinations by reflecting its unique needs and demands. On the other hand, in order to attract talented people into the civil service, the government has the policy to allow the head of agency to recruit highly qualified candidates (excellent university graduates or PhD degree holders) without conducting examinations.

Second, there was a change in grade promotion of civil servants. Before the PAR, the grade promotion of civil servants was solely based on seniority. Under the new regulation, civil servants who want to be promoted should satisfy two essential conditions: seniority at a certain level and passing a competitive examination. However, some criticize that such changes have mainly impacted on the formality of the examination rather than the improved quality of civil servants.

Third, the appointment of civil servants to leadership and managerial positions also changed. Some provinces such as Ho Chi Minh City, Hai Phong City, Da NangCity, and Quang Ninh introduced a competitive examination for selecting directors and managers since 2005. The initial results of the pilot showed that it is a good way to identifying and selecting qualified candidates. However, some critics indicate that there remain some confusions and difficulties in replicating the pilot results.

Fourth, another change is the remuneration system. For the reform of the remuneration system, the Vietnam government set up a Steering Committee of Remuneration Reform, headed by a Deputy Prime Minister. The Committee made a great effort to increase salary levels from 180,000 VND (1999) up to1,300,000 VND (2017), and the minimum salary level has been adjusted more than seven times. However, the challenge still remained. In spite of such effort at the adjustment, the overall level of salary of civil servants is still very low compared to the cost of living. Assuring the appropriate level of salary is a challenge to the Vietnam government.

Fifth, one could observe the improvement of training and retraining programs. Based on the Decision No.1374/QD-CP, over 2,900,000 cadres and public servants participated training and re-training programs during 2011-2015 period. Especially, the number of retrained people in skills was 1,870,000, nearly 65% of the total number of trained cadres and public servants. The figure 3-3 explains the recent trend (Hai, 2016).

Sixth, one of the major HRM issues in Vietnam is staff reduction. The Resolution No. 39-NQ/TW by the Central Executive Committee of CPV set the target that at least 10% of the payrolls of all units and many local ministries and branches should be streamlined by 2021.

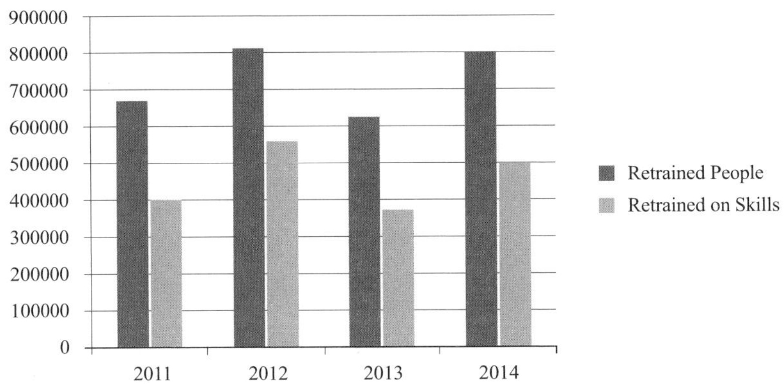

Source: Hai, H. Nguyen (2016, p.253) Public Administration Reform: Theory and Practice, National Politic Publisher.

Figure 3-3 Number of retrained people for the period 2011-2014

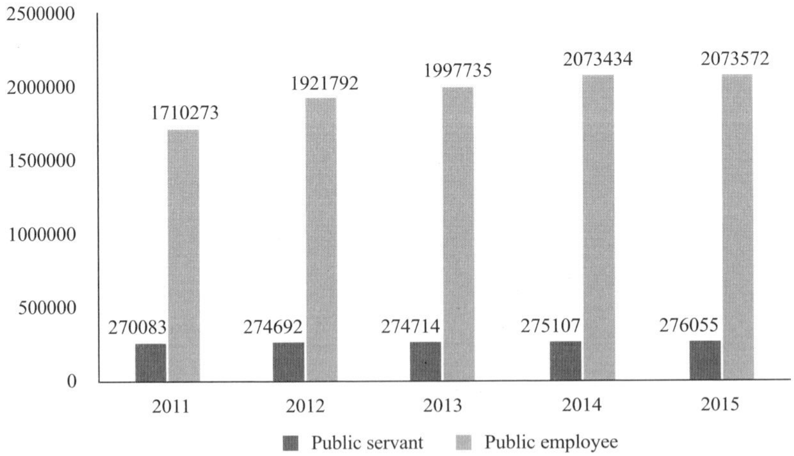

Source: Report of the Ministry of Home Affairs (2016)

Figure 3-4 Number of public servants and public employees during 2011-2015

Through the downsizing, the Vietnam government seeks to improve the quality of human capital in the public sector and to improve the treatment of public officials. By removing redundant staff, one can expect that the overall managerial efficiency will be enhanced while saving government resources. However, the existing result of the reform does not seem to be very successful. The policy target, 15% staff reduction, was not achieved yet, while the body of state agencies and non-business units has been increased. In detail, the number of newly hired public servants was 238,668 in 2007, and the number was 275,620 in 2014 (15% increase). The number of staffs in public service units was also rapidly increased from 1.63 million in 2010 to 2.31 million in 2014. As Figure 3-4 illustrates, the total number of public servants and public employees has shown a steady increase between 2011 and 2015.

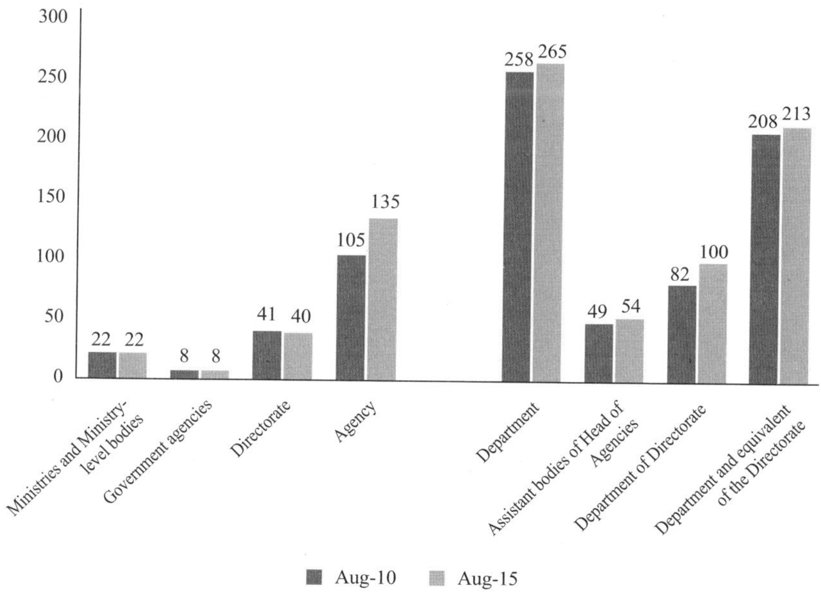

Source: Report of the Ministry of Home Affairs (2016)

Figure 3-5 Number of central administrative units during 2010-2015

In addition to the number of public servants and public employees, both the number of central administrative units and the number of local administrative units have been increased since 2010 (Ministry of Home Affairs, 2016). Figure 3-5 compares the number of central administrative units between 2010 and 2015. One can find that most units expanded in its number. Similarly, the number of local administrative units has been increased since 2001. The number of District was increased from 627 in 2001 to 713 in 2015. The number of Ward was increased from 10,543 in 2001 to 11,164 in 2015.

Finally, regarding the downsizing, one also needs to take caution in its implementation. The efforts for downsizing throughout the world have not been always successful. Most importantly, for successful downsizing, there should be empirical data and evidence for the detailed downsizing plan. That is, one should be able to provide evidence for how many employees and what kind of employees from what specific agencies should be downsized. Without such empirical evidence, there will be backlash from the employees and the organizations will suffer from the equity issue. One may also observe unexpected results. For example, if the result of the downsizing is the turnover of high performers who are near the retirement age while retaining low performers, that may further decrease the effectiveness of public service. Considering the existing result and the potential risks of the downsizing, rightsizing might be a better solution than standardized downsizing according to an allocated quota for each organization. A more cautious approach seems to be required for the Vietnam government in conducting the downsizing.

Based on the achievements and remaining challenges of the Vietnam HRM reform, one should consider how to make the current achievement more fruitful and sustainable as well as how to overcome the existing challenges. The six HRM reform initiatives that will be introduced in the following chapter are closely related to those issues, and they are helpful in addressing them. For example, to sustain a diversified recruitment system that can assure the attraction of talented people, the open recruitment system that the Korean government is using may provide some useful guidance. To further strengthen the performance of civil servants, the performance evaluation system that the Korean government uses can also be a useful point of reference for the Vietnam government. Assuring the accountability of high-level officers, the Performance Agreement that is applied for the high level officials in Korea can be considered as one alternative.

IV. Major HRM Reform Initiatives

1. HRM Reform Initiatives for TAP Government

1.1. Global HRM Trend and TAP Government

As discussed in the above section, the global reform trend in HRM field can be summarized as follows: 1) hybridization of the career-based system and position-based system, 2) emphasis on performance, 3) special attention to senior management, 4) a reduction of protection, immunity, and privilege, and 5) decentralization of HRM policies. Considering the purpose of these elements, one can easily think of the relationship between the elements and TAP government. Many of the elements are directly related to enhancing performance. That is, ensuring a well performing government is one of the priorities of recent HRM reforms. Simultaneously, those elements are also relevant to transparent and accountable government. A part of the reason of reducing privilege of public officials is to make more transparent, corruption-free government. The purpose of the decentralization is to make each department and local governments more accountable, while also increasing their performance. Finally, consistent with the Vietnam 2035 report, building a TAP (Transparent, Accountable, and Performing) government can serve as a foundation to design HRM reform initiatives. The importance of the three values included in the acronym– transparency, accountability, and performance –will persist in the future. The acronym also serves as an ongoing objective, in that no country can perfectly achieve the values to the fullest potential.

1.2. Reform Initiatives to Make a TAP Government

Then, what kinds of HR reforms are necessary to make a TAP government? The reform initiatives should help to achieve the three major goals of transparency, accountability, and performance. Prioritizing those goals prompts the nomination of six initiatives that need attention from the Vietnam government: 1) preparation of a system for evidence-based management, 2) establishment of a career civil service system, 3) strengthening administrative ethics, 4) promoting competence of street-level bureaucracy, 5) performance evaluation and management, and 6) introducing position classification system elements.

These initiatives are also linked to the global trend of HRM reforms. For example, the first initiative, preparation of a system for evidence-based management, is related to the global trend emphasizing performance. The introduction of the position classification system, the sixth element, is closely related to the global trend of hybridization. The evidence-based management system is related to transparent government, while the establishment of career civil service system reflects accountable and performing government. Addressing administrative ethics is critical for accountable and transparent governance, and facilitating the competence of street-level bureaucracy contributes to establishing a well-performing government. Both conducting performance management and introducing position classification system elements seek to enhancing performance of government. Thus, fulfilling these six initiatives is directly related to achieving a TAP government.

To maximize the effectiveness of HRM reform, we suggest that the first four initiatives are conducted first, and the 5th and 6th initiatives are implemented subsequently. The main reason for this is to stabilize and solidify the career civil service system while minimizing conflicts among different initiatives. Accordingly, we believe that the first four initiatives have a high priority in conducting HRM reform to solidify the overall career civil service system. The last two initiatives will be successful when the current Vietnamese HR system, which is based on a rank-in-person system, is stabilized by fulfilling the first four initiatives. The initiatives are explained in turn in the following sections.

2. Preparation of System for Evidence-based Management

An evidence-based HR management system is a basic condition of a TAP government. To make a transparent, accountable, and performing government, all decisions should be made based on empirical evidence. Otherwise, public managers cannot make the best HR decisions, and those decisions often become arbitrary and fail to assure fairness. That is, HR decisions without empirical evidence fail to meet either efficiency or equity criteria. Accordingly, systematic data gathering is the basic requirement for an effective HR system. The preparation of the system begins with the systematic gathering of personnel data

In implementing evidence-based management, the U.S. Office of Personnel Management (OPM) can serve as a role model that demonstrates the best practice of evidence-based management. The OPM is in charge of collecting statistical information of the federal civilian workforce. Based on Enterprise Human Resources Integration (EHRI) Data Warehouse, the OPM operates the online tool called "Fedscope" (www.fedscope.opm.gov). By utilizing the website, the general public as well as government agencies are able to access, classify, and visualize the personnel data of over 2 million federal civilian employees. The data contains various aspects of personnel information, including gender, race, length of service, type of occupations, agency of employment, salary level, supervisory status, type of appointment, work schedule, etc.

In addition to such "hard" data of personnel, the OPM has regularly conducted surveys to diagnose the status of federal employees. In 2002, the OPM began to conduct government-wide survey called "Federal Human Capital Survey (FHCS)." While the name was changed to "Federal Employee Viewpoint Survey (FEVS)" in 2010, the survey has continued to show the evaluation of federal employees for various aspects of their workplace and supervisors. Still, the survey serves as a useful tool to measure whether each agency is characterized as a successful organization based on its employees' perception. Based on the empirical data, the OPM analyzes the trend of employee perceptions as well as catches the current HR issues to be addressed. Those analyses provide critical information to make major HR policies and legislative changes.

3. Establishment of Career Civil Service System

3.1. Main Characteristics of Career Civil Service System

The career civil service system is "a personnel management system intended to recruit and retain outstanding young talents with a high sense of honor and integrity for public office" (Choi & Park, 2013, p22). That is, the system seeks to find young people with a high level of potential, despite their lack of experience. Thereby, the system aims to raise those young people into leaders in the public sector by letting them consider public service as their lifetime career with a long-term perspective (Choi & Park, 2013, p25).

Because of the global financial difficulties, some countries transformed the basic mechanism of career civil service and lowered the level of job security of civil servants. However, one should consider whether the unconditional cutback will be advantageous in the long term. Although downsizing was applauded and accepted as a good solution, the best solution might differ by context. Currently, the concept "rightsizing" is considered as a more appropriate solution. Thus, each country needs to evaluate whether their current workforce is at an appropriate level to successfully conduct government policies with sufficient competency. Moreover, the pros and cons of a career civil service system should be discussed.

The main advantage of the career civil service system is to assure the stability and consistency of public service because most public officials serve in their lifetime. The system trains generalists who can deal with diverse tasks with a comprehensive perspective. That characteristic provides an opportunity for public officials to experience various areas of government works, which helps them have a wider view and ability of coordination and integration (Oh,

2009). As a result, public officials can have pride in their careers because the government heavily invests in their training and development by treating them as core human capital of the state (Lee, 2007). On the other hand, because the system focuses on developing generalists, it has weakness in terms of increasing professionalism within the public service. To overcome this weakness, many countries with the civil service system try to introduce some position-based system elements. Korea is such a case, and Vietnam should consider doing so.

3.2. Necessary Conditions to Establish Career Civil Service System

To establish the civil service system, there are certain conditions to be met: 1) high social evaluation of public service, 2) successful recruitment of competent young generations, 3) effective development system, 4) appropriate compensation and pension system, and 5) long-term supply and demand plan for recruitment (Kim & Kim, 2000).Accordingly, whether the country fulfills those necessary conditions should be carefully diagnosed before introducing position classification system elements into the system. As we will discuss later, the career civil service system is based on the rank-in-person system, which contradicts the position classification system to some extent. Although many countries, including South Korea, seek to introduce some elements of position classification system to enhance the professionalism in the public sector, those reform initiatives were not always successful. Accordingly, the Vietnam government may want to have a cautious approach, and establishing and stabilizing of the existing rank-in-person system need to be prioritized.

4. Strengthening Administrative Ethics

Lots of practitioners and scholars have indicated the importance of administrative ethics. Various reports illustrate that corruption is detrimental to national development and political legitimacy. In addition, the negative effect of corruption is magnified for the poorest people in the country (OECD, 2006; Transparency International, 1998; Transparency International, 2007; UNDP, 2008; World Bank, 2006). Similarly, the UNDP (2008, p.1) listed negative effects of corruption, including "1) weakened national institutions, 2) inequitable social services, and 3) blatant injustice in the courts – along with economic inefficiency and unchecked environmental exploitation." It also emphasizes that poor populations who heavily rely on public services (but are unable to pay bribes) will suffer most (UNDP, 2008).

Angel Gurría, the Secretary General of the OECD, emphasizes that "in all countries and at all levels of society, corruption threatens to distort social and economic interactions, reducing efficiency and increasing inequality by favoring the well-positioned. As a result, the cost of doing business increases, public resources are wasted and the poor are pushed aside. The crisis has also led to a loss of trust and confidence in the economic system as a whole. A coherent, coordinated and effective commitment to fight corruption and promote integrity is now crucial to restore citizens' confidence and pave the way for stronger, cleaner and fairer growth." (OECD, 2016, p3)

The OECD has made various efforts to support the fight against the corruption. For example, it began the "CleanGovBiz" initiative to support governments, business, and civil society in their fights against corruption. The initiative aims to gather the relevant tools of anti-corruption, facilitates the coordination among participants, and monitors the progress (OECD

CleanGovBiz homepage, access to site 2017.07.11). Another example of an international institution that fights against corruption is the G20, which is a forum of 19 countries and the European Union. The G20 established the 'Anticorruption Working Group' in 2010. The group developed the tools to strengthen members' legislative, regulatory, and institutional frameworks that improve the overall integrity (G20 ACWG, 2015). Sometimes, the G20 and OECD have cooperated to eradicate corruption. For example, the OECD helped the G20 develop the High-Level Principles on Financial Disclosure as well as the Anti-Corruption Open Data Principles (OECD G20 homepage, access to site 2017.07.11).

5. Promoting Competence of Street-level Bureaucracy

Street-level bureaucracy can be defined as public employees who provide public services at the front-lint by directly interacting with citizens (Lipsky, 2010). Accordingly, street-level bureaucrats include teachers, judges, police officers, health workers, social workers, public defenders, and more. Common characteristics include that 1) they can provide benefits and sanction directly to citizens, 2) they can make discretionary decision-making, and 3) they exercise autonomy from management to some extent (Adami, 2014).

The role of street-level bureaucracy becomes more and more important because, in the modern society, government should deal with the fiscal deficit problem while at the same time satisfying citizens' high service needs. That is, street-level bureaucrats are required to deliver effective public service with constraint resources. Based on their common characteristics, street-level bureaucrats play important roles in shaping public policies based on their discretion (Adami, 2014). In addition, they are the first contacts through which citizens experience government services.

In spite of the importance of their roles, work conditions of street-level bureaucrats are deteriorated by financial difficulties. Street-level bureaucrats usually suffer from lack of resources and excessive workload. They often conduct emotional labor when interacting with clients. Accordingly, proper management of street-level bureaucrats is required to provide effective government services in the long term. Considering its importance, building the competency of street-level bureaucrats needs to be one of the priorities of HRM reform. The management of street-level bureaucrats is closely related to HR issues in the local governments in that many local government employees tend to serve as street-level bureaucrats in the field and have frequent interactions with citizens.

6. Performance Evaluation and Management

Behn (2002, p.20) defines performance management as "the collection of organizational, managerial, and leadership strategies that are designed to get the people within a public agency—and their essential collaborators—to achieve specific public purposes." When one narrows down the concept into HR field, performance management can be defined as a process of managing employee performance by planning, monitoring, evaluating, and rewarding individual contributions (Cho & Lee, 2012, pp.239–240)

In line with New Public Management (NPM) prescriptions, performance management has been noted as a key element to improve government performance in many countries (Nielsen, 2014). For example, the U.S. OPM nominates the capacity of conducting performance management as a core element of good managers by stating that "good managers have been speaking and practicing effective performance management all their lives, executing each key component process well. They not only set goals and plan work routinely, they measure progress toward those goals and give feedback to employees. They set high standards, but they also take care to develop the skills needed to reach them. And they use formal and informal rewards to recognize the behavior and results that accomplish their mission" (OPM homepage, access to site on 2017.07.11). Scholars have begun to evaluate performance management systems within their respective fields, providing evidence on the impact of performance management. Representatively, Garrish (2016) analyzes the impact of performance management systems on performance of public organizations through a meta-analysis of studies in each of these fields. The research demonstrates that performance management actually leads to higher performance in public organizations regardless of the fields.

7. Introducing Position Classification System Elements

The career civil service system is based on the rank-in-person system. The main idea of the career civil service system is that the government attract young and competent people, and make them work for the government with pride and eager during their entire careers. The HR system that accommodates this need is the rank-in-person system. Accordingly, it focuses on personnel characteristics in recruiting public officials. That is, how much potential and competency a person has is the main recruitment criterion. On the other hand, the position classification system is based on the classification of jobs by their main function, level of specialty, difficulty, and responsibility. In recruitment, the system finds people who meet the requirements of the specific positions (Choi, 2015). That is, the focus is on the position rather than person. While the system has the advantage in finding people with required expertise, the stability is low because the person is replaceable whenever another person is available. No HR system is perfect, and most countries seek to combine the two systems. However, as we reviewed, the two systems are contradictory and one will face some challenges in the process of combination, which South Korea also experiences.

The career civil service system has shown good achievements, and Korea has also enjoyed the advantages of the system. Based on the hierarchical rank system, the government departments were efficiently operated and many policy goals were successfully achieved (Yoo & Park, 2013; Choi, 2015). However, the change of the administrative environments requires other elements of the HR system that the career civil service system does not effectively provide. For example, the current administrative environment requires high levels of flexibility, openness, and professionalism. To overcome the limitation of the career civil service system, countries based on the system have sought to introduce some elements of the position classification system throughout the HR system. That is, by "position classification system elements," they include HR reform initiatives that emphasize enhancing expertise and professionalism. Representative examples include the open position recruitment system and the Senior Civil Service (SCS) system. The explanation of those elements will be found in section V, which explains the Korean experience.

V. Experience of Korea

1. Evidence-based Management

1.1. Electronic Personnel Management System: E-Saram

E-Saram is a standardized electronic personnel management system that supports government-wide personnel policies and operations by the Ministry of Personnel Management (MPM). The system computerizes the overall process of personnel administration from employment to retirement. Using the system, each government agency electronically manages a variety of personnel-related tasks such as transfer, promotion, pay and leave, etc. Furthermore, various data and statistics produced by the system are utilized for personnel policy-making at the MPM. In 2014, the e-Saram mobile service was launched, which further enhances the accessibility of the system. In 2015, the salary calculation and expenditure processing system were integrated through linkage of e-Saram and dBrain (accounting system). Based on data collected through the e-Saram system, the MPM publishes the Statistics of National Public Officers every June.

1.2. Census of Civil Servants

Since 1969, the Korean government has regularly conducted a comprehensive investigation of all public officials including central and local governments to improve the personnel system based on empirical evidence. Recently, the census has been conducted every five years, and the most recent investigation was done in 2013 by the Ministry of Security and Public Administration (MOSPA, currently Ministry of the Interior (MOI)). It utilized the electronic management system, which enhanced the efficiency and respondents' convenience as well as assuring personal information protection. The investigation items include work-related issues such as satisfaction of public service, foreign language ability, career development, training, education as well as private issues including family relations, welfare, home ownership, commute time, etc. However, the interval of investigation is quite long (five years), which makes it difficult to reflect social changes promptly. In addition, the items mainly focus on general information, which has limitations for provision of practical implication in personnel management.

1.3. Public Employee Perception Survey (2012-current)

To provide implications for an effective HRM system, the Korea Institute for Public Administration (KIPA) has conducted the survey since 2012 (Cho, 2016). The survey is distributed to both central and local government employees. In the 2016 survey, questionnaires were distributed to 42 central administrative agencies and 17 local governments. The total number of respondents was 2,070, among whom 1,370 came from the central administrative agencies and 730 from local governments (Cho, 2016). Based on the survey result, the KIPA has examined the perception of public employees on various aspects of their work-life and management. As the data cumulated, it began to analyze the trend of perceptual changes across years. The data is expected to serve as a basis to diagnose the status quo and suggest managerial prescriptions.

2. Main Characteristics of the Korean Career Civil Service System

2.1. Career Civil Service System

The status of Korean public officials is guaranteed unless they are involved in an illegal act or corruption (Civil Service Act Art. 73-3). In order to ensure stable and fair management, the status of public official is guaranteed through constitution and law based on the meritocracy principle (Kim, 2013). Article 7 of the Constitution guarantees political neutrality and the status of public servants to all citizens, and this applies to both national and local public officials. With the guaranteed status, the Civil Service Act ensures that public officials should keep working hours and that all work-related materials remain confidential (Civil Service Act. 58 Art. 60). In addition, they cannot hold another job, and accepting donations or treats is strictly regulated (Civil Service Act Art. 61 Art. 64 Art. 65). In summary, the HR system of the Korean government is based on the career civil service system. The system corresponds to the rank-in system.

2.2. Rank-in System with Supplement of Position Classification System Elements

Whether a basic government HR system is based on the rank-in system or position classification system makes a big difference because it affects all major dimensions of an HR system, including selection, promotion, incentive programs, and training (Choi, 2015). As explained above, the Korean government sought to establish the career civil service system, and employed the rank-in system accordingly. On the basis of the rank-in system, like other nations, the Korean government operates a hybrid system by supplementing it with elements of position classification system (Choi & Park, 2013).

2.3. Selection Process based on Merit Principle

The selection process is based on the merit principle. The Korean government operates the nine-grade system with three kinds of recruitment exams. Based on open competition, exams for grades 5, 7 and 9 are administered every year through written tests and interviews (Park, 2015). Level 5 (high level officials) recruits personnel in the areas of regular service, administration service, technological service, and foreign service; level 7 (middle level officials) and level 9 (low level officials) selects personnel in administration service and technological service areas (Choi & Park, 2013).

Although the recruitment is basically based on a closed system (three entries in grades 5, 7, and 9), the Korean government partly introduced the open system at higher levels. High-level public officials (above level 3) are called the Senior Civil Service (SCS). Although many SCS members are public officials who entered in grade 5 and were promoted, there are also SCS members who came from outside government via the open position recruitment system. The system intends to secure talented people from outside government and to enhance the expertise in the public sector.

Some scholars evaluate that the introduction of the "open position recruitment system" in 1999 and the introduction of the "part-time public service system" in 2002 somewhat weakened the identity of public officials (Kim, 2013). The "part-time public service system" enables the chief of the department to hire employees for 15 to 32 hours per week, and their tenure is not guaranteed while the contract can be renewed (Shin & Kang, 2003). Accordingly, the government needs caution when introducing some elements of the position classification system. That is, balancing between stability and efficiency is necessary. The discussion of the elements of position classification system will be provided later.

2.4. Appropriate Compensation and Pension System

Regarding salary, the Korean government employs the salary step system. Although the salary level itself is not very high when compared to private equivalents, lower-level government officials can be recipients of 31 types of benefits. On the other hand, public officials whose grade is over level 4 are regulated by the annual salary system. In case of high-level officials except political appointees, their salary level is determined by their performance (Choi & Park, 2013). The government provides diverse welfare programs through the personnel welfare system, which offers sixteen types of welfare support including housing support, education loans, medical expenses, parental expenses and insurance, etc (Yoo & Park, 2013).

The Korean government operates the pension system based on a special occupational pension scheme for the career civil service. The two major principles include the social insurance principle and the support principle. The former regulates that the government and public officials take equal responsibility, which adopts the contributory system. The latter principle aims to contribute to social welfare of public officials and their families by compensating the low level of salary. In summary, based on the two principles, the Korean government contributes to the pension with an equal portion of public officials and public finance used in case of budget shortage (Lee &

Song, 2016). Government employees who retire after working over 20 years or who retire early because of an injury or disease from the workplace are entitled to receive a single lump-sum payment or pension (Choi & Park, 2013).

3. Administrative Ethics

3.1. Current Status and Existing Reform Efforts in Korea

Assuring administrative ethics is an important issue in Korea; there have been various efforts to eradicate corruption, from which Korea still suffers. According to the 2014 Corruption Perception Index (CPI), which is published annually by the Transparency International, Korea was ranked 43rd out of 175 countries with 55 CPI (Transparency International, 2014). When one considers that the ranking is 27th out of 34 OECD countries, administrative ethics issue remains critical in Korea (Im & Lee, 2015).

The Korean government seeks to ensure administrative ethics by providing a Code of Conduct and conducts several regulations for high-level public officers. The Public Officials' Code of Conduct in Korea reads as follows. "As a public servant who serves the Korean people, a public official has a duty of good faith, kindness and fairness, secrecy, integrity, political impartiality and is prohibited from seeking profit, and taking part in collective action. Those who violate their duty may face disciplinary actions from reprimand, pay reduction, suspension, demotion, dismissal to expulsion, depending on the level of violation, and monetary sanctions in case of irregularities involving money and valuables. We also have a system that prevents public officials from illegally increasing property by using their position and ensures the fairness of the execution of official duty." (Presidential instruction No. 352).

In addition, according to the law of the registration of property, Public officials of Grade 4 or above have to register all their and their families' property, and high-ranking officials in the Senior Civil Service (SCS) must disclose their property. If they have any property that turns out to be falsely registered or omitted, they are subject to fines or disciplinary actions. This system seeks to strengthen transparency and openness and prevent the possibility of corruption in advance, thereby strengthening public ethics (Im & Lee, 2015).

Another regulation is the blind trust of stock. If high-level public officials over Grade 4 hold job-related stocks worth over ₩30 million won, they have to sell these stocks or transfer them into a blind trust. However, they are allowed to hold stocks that are deemed irrelevant to their job. This system seeks to prevent the pursuit of individual profit by acquiring stocks related to job through their positions (Im & Lee, 2015).

Korean public officials are also restricted in terms of employment. During the first three years after they retire, public officials of Grade 4 or higher cannot get a job at organizations related to the agencies for which they have worked for the last five years; the aim of this is to prevent public officials giving preferential treatment to a specific company for the purpose of gaining employment after retirement. This regulation was introduced in July 2011 (Im & Lee, 2015).

A new law was recently launched in Korea to prevent solicitation; the law on the prevention of solicitation has been applied to a wide variety of people including public personnel. One of the law's main points is that all solicitation is prohibited, with the exception of spending for the purpose of ensuring effective job performance, social intercourse, and ritual. Even in such cases, expenses are limited: ₩30 thousand KRW for a meal, ₩50 thousand KRW for a gift, and ₩100 thousand KRW for a gift for family occasions.

3.2. Remaining Challenges in Strengthening Administrative Ethics in Korea

According to Ko (2017), most of the anti-corruption policies since 2011 have focused on revising the existing system rather than making any radical changes. Representatively, the Anti-Corruption & Civil Rights Commission, the government agency responsible for dealing with corruption issues, has maintained its major policies as it has enacted relevant laws, monitored and detected corrupt practices, enforced the Code of Conduct for Public Officials, and conducted anti-corruption education (Ko, 2017). However, maintaining the traditional approach may not lead to expected outcomes. The fact that many corruption problems are still observable, even though it has been long time since the relevant institutions have been established implies that the system alone cannot completely solve the problem. Beyond the mere adoption of any institution or system, the whole society should facilitate ethical culture of ethics based on voluntary participation rather than hierarchical control.

In addition, one may want to consider providing positive incentives for the ethical behavior of public officials. The current management of administrative ethics in Korea heavily depends on control and punishment mechanisms; the system might be effective at guaranteeing the minimum level of administrative ethics. However, it fails to facilitate ethics beyond the minimum level. Providing positive incentives should be considered to enhance administrative ethics overall. That is, giving public officials who demonstrate a high level of ethical behavior incentives such as rewards and promotion opportunities may improve the overall ethical awareness and behavior of those in public service (Im & Lee, 2015).

4. Street-level Bureaucracy

4.1. Status of Street-level Bureaucracy in Korea

Since the 1980s, the overall trend of public sector reform has been to improve public performance. Many local governments have competitively introduced reform initiatives to improve organizational performance (Lee et al., 2011). At the local government level, the roles of street-level bureaucrats have been critical in that many services have been conducted through their services. Various reform initiatives have been adopted by local governments in Korea, and one can observe both successes and failures; the following section contains representative examples of local government reforms in Korea.

4.2. Performance Points System by Seoul Metropolitan Government

The Seoul Metropolitan Government introduced the so-called "New Personnel System" in 2007 to develop a creative and productive organizational culture (Cho, Ahn, Song, & Nho, 2014). The performance point system was designed to manage high performers, and operated between 2007 and 2012. The government provided performance points to high performing employees and employees could accumulate points and use them in various ways such as to gain promotions, transfers, training opportunities abroad, etc. (Seoul Metropolitan Government, 2007).

However, some problems arose; first, it was difficult to clearly measure each employee's contribution. Some bureaus intentionally gave points to employees who were expected to be promoted, and free-rider problems were observed. Meanwhile, some other bureaus distributed points equally to all employees. All of these cases went against the system's original intention (Seoul Metropolitan Government, 2012). Further side-effects included that some employees neglected their duties to earn performance points and some bureaus that focused on implementation had intrinsic difficulties earning performance points, which raised the equity issues and discouraged employees from working at such bureaus.

4.3. Corrective System by Seoul Metropolitan Government

Besides the Performance Points System, the Seoul Metropolitan Government also prepared a reform initiative to manage low performers. The Corrective System, which was nicknamed the "3% kick-out" system, operated between 2007 and 2010. The system received strong support from citizens (67.9%) and the heads of local government (72%), but intense resistance from the civil servant union. The rule that public servants who did not improve their performance even after the training would be dismissed led to controversy regarding the guarantee of public employment status. Thus, the system was finally terminated after three years.

The objective of the corrective system was to improve organizational performance. The system provides opportunities for low performers to introspect and re-build themselves through re-training programs. At the organizational level, the system seeks to make organizations more productive by increasing competition among members. The system's general process is as follows. 1) Each bureau nominates low performers for candidates for transfer to other bureaus. 2) Bureaus select employees with whom they work. 3) Employees who were not invited by any bureau are asked to file relevant documents that demonstrate their competence and evaluation records. 4) Based on the auditor's evaluation of those documents, the evaluation committee determines who will be the target of low-performer training programs (3% of employees). 5) After six months of training, the low performers are expected to return to work.

The system showed several positive results; for example, a substantial proportion of the lowest performers left the organization. Among the 190 employees designated as low performers during first two years, 51 left the organization (36% of the first designation, 80% of the second designation) (ChosunIlbo, 2009.3.7). Some employees who were designated low performers and successfully completed the training program showed dramatic changes and demonstrated good performance afterward (JungangIlbo, 2007.12.31). Despite these positive results, the system also revealed several limitations at the management level. At first, part of the training program included low quality work such as picking cigarette butts, weeding, and removing chewing gum from the streets. In 2008, the National Human Rights Committee of Korea judged that such activities may violate human rights, and recommended corrections. Thus, the Seoul Metropolitan Government changed how it operated the system. As Figure 3-6 shows, the portion of fieldwork was reduced and the training portion steadily increased. After a few years, the system was terminated through employees' continuous resistance.

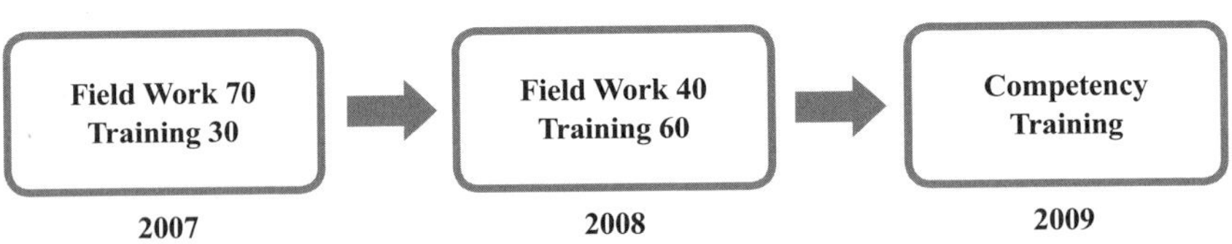

Source: Seoul Metropolitan Government (2009)

Figure 3-6 Changes of System Operation by Year

One can also find some unexpected negative effects in the system. Although its original purpose was to remove low performers, the Seoul Metropolitan government allocated a quota to each bureau, and each was forced to select low-performers, even in bureaus where every member worked hard. In addition, employees who were designated as low performers were stigmatized within the organization, which severely damaged their pride. Considering these negative influences of the system, a more cautious approach was required to manage low performers.

5. Performance Management

5.1. Performance-based HRM Reform

HRM reforms of previous governments in Korea have actively used the paradigm of "openness and competition" and "performance and responsibility" as new public administrative reforms. Specifically, the previous government has tried to change the reward and promotion aspect of the existing seniority-based system in the direction of performance and competency standards. In particular, the implementation of a multi-faceted evaluation system and the introduction of a senior civil servant system were introduced to promote the distribution of emphasis on competition and performance in the public sector. This personnel reform was aimed at moving away from existing personnel management, which emphasized uniformity of remuneration system based on seniority and warmth.

5.2. Performance Agreement System and Job Evaluation System

One can classify Korea's performance evaluation system into two categories: Performance Agreement System and Job Evaluation System. Depending on the rank of public personnel, the applied system is determined in that the Korean civil service has a grade system that reflects a strong tradition of seniority (Kong, Kim & Yang, 2013). The Korean government classifies civil servants into nine grades, where Grade 9 is the lowest, entry level grade. Employees Grade 4 or above are subject to the performance agreement system, whereas employees who are Grade 5 or below are regulated by the job evaluation system (Kong, Kim & Yang, 2013).

The Performance Agreement System is based on agreements between evaluators and personnel who are evaluated for performance goals and critical criteria to measure their performance. To establish the HR system based on merit and performance in the long term perspective, for officials above grade 4, the Korean government uses personnel records card system that collects all kinds of evaluation and audit records in a comprehensive and cumulative manner (Choi & Park, 2013). The Performance Agreement System follows the operation process of strategic planning, setting objectives for directors and managers, mid-year review, rewards, and feedback. The system begins with the strategic planning in that it sets both the core mission and sophisticated strategies to achieve it, which serve groundwork for performance management. The objective setting stage contracts the chief directors' performance objectives for each core task as presented in the earlier stage (Kong, Kim & Yang, 2013).

While the performance agreement system applies to high-level officials above Grade 4, mid- and low-level officers who are Grade 5–9 are ruled by the job evaluation system. Each employee is evaluated for his or her performance each year, and the evaluation becomes the basis for important HR decisions (Kim, 2009). This job evaluation commonly reflects three elements: job appraisal scores (70%), seniority-based scores (30%), and weight (5%) (Kim, 2009).

5.3. Performance Benefit System

Performance bonuses are paid according to the evaluation results of job performance contracts (December 31 each year) (Kang &Bae, 2012). Figure 3-7 explains the overall determination process for performance salary. First, evaluators conduct absolute evaluation based on the performance contract. Based on the absolute evaluation result, the relative evaluation is conducted to rank the evaluated personnel. Finally, a pay-for-performance committee determines the performance pay for each person.

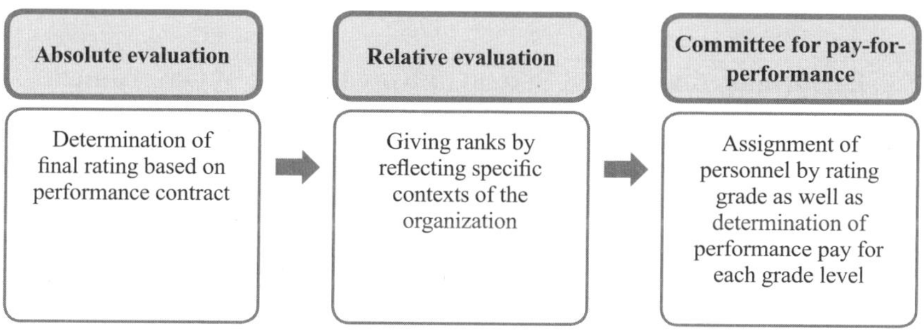

Source: Homepage of Ministry of Personnel Management(http://www.mpm.go.kr/mpm/info/infoBiz/bizSal/bizSal03/)

Figure 3-7 Performance Salary Determination Process

The overall scheme of the performance bonus is explained in Table 3-2. It has four ranks: S, A, B, and C. Only the upper 20% of employees receive an S grade, and they enjoy a 172.5% bonus. Meanwhile, the lowest 10% employees who receive a C grade do not receive any bonus. The standard amount for bonus is differentiated by grade. For example, the standard amount for a Grade 5 employee is approximately ₩3,800,000 KRW ($3,400 USD), and that for a Grade 7 employee is approximately ₩2,800,000 KRW ($2,500 USD).

Table 3-2 Performance bonus differential payment standard

Rank	S	A	B	C
Person ratio (%)	Upper 20%	20% to 60%	60% to 80%	Lower 10%
Payment rate (%)	172.5%	125%	85%	0%

Source: Administrative Rules of Ministry of Personnel Management (2017)

The performance-related pay system's main goals were: (1) to create a hard-working atmosphere in public service; (2) to attract competent and professional talent from the private sector; and (3) to spread a competitive attitude in government so that every civil servant can carry out their other tasks with liveliness and creativity (Kim, 2014).

5.4. Performance Appraisal System in Korean Central Government

Performance Agreement System (for high-rank officials): The Korean government conducts a "Performance Agreement System" for high level public officials that is based on agreements between individual officials and their supervisor. The evaluation criteria include job-related competence, individual performance, and organizational performance. The performance evaluation is conducted based on this agreement, and the evaluation result is applied to critical HR decisions such as performance pay and promotion (Kim, 2003; OECD, 2005). Allowing differentiated agreements means that the system is intended to incorporate different types of work and task characteristics. Regarding task characteristics, one person may have more qualitative targets than others if his or her work is policy-oriented. On the other hand, agreements for personnel in the service delivery department might have more quantitative performance indicators (Kim, 2014). Below is an example of performance agreement for the position of managing the performance management system.

[Template No. 1]

Performance Agreement

□ Evaluation period: Year 2014

	Department	Position	Name	Signature
Person subject to evaluation				
Evaluator				
A and B complete the following performance contract by mutual agreement to achieve the organization's mission and objectives.				

□ Individual performance objectives

No.	Performance Objective	Evaluation index		Action Plans
		Evaluation index (Including measurement methods)	Target points	
1	Assistance for settlement of the performance evaluation system	Level of compliance with the performance evaluation procedure	80%	▪ Orientation of the performance evaluation system ▪ Facilitation of the use of performance manager training manuals ▪ Monitoring operational conditions and finding best practices ▪ The preparation of a feedback system for performance management ▪ Development of cyber curricula for performance managers
		Enhance the recognition of the necessity for performance management	60%	

<table>
<tr><td rowspan="2">2</td><td rowspan="2">The establishment of a comprehensive performance information system</td><td>Use of Balanced Score Card (BSC)</td><td>80%</td><td rowspan="2">▪ Preparation of BSC manuals and orientations
▪ Link establishment between BSC and related systems
▪ Monitoring BSC operations and conducting a satisfaction survey
▪ Improving the BSC system</td></tr>
<tr><td>Satisfaction with BSC operations</td><td>60%</td></tr>
<tr><td>3</td><td>Improvement of the 360° feedback system</td><td>Establish an improvement plan for the 360°feedback system</td><td>Keep scheduled deadlines</td><td>▪ Preparation of the improvement plan focusing on competency evaluation
▪ Conducting a satisfaction survey for professionals and internal public servants</td></tr>
<tr><td rowspan="2">4</td><td rowspan="2">Support for employees‘ career development</td><td>Average hours of learning by employees</td><td>100 hours</td><td rowspan="2">▪ Encouraging employees to participate in regular learning and training sessions
▪ Conducting interviews and coaching each month</td></tr>
<tr><td>Number of performance interviews and coaching sessions</td><td>Five times</td></tr>
<tr><td>5</td><td>Support for employees' vacation usage</td><td>Improvement of vacation use (Growth rate compared to the previous year)</td><td>10% increase</td><td>▪ Establish an action plan to encourage the use of vacation time</td></tr>
</table>

The General Performance Appraisal System (for mid- and low-rank officials): The Korean government‘s general performance appraisal system has a rating scale based on two aspects: ―(1) job performance in major performance goals or major tasks in terms of job difficulties, completeness, and timeliness; and (2) job-fulfilling abilities (e.g. competencies such as planning, communication, teamwork, execution, innovation, customer-orientation)‖ (Kim, 2014, p.15). The template for the general performance appraisal is as follows.

[Template No. 2]

Civil Servant Performance Evaluation Form

□ Evaluation period:

Name	Department	Position	Rank	Employment Date for the current rank	Date of holding the current position

□ Main Task and Responsibilities

□ Job Performance Evaluation (point 50)

No.	Performance goals or unit task	Percentage of work (%)	Key Performance	Evaluation results	Subtotal score
				Overall performance/ Level of task completion	
1				Five point Likert scales	
2				Five point Likert scales	
3				Five point Likert scales	
4				Five point Likert scales	
Total score					

□ Job-fulfilling Abilities (point 50)

No.	Evaluation Factors	Points	Description of abilities	Rating	Subtotal score
1	Planning	9	▪ Predict problems and create actionable plans with creative perspectives. ▪ Make a clear plan that enables effective explanations.	Five point Likert scales	

2	Communication	6	▪ Make well organized and concise documents that clarify the main points. ▪ Explain in a logical and persuasive manner	Five point Likert scales	
3	Negotiation	6	▪ Understand the other party's intention and persuade them . Coordinate conflicting interests	Five point Likert scales	
4	Execution	5	▪ Be responsible for tasks and achieve them successfully ▪ Overcome environmental disadvantages with passion	Five point Likert scales	
5	Rapidness	5	▪ Conduct tasks without delay and meet deadlines ▪ Concentrate on a given task and complete work faster than the expected schedule	Five point Likert scales	
6	Teamwork	8	▪ Respect others and create a cooperative atmosphere with team members. ▪ Readily accept appropriate demands and constructive criticism.	Five point Likert scales	
7	Integrity	5	▪ Avoid deleterious actions such as beginning an absence without notice ▪ Have a dedicated attitude to both given tasks and the organization.	Five point Likert scales	
8	Customer-orientation	6	▪ Have an attitude of wanting to understand what the public want and seek to satisfy such demands	Five point Likert scales	
Total score					

□ Overall Evaluation

Rating and Score	Evaluator Comments
	※Describe work performance, managerial abilities, etc.

6. Elements of the Position Classification System

The Korean government has used the rank-in system as a basis to establish the career civil service system. Like other nations that have adopted the system, Korea has also sought to introduce some position classification elements to overcome the rank-in system's limitations. The open position recruitment system and senior civil service (SCS) system are representative.

6.1. Open Position Recruitment System

One major effort is enhancing the professionalism of public services by recruiting competent personnel from the private sector. Although the recruitment of public officials is based on a closed system (three entries at Grades 5, 7, and 9) where people are selected by through an open competitive exam, the Korean government also introduced an open recruitment system for higher level public officials in 2000 (Choi, 2015). The open position recruitment system seeks to increase knowledge sharing while facilitating the flexibility of utilizing human resources at the national level. At the organizational level, the system aims to recruit the competent personnel that organizations need in a timely manner and overcome the limitations of a closed recruitment system by diversifying recruitment channels and introducing position-based management.

The system has shown its achievements in recruiting personnel from the private sector. In February 2000, the Korean government began using the system by designating 130 chief/director positions as open positions. Currently, open positions are designated by each department (Within 20% of total SCS and director positions). In February 2016, 442 positions (173 SCS positions and

269 director positions) were designated. Figure 3-8 explains the recent trend of hiring through the open position system; out of the positions designated as open, approximately 45% were filled by outside personnel in 2009. This percentage decreased to below 35% in 2014 and bounced up in 2015. The graph indicates that not all open positions are filled by personnel from the private sector; more than 50% of open positions are filled by insiders.

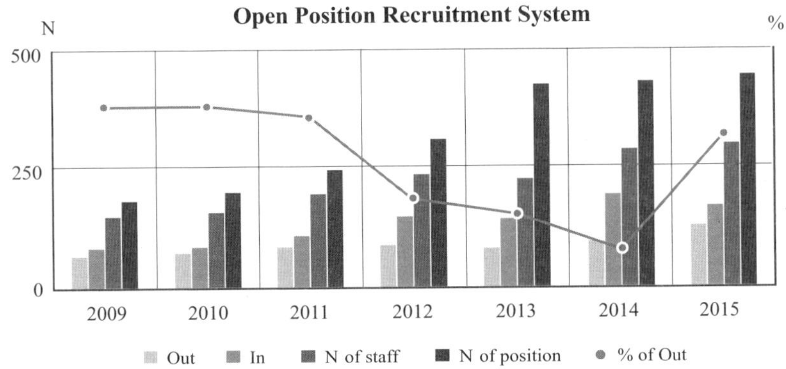

Source: National Public Service Personnel Statistics

Figure 3-8 Open position recruitment after 2009

The system does have some challenges and limitations. Newcomers from the private sector often experience difficulties in working in government. According to Lee et al. (2016), the main causes of difficulties include personal maladaptation, the closed organizational culture, and the instability of short-term contracts. In addition, by employing two kinds of recruitment system—open competitive exam recruitment and open position recruitment—factions may emerge by recruitment routes. More seriously, because of the perceptions that open positions for higher level officials are "temporary," there has been the limitation that people from the private sector may not take main roles within organizations (Choi, 2015). Another issue is whether talented people are attracted to open positions in government. Several scholars who participated in the recruitment process indicated that job candidates from the private sector were not quite as competitive, so that there was little chance of their recruitment. That might be part of the reasons why most open positions were filled by insiders who were existing public officials rather than private sector personnel. In 2014, private personnel were recruited to11 positions out of 162 open positions (Choi, 2015). A related problem is whether government agencies are willing to provide critical positions to their open positions. In the past, the decision about which positions would be open was reliant on each agency's decisions. Accordingly, most agencies designated positions that were not very attractive as open. Currently, the Ministry of Personnel Management designates several positions as open on their own while still giving each agency some discretion to address this weakness.

Considering these limitations, one should be cautious about introducing similar systems. First, selecting open positions by job type rather than by ministries' decisions might work better. That is, before determining which positions will be open, the job characteristics, difficulties, and responsibilities must be analyzed in terms of comparable private sector positions. In addition, conducting mentoring services for newcomers from outside is required. Both formal and informal mentoring will be critical for those people to settle in the public sector successfully.

6.2. Senior Civil Service (SCS) System

The objective of the Senior Civil Service (SCS) is to improve the government's competence by holding senior officials accountable for individual and organizational performance. The main idea is to pool high-level officials and match those employees to positions that maximize their competence and expertise across agencies. That is, the system seeks to strengthen accountability for performance by selecting and developing senior officials from an expanded government-wide pool and from outside the government.

The total number of SCS was 1,764 at the end of 2015. 54.6% of SCS members are elite officials who had entered the government via Gosi (a Grade 5 entrance exam). The SCS had a male dominant composition (Male 96%, Female 4%), SCS members had changed their positions 2.7 times during their SCS period, and the average period for which a position was held was 12.3 months. When considering the short period for which positions were held, SCS members may still have difficulties fully showing their potential.

Regarding the composition of SCS members, 20% were supposed to be selected by Open Position Recruitment System and 30% by the Job Posting System. That is, a candidate who meets the job requirement will be selected regardless of his or her affiliation, which is expected to ensure interagency competition. The remaining 50% are determined by the Minister's discretion. The SCS system conducts a strict screening process; becoming an SCS member, candidates should complete the SCS Candidate Development Program and pass the Competency Assessment. After successfully fulfilling these requirements, they can become SCS members.

After becoming SCS members, their performance is evaluated by job performance agreements. Each SCS member makes an individual performance agreement including performance objectives and measures, and agreements are determined after discussion with the member's direct supervisor. Commonly, their annual performance appraisal has five different ratings (Very excellent,

Excellent, Average, Insufficient, Very insufficient). The total salary of SCS is determined by three elements: basic pay, job pay, and performance pay. Basic pay is determined by each employee's grade. Job pay is determined by the job's level of difficulty and importance rather than by seniority or grade. There were five levels, but this was recently reduced to two. Finally, performance pay depends on the performance appraisal based on job performance agreement. The Korean government seeks to widen the performance gap; the maximum difference between the lowest and the highest rating is currently about $15,000 USD.

VI. Policy Recommendations

1. Sequence of HRM Reform

For better results of the HRM reform, we provide a reform plan as a sequence of three stages. If the six HRM initiatives discussed above are conducted simultaneously, that might lead to unexpected negative results and the reform's effects might not be fully realized. Accordingly, this chapter illustrates what initiatives must be prioritized and which initiatives serve as a foundation for others to demonstrate their full potential. As a preliminary prescription, we provide three steps to conduct HRM initiatives as follows: 1) the stabilization of the career civil service system, 2) the establishment of evidence-based management, and 3) full implementation of performance management and the adoption of position classification system (open system) elements. In practical terms, the first and second steps work as the foundation of the third step. That is, the first and the second steps can be conducted simultaneously. However, when resources are constrained, one may delay the establishment of evidence-based management system while prioritizing the stabilization of the career civil service system. In summary, the four initiatives serve as a basis for the third step initiatives as shown in Figure 3-9 below.

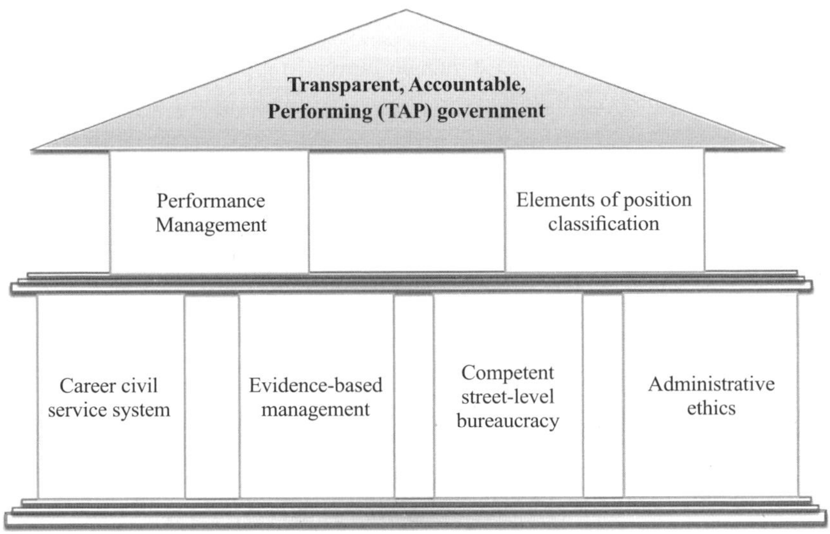

Figure 3-9 Scheme of HRM reform

First, stabilizing the career civil service system should be prioritized. Management based on merit is required, and assuring a high standard of administrative ethics is necessary for successfully adopting other reform initiatives. Providing a competitive salary to public personnel is also important for ensuring a high standard of morale. Currently, the Vietnam government has implemented cut-backs among public officials to enhance the efficiency and performance. When considering that the current salary level is insufficient, the Vietnam government may want to use the budget it has saved through cut-backs to increasing salary levels. Finally, making public service attractive, enhancing the pride of existing public personnel, and developing public personnel who are respected by citizens for their high standards of morale and competence are critical to establish the effective career civil service.

Second, the Vietnamese government must establish a system to regularly collect data about public personnel. This will make a foundation for evidence-based management. Understanding the distribution of public officials and evaluating their current status will help make future recruitment plans. For example, the database will clarify what types of expert are currently required in government, what professionals will be needed over the next 10 years, etc. Another required task is classifying the major tasks of public personnel and preparing specific job descriptions for each Ministry. Related to the current cut-back efforts, each Ministry is required to prepare job descriptions to justify their personnel. The preparation of job descriptions is also helpful for other purposes. For example, one can systematically classify required tasks within an organization to successfully conduct its mission. The job description also illustrates each job holder's core competences. Such information will serve as a basic standard with which to evaluate the performance of public personnel, and becomes a basis for effective performance management. This is also a pre-condition for the introduction of certain elements of a position classification system.

Finally, after stabilizing the career civil service system and achieving sufficient preparation for evidence-based management and detailed job descriptions, adopting a performance management system and introducing elements of a position classification system will be executable. When accompanied with sophisticated performance measurements, performance management can be a quite useful tool with which to enhance individual and organizational performance. In utilizing performance management, the

Vietnam government wants to connect its management to its core vision. For example, each Ministry's performance objectives should be aligned with the overall vision of the government. Similarly, each bureau's performance targets should be aligned with the vision of the Ministry. In addition, some elements of position classification systems will be helpful for increasing expertise in the public sector, which will supplement the shortcomings of the career civil service system.

Maintaining this sequence is desirable to maximize the effectiveness of HRM reform. For example, performance management (third phase) may not achieve its expected effects if the job descriptions (second phase) are poorly prepared. As discussed, if job descriptions are not prepared, one will have difficulties designing proper performance measurements. Without stabilizing the career civil service system (first phase), introducing an open system (position classification system) (third phase) will cause confusion among public officials. For example, introducing an open position recruitment system may not attract competent personnel from the private sector if the salary level is not competitive. Likewise, unless a merit-based system has been well established (first phase), public officials will not accept the performance evaluation results (third phase). Finally, the effectiveness of reforms will be maximized when the sequence is well maintained.

2. Prescriptions in Specific Areas

2.1. The Establishment of a Bureau for Evidence-based Management

As a specific prescription with which to implement the reform sequences discussed above, the Vietnam government may want to consider establishing a bureau that is responsible for data gathering and analysis while also providing HR strategies. Under a certain Ministry (Currently, the Ministry of Home Affairs seems the appropriate Ministry), the bureau will collect the comprehensive personnel data and share this with other Ministries. Regarding data collection, the "FedScope" website (www.fedscopt.gov) as operated by the U.S. OPM may serve as a role model to benchmark. . Establishing the database will serve as a foundation for evidence-based decision making. One may not conduct the evidence-based decision making for every single decision, but it is required for critical HR decisions for better outcomes and for making the TAP government.

Besides, the Vietnam government may consider building a bureau that creates strategic plans for HRM, , which does not currently exist The bureau will use the generated empirical data to diagnose the current status and make a recruitment plan with which to sustain and enhance the government's human capital. Making an appropriate and comprehensive plan will require that the bureau makes strong networks with other Ministries; the bureau will collect job descriptions from each Ministry and analyze them in a systematic manner to determine which expertise and what types of personnel each ministry require. The analysis result must be reflected to establish both long- and short-term strategic plans for HRM. Having this forecasting capability will help the government recruit more competent people in a timely manner.

2.2. Cautious Cut-backs with Strengthened Administrative Ethics

One major upcoming HRM issue in Vietnam is downsizing. As we discussed previously, a cautious approach is required for successful downsizing. The downsizing issue is not confined to the physical reduction of staffs. The issue is related to other HR dimensions such as recruitment, promotion, performance management, etc. More fundamentally, it is also related to the restructure of central and local governments and the establishment of border line between the public and the private sectors. Considering that the number of public officials has recently increased (particularly at the local level), one can admit the necessity of downsizing; the issue is how it should be conducted. We believe that the preparation of evidence-based management will be helpful for conducting downsizing. Job descriptions and the detailed demographic information of each Ministry and bureau will serve as basic evidence and more appropriate decisions for downsizing will be made based on the database.

Another initiative is to assure administrative ethics, which is related to competitive payment. Ensuring a high level of ethics among public officials so that they can serve as role models will require that the government treats them better so that they are more resistant to bribery. Still, the current salary level of public employees in Vietnam is not comparable to their counterparts in the private sector. The government may want to consider using resources saved through downsizing for the benefit of public officials to break the chain of corruption. Simultaneously, stricter punishments for corruption should be implemented. The Vietnamese government may want to consider strengthening their auditing function by establishing an independent audit agency, which is the case in Korea. The Vietnamese government can also consider establishing laws that specifically regulate bureaucratic behaviors and transactions like Korea (setting maximums of $30 for meals, $50 for presents, etc.), but this requires a cautious approach. Vietnam's contexts and situations should be fully considered.

2.3. Introduction of Position Classification System Elements with Caution

To increase the expertise and professionalism within the government, the Vietnam government may consider introducing some elements of position classification systems. One representative example is Korea's Open Position Recruitment System (Open Civil Service System). However, cautious investigation must first be conducted to evaluate whether the system will be beneficial in Vietnam. The expectation of introducing the Open Position Recruitment System is to attract talented people from the private sector and enhance expertise among those in the public sector. The system has had some achievements in Korea. However, as discussed previously, some challenges remain. For example, one primary issue is whether talented people are attracted to open government positions. Several scholars who participated in the recruitment process indicate that job candidates from the private sector are less competitive, so that there is little chance of their recruitment. This view is reflected by the fact that out of 162 open positions in 2014, only 11 private personnel were recruited (Choi, 2015). In addition, another issue is whether government agencies are willing to allocate critical positions to open positions. In the past, the decision about which positions would be open was reliant on each agency's decision, and most agencies designated positions that were not very attractive as open. The MPM currently seeks to ameliorate this issue by designating several positions as open on their own while still giving each agency some discretion. The Vietnam government may avoid the pitfalls that Korean government has experienced if they evaluate the following factors before adopting the system: 1) whether such a system will be beneficial, 2) whether there will be some unexpected side-effects, 3) how to overcome any obstacles, and 4) how to structure incentives to help the system succeed.

3. Summary and Conclusion

The current chapter first reviewed global HRM trends and suggested the concept of Transparent, Accountable, and Performing (TAP) government as an ideal status that the Vietnam government might pursue. Then, the report provided six reform initiatives in the HRM area to help realize the TAP government concept. The six initiatives include 1) preparation of a system for evidence-based management, 2) establishment of a career civil service system, 3) strengthening administrative ethics, 4) promoting the competence of street-level bureaucracy, 5) performance evaluations and management, and 6) introducing position classification system elements. It then discussed what specific systems and practices have been performed in Korea for each initiative. The chapter sought to provide some practical implications to the Vietnamese government by discussing the sequence in which reform initiatives should be introduced and some prescriptions for specific areas.

This chapter's intention is not to argue that the systems and practices that the Korean government is using or has used before are superior and should be adopted by the Vietnamese government. Every system and practice has its own positives and negatives, and no one system fits all nations. A particular system may work very well in one country and fail in another. In addition, the systems and practices that the Korean government currently employs are not perfect; they have shown some achievements, but they still have limitations and challenges.

This report's objective is to inform both the benefits and costs of Korean HRM practices, and let the Vietnamese government find the best way to reform the HRM system. Some practices may fit Vietnam well, and might be adopted without revisions. However, other practices may need substantial transformation to reflect Vietnam's specific unique contexts. Finally, utilizing this report's information and making actual HR policies that reflect the Korean government's experience will rely on the decisions of the Vietnamese government. The authors hope that the Vietnamese government will be successful in its HRM reform by understanding both the achievements and challenges of the Korean experience.

CHAPTER FOUR:

Public Expenditure Management Reform

Seungwon YU
Professor, Department of Public Administration, Korean National Police University

CHAPTER FOUR:

Public Expenditure Management Reform

I. Coverage of this research

The analysis of this research targets Public Expenditure Management (PEM) reform and thus includes PEM reform measures such as Medium-Term Expenditure Framework (MTEF) and program budgeting. However, the issues on the revenue side such as tax reform are excluded from the research.

The analysis of this research targets Vietnam's central government; therefore, it includes each ministry under the central government. However, local governments and public enterprises are excluded from the analysis based on the System of National Accounts of UN and Government Finance Statistics of IMF.

II. What should be reformed to enhance PEM in Vietnam?

Vietnamese public finances have poor efficiency with the fiscal deficit's large scale and increases in government debt. Therefore, despite the expansion in the public finance scale, the contribution of public finances to economic growth remains low. PEM reform is strongly required to overcome this phenomenon.

Various PEM reforms can be introduced or performed as follows: MTEF, Top-down Budgeting, Program Budgeting, Performance Management, Budget Coverage Expansion, Integrated Information System, the Rearrangement of Public Finance Statistics, Accrual Basis Government Accounting, Project Management (total cost management, preliminary feasibility tests, etc.).

The 2015 State Budget Law that took effect on January 1, 2017 provided for MTEF and Vietnam had previously piloted MTEF in four ministries and three cities and provinces from 2004 to 2009. This is a good attempt at Vietnamese public expenditure management reform, in that MTEF is acknowledged as essential for strategic budget allocation policies and the enhancement of fiscal soundness. However, the reality is that Vietnam still lacks experts who are capable of developing and implementing MTEF. The government has not considered the linkage between MTEF and the annual budget, which is a precondition for the success of MTEF. Appropriate measures are needed to solve issues. They also said that the Vietnamese government had not prepared for public expenditure management reform policies other than MTEF.

There are PEM reforms whose introduction the Vietnamese government cannot delay. For example, many funds such as the Vietnamese public insurance fund have not been included in the budget coverage. This may result in underestimating the size of the budget deficit and government debt. Off-budget funds are not reviewed by the Vietnamese national assembly, and so it may not easy to control the reckless management of off-budget funds, if any. In addition, the Vietnamese government has recently assigned approximately five percent points of the budget deficit to GDP each year on average. Thus, the Government should have as significant an increase in the ratio of government debt to GDP as the increase in the budget deficit, unless there is no redemption of government debt. However, statistics from the Vietnamese government show that the government debt has recently increased by just two percent points on average each year. If public finance statistics were rearranged, numbers for the budget deficit and government debt may change.

The Vietnamese government is not required to introduce or perform all the PEM reforms mentioned above. A few of the PEM reforms that are expected to have poor effectiveness or efficiency in Vietnamese reality can have a delayed introduction, even if the PEM reforms themselves are evaluated as important.

It is necessary for the Vietnamese government to prioritize PEM reforms and analyze related methods in depth. However, academic research has not cast light on the strategies, action plans, and methods in the PEM reform field. International organizations such as the IMF and World Bank have presented each country's updated status for PEM reforms without suggesting an overall strategy or action plan for introducing the reforms. There is also a lack of detailed experience sharing in the field. Fortunately, Korea has a long history of PEM reform and has introduced or performed almost all PEM reforms. The writers of this paper well understand the principles and application methods of PEM reforms. Despite the limitations of academia and international organizations, the writers' expertise and Korea's trial and error approach can help the Vietnamese government prioritize PEM reforms and prepare actual introduction strategies and action plans.

III. Evaluation of and Lessons from the Korean Experiences in Public Expenditure Management Reforms

A few criteria for evaluating the experience of Korea's PEM reforms can be considered. It is necessary to consider how much time is needed for each reform to take effect as well as visible and invisible calculable costs for the introduction. Some reforms may take a relatively short time or low cost to implement. However, the introduction time and cost can be considerable, depending on the complexity of each system or the goal of the system. It is also necessary to consider a link with other reforms. In the case of reform measures with strong links with other reform measures, it is necessary to introduce them first to attain a synergy effect with other reforms. If a reform has not been not introduced even though it has a strong link with other existing reforms, the existing reforms may not be effective. We can also consider whether the reforms are fundamental to the PEM. For example, the budgeting coverage expansion or the rearrangement of public expenditure statistics is not popular among common people or government officials. However, because they are very basic reforms in financial management, the reforms must be introduced regardless of the cost or time required to introduce.

When we evaluate the Korean public expenditure management reform, we should focus on both whether the individual reform policy has been successful and whether the reform policies have operated in balance from the overall point of view. For the evaluation, we will analyze in this paper a process by which the Korean reforms were progressed and issues which were seen in that process, and we will evaluate the Korean reforms from the overall point of view and the individual point of view. Based on the evaluation, we will try to suggest some lessons that can be applied to Vietnam.

- Time to take effect
- Cost of introduction
- Link with other reform policies
- Whether it is a basis of public expenditure management

Figure 4-1 Criteria for evaluating the experience of Korea's PEM reforms

1. Evaluation on the Korean PEM Reforms

Here are evaluations of a few representative Korean PEM reforms.

1.1. Medium-Term Expenditure Framework (MTEF)

In Korea, it took a short time for the MTEF to take effect. Since the introduction of the revised MTEF in 2004, each ministry has established a single-year budget under a medium-term plan. In addition, considering that a new project should be included in an MTEF before being included in an annual budget, the MTEF is in effect the introduction. The cost of introducing the MTEF was not large. Because Korean public officers had acquired some techniques for managing the costs, benefits, and performance of each project, it has not been difficult for each ministry to calculate the project financing from the medium-term viewpoint. MTEF has a strong link with other PEM reforms. This is because medium-term financial needs of all projects should be identified, and top-down budgeting and performance management should be planned from a medium-term perspective.

1.2. Program Budgeting

The program budgeting is a system in which the budget is implemented focused on program units. It has been taking a long time for Korean program budgeting to become effective; efforts are still underway. For a program budgeting to be effective, the budget should be managed based on a program unit, which is a national strategic unit. However, the budget is mainly managed based on a project unit, which officials regularly have strong preference for. It takes a considerable amount of time to convert the basic unit of managing budget from the project to the program. The cost of introducing program budgeting was high in Korea. It took about two years, including the pilot test period, to reclassify all ministries' budget classifications into the program-activity-project approach. The program budgeting has a very strong link with other budget systems. The Korean government has envisioned the program budgeting as an enabler for other budget systems to work. MTEF, top-down budgeting, performance management, and an accrual-based government accounting system were planned to operate on a program unit basis. For this reason, the program budgeting corresponds to the basis of other PEM reforms.

1.3. Budget Coverage Expansion

Budget coverage expansion in Korea is taking a long time to show its effect. It is still in the process. A big cost was incurred for the introduction of the reform. It is very difficult to judge whether an individual institution is included in the public sector or the private sector based on criteria, or whether it is actually a general government or a state-owned enterprise. In addition, the Korean government experienced that some provisional judging criteria were exposed to the big news media before finalizing official judgment criteria. As a result, work for the budget coverage expansion reform was delayed by about two years due to the opposition pressed by some relevant institutions and the majority-opposition party. Because each institution can be included in or excluded from government budget coverage due to the criteria, each related institution was very sensitive to the criteria. The reform is strongly connected to other budget systems. This is because the public sector or any institution belonging to the general government must follow the government's fiscal policy. For this reason, this policy corresponds to the basis of other PEM reforms.

1.4. Performance Management

It takes long time to witness policy effect of performance management in Korea. Performance plans and performance reports have been reported to Parliament and performance evaluations have been performed for each project. However, the performance of the performance management has not been high, because performance indicators do not fully reflect the goals of each ministry or each project, and the targets of the indicators are not high. In other words, the performance management looks good, but it is not good in reality. In addition, it took great cost to introduce the performance management. This is because government officials spent a considerable amount of time in creating performance indicators for each project and performance plans and performance reports. In addition, the Korean government had to use external experts in order to improve the credibility of performance information prepared by government officials themselves. This PEM reform has a high connectedness to other budget systems. For example, the performance management can be carried out based on the program units under connection with the program budgeting, and the MTEF can be strengthened through performance information produced by performance management.

PEM reforms	Time to take effect	Cost of Introduction	Link with others
MTEF	Short	Small	Strong
Program budgeting	Long	Big	Strong
Top-down budgeting	Long	Big	Strong
Performance management	Long	Big	Strong
Budget coverage expansion	Short	Big	Strong
Integrated information system	Short	Big	weak
Rearrangement of public finance statistics	Short	Small	weak
Project management	Short	Small	weak
Accrual basis government accounting	Long	Big	weak

Figure 4-2 Evaluation on an individual PEM reform policy (Korean experiences)

2. Lessons from the Korean PEM reforms

The Korean experience of PEM reforms has down sides as follow. The Vietnamese government should be cautious to minimize the trial and error experienced by Korea.

Firstly, an individual PEM reform was carried out separately without consideration of the linkages between PEM reforms. For example, when introducing the MTEF, the MTEF budget classification and the annual budget classification were different. As a result, it was difficult to apply the medium-term strategies reviewed through the MTEF to annual budgets. In addition, when introducing the top-down budgeting, Korea did not consider linkage with the MTEF already introduced. This is because the Government considered a ceiling in the annual budget, not the ceiling in the MTEF. When introducing a performance management system, Korea did not consider the linkage with the annual budget. It also failed to consider the linkage between the performance management classification and the budget classification.

Secondly, the Korean government has paid little attention to the PEM reforms, which take a long time before the reform takes effect. For example, program budgeting is a budget system that implements the budget focused on program units. To attain the goal of the program budgeting, the budget should be classified into program units, activity units, and project units, and the budget systems such as an MTEF, top-down budgeting, and performance management should be implemented, focused on program units. The Korean government has been successful in classifying the budget into program units, activity units, and project units. However, it is evaluated that the implementation of the budget focused on program units is so difficult that the Korean government has not endeavored much in the implementation.

Thirdly, when introducing an individual PEM reform, the Korean government has implemented the reform with the intent to accomplish every goal of the reform at once, without considering the gradual phased development of the reform. Korea did not set up a master plan for phased implementation of related PEM reforms, nor did it consider step-by-step linkages with other PEM reforms. For example, to successfully implement top-down budgeting, a program unit must be established by which the fiscal authority of Korean government can afford the ceiling. However, the Korean government has introduced top-down budgeting without setting up program units, and has not considered plans to afford a ceiling by program unit so far.

Table 4-1 Lessons from the Korean PEM reforms

• Little consideration paid to the link with other PEM reforms
• Relative unconcern for PEM reforms that take long time to take in effect
• Not performed in a step-by-step way

IV. Strategy and action plans of public expenditure management reform in Vietnam

Based on the above analyses, we examine here PEM reform strategies and action plans applicable to Vietnam.

1. Redirect the way of managing public resources

First, improving financial discipline in general and public expenditure discipline in particular in recommended. The State Budget Law 2015 stipulates budgeting in the medium-term expenditure framework and performance budgeting. This is a great step, reflecting the thinking of Vietnam's fiscal integration with world standards. However, the problem is that even if Vietnam uses an annual budgeting method, with such a short-term nature, public expenditure discipline was not ensured to be strict, resulting in expenditure over budget estimation. Therefore, there is reason to be concerned about this continuing (and likely to repeat) regarding the medium-term expenditure framework (3 to 5 years). In other words, if there is a good tool but the financial discipline is not strict, the tool does not work well. Therefore, we recommend that state agencies that implement the budget of Vietnam must strictly implement financial discipline, so that the effectiveness of implementation of the new state budget law is guaranteed.

Second, a national financial information service agency should be established to ensure the handling of sensitive financial data and ensure the accuracy and consistency of data when published. In addition, the national financial information service agency will also facilitate the provision of financial information to organizations and individuals in society; they can thereby make business decisions in line with the macroeconomic situation of the country, contributing to the establishment of a developmental government. In this regard we can refer to the model of Korea Public Finance Information Service (KPFIS).

Third, reform the growth model in Vietnam, transforming from a broad-based growth model to an in-depth growth model based on technical efficiency, allocation efficiency, and scientific-technical progress towards sustainable growth. In order to quickly shift growth model from breadth to depth, economic restructuring is a viable option in the first stage; thereby, the resources of the economy are reallocated in the most efficient way to facilitate economic model innovation.

Fourth, the use of statistical methods in accordance with international standards and practices.

Fifth, the restructure of state budget expenditures in the direction of reducing recurrent expenditures, especially emphasis on staff streamlining, quickly and resolutely reduce the number of people who receiving budget salary, thereby reducing the salary burden for the state budget.

Sixth, the restructuring and equitization of SOEs, SOEs' self-accounting system, eliminating inputs privileges of SOEs, and creating an equal business environment for all economic sectors. Valuing of land at market prices for all transactions between the State and SOEs. Using the modern business administration for SOEs to separate state ownership from enterprise management, thereby reducing the consequences of poor performance and public debt of these enterprises.

Seventh, establishing the national financial transparency and oversight mechanism. Lack of transparency is one of the major causes of corruption in Vietnam. Fiscal transparency will help to ensure financial discipline, providing a more complete assessment of financial risks, giving timely solutions to prevent these risks and improving the financial management capacity of the government.

2. Which PEM Reforms to Carry Out in Vietnam

When deciding on which PEM reforms to adopt at present in Vietnam, Vietnam's environment and preferred criteria should be considered first. First of all, in Vietnam, many PEM reforms have not been implemented in earnest, and the contents of the PEM reforms have not been sufficiently introduced. Vietnam is currently working hard to implement MTEF under the Law on State Budget 2015. However, there is no concrete plan to introduce various other PEM reforms such as program budgeting, performance management, top-down budgeting, etc., and it seems that consensus on the contents of the PEM reforms has not been reached in Vietnam. In other words, the pros and cons of each PEM reform, and the success possibility of each PEM reform have not been analyzed or verified in Vietnam.

Another consideration is that the Vietnamese government is not planning to implement comprehensive PEM reforms like the four major PEM reforms of South Korea. Thus, it can be expected that an individual PEM reform will be introduced separately until the time when the Vietnamese government implements comprehensive PEM reforms in the future. Apart from these circumstances, foreign governments or international organizations may recommend a sporadic PEM reform measure. At this time, even if the Vietnamese government does not consider the introduction of the PEM reform measure, the PEM reform is likely to be introduced if foreign governments or international organizations prefer or emphasize it. However, this is beyond the scope of this report and is not discussed herein.

Under the above circumstances, the following figure can be used as the criteria that distinguish between the introduction and non-introduction of many PEM reforms by the Vietnamese government.

Vietnamese environments to consider	- Little experience of PEM reforms - Little consideration to implement comprehensive PEM reforms
Criteria for deciding preferred PEM reforms	- PEM reforms that can be implemented in simpler and easier way - PEM reforms that can be effective in shorter time - A more independent PEM reform with less link with other PEM reforms

⇩

PEM reforms which can be introduced at present	- MTEF - Rearrangement of fiscal statistics - Project management
PEM reforms which should be cautious in the introduction at present	- Performance management - Program budgeting - Top-down budgeting - Accrual basis government accounting
PEM reforms which may or may not be introduced at present	- Budget coverage expansions - Integrated (advanced) budget information system

Figure 4-3 Core PEM Reforms Which Can Be Introduced at Present Based on Vietnamese Environment and Criteria

3. How to Implement the Core PEM Reforms in Vietnam?

In the following, we will focus on core PEM reforms, which are recommended to be introduced in Vietnam, and performance management, which Vietnam HCMA has requested to review. We would like to outline some things to consider when introducing the core PEM reforms, etc.

3.1. Medium-Term Expenditure Framework (MTEF)

Considering the limitations in Korean experience when introducing an MTEF and the characteristics of the MTEF, the Vietnamese government should consider the following three points when introducing an MTEF.

First, when introducing an MTEF, it is necessary to steadily implement it from the basic level without being greedy. It is desirable for the Vietnamese government introduce the MTEF to the basic level of an MTFF. For reference, the World Bank has examined the extent to which countries around the world have introduced MTEFs. As of 2008, 88 of the South Asia countries introduced MTEFs (even formally), of which 63 countries (72%) adopted MTFFs and 25 countries (28%) were in the more advanced form of MTBTs (World Bank, 2013). In order to introduce the MTBF scheme, medium-term funding should be allocated based on the priority between government sectors and programs. To this end, the prerequisite that the budget classification system should be set well must be satisfied. In other words, a program budgeting should be introduced with well-made budget classification. This report does not recommend introducing it considering the current environment in Vietnam. For reference, MTEF can be divided into three levels depending on extent of introduction of the system: MTFF, MTBF, and MTPF.[11].

Secondly, it is necessary to make the MTEF's budget classification and the yearly budget classification the same. At the very least, the units of government sectors and sub-sectors must be the same in the MTEF classification and the yearly budget classification. In order for the medium-term fiscal forecast to be reflected in the yearly budget, the MTEF and the yearly budget should have the same budget classification. Otherwise, there is no device to link the MTEF with the yearly budget, so MTEF is highly likely to fall into a formal system. If Vietnam is oriented towards an MTBF, MTEF and yearly budget classification should be the same in the full units of sector, sub-sector, program, activity, and project classification. If Vietnam is oriented towards an MTFF, then it is only necessary to make same in the units of sector and sub-sector. In Korea, approximately 30 years after the introduction of the MTEF, it became same as the yearly budget classification. Until then, the effectiveness of Korean MTEF had been weak.

Third, various measures should be carried out to increase the effectiveness of MTEF. There are many ways to do this. One of the recommendations is to make sure that when the medium-term outlook forecasted by the Vietnamese government is different from the actual results, the government should report the difference to the party or the National Assembly. If the gap between the

11 An MTFF is a medium-term fiscal framework. This encompasses the top-down specification of the aggregate resource envelope and the allocation of resources across spending agencies. Putting in place an MTFF is desirable regardless of a country's level of budgeting capacity. An MTBF is a medium-term budgetary framework. In addition to the features of an MTFF, an MTBF includes both the bottom-up determination of spending agency resource needs and reconciliation of these with the resource envelope. MTPF is a medium-term performance framework. Starting from an MTBF, an MTPF completes the shift in focus from inputs to outputs, with an emphasis on the measurement and evaluation of performance. An MTPF, and therefore a full-fledged MTEF, is a pinnacle reachable only by those countries that have implemented a well-functioning MTBF. Source: World Bank. (2013). Beyond the annual budget-Global experience with medium term experience frameworks.

medium-term outlook and the actual outcome is to be reported to the outside, the Vietnamese government will strive to improve the accuracy of the medium-term forecast. If the above matters are mentioned in the law, the effectiveness will be higher.

Table 4-2 A few points to be considered when introducing MTEF in Vietnam

• To steadily implement the MTEF from the basic level without greed
• To make the MTEF's budget classification and the yearly budget classification the same
• To introduce various measures to increase the effectiveness of the MTEF (e.g. To report the gap between the forecast and the results of the MTEF to the Parliament, etc.)

3.2. Rearrangement of public finance statistics

Considering Korea's experience, there are three things to consider when implementing the rearrangement of public finance statistics.

First, if Vietnam attempts to rearrange all public finance statistics, the probability of success of the reform may be low. It is desirable to rearrange only core financial statistics through selection and concentration. It would be good to rearrange micro-statistics after rearranging macro-statistics in terms of securing the driving force and raising credibility in the rearrangement of public finance statistics. The financial statistics that should be included in the rearrangement as macro-statistics are government debt or liability statistics, government expenditure size statistics, and public-sector workers statistics. At present, the government debt or liability statistics of the Vietnamese government seem to have room for improvement. If government debt statistics are underestimated compared to international standards, it may lead to various problems. Under-estimated government debt or liability statistics can further reduce external credibility and hinder the overcoming of a crisis, if any.

The size of government spending should also be estimated by applying the same financial coverage used in calculating government debt or liability statistics. If the standard in calculating the government expenditure size is different from that used in calculating government debt or liability statistics, either may be under-estimated and the other over-estimated. To solve this problem, the coverage of central government, local government, general government, and the public sector should be set in accordance with international standards, and the same criteria should be applied when estimating the amount of government expenditure and government debt or liability.

In the case of public sector workers' statistics, it is necessary to apply the same public finance coverage as that used in estimating government spending and government debt or liability. At present, the government of Vietnam is said to have a high proportion of public sector employees, and the proportion of personnel expenses paid to them is high. In order to prepare counter-measures against these problems, it is necessary that all the statistics on the public-sector workers are accurately derived as basic statistics.

In order to properly carry out the rearrangement of the government expenditure, government debt or liability, and public-sector employee statistics, it is necessary to rearrange or expand the public-sector coverage. This is not an easy task from the experience of Korea. In the case of Korea, many public finance experts participated to perform the task for a long time. However, if the public-sector coverage is rearranged or expanded, it affects all PEM reforms. Thus, if this task is successful, financial accountability and efficiency can be significantly improved.

Second, there is a need for supplementary measures to smoothly carry out additional upgrades or other rearrangement of public finance statistics in the future. It is necessary to establish a public finance statistical information system or to build a public finance statistics database. At least, a public finance statistics database should be established, and it should be disclosed to the general public via the web. It can improve the quality of statistics by increasing the accuracy of the statistics. In addition, it is possible to prevent the improved database from being retreated to the state before the improvement. This can be done by upgrading the existing Vietnamese public finance information system or by building separate public finance database.

Third, a separate organization or experts are needed to manage only the public finance statistics, which will be helpful in implementing the two things mentioned above. It is possible to consider establishing a public finance statistics center as an organization attached to existing Vietnam research institutes or public-finance-related think tanks. In the case of Korea, the financial intelligence agency was established as an affiliate of the Korean public finance authority. This organization is managing the public finance information and statistics by operating a financial statistical system as a sub-system of dBrain, an integrated public finance information system of Korea.

Table 4-3 A few points to be considered when rearranging public finance statistics in Vietnam

• To rearrange core financial statistics by selection and concentration (e.g., government debt or liability, government expenditure, and public-sector employees)
• To establish a public finance statistics information system or database
• A separate organization or experts needed to manage the public finance statistics

3.3. Project Management

Currently, the Vietnamese government's expenditure growth is very high. However, capital expenditures are not expanding as much as the current expenditures. In other words, capital expenditures are likely to increase in the future. Project management should be introduced to effectively manage this expansion of capital expenditure. In order to increase the effectiveness of project management, specific measures should be prepared to efficiently manage projects over a certain scale before an official introduction of the projects. Vietnamese government needs to pay attention on the three things based on Korea's experience.

First, measures should be prepared for pre-feasibility tests on projects of a certain size or bigger. Public finance authority or related agencies should carefully examine the policy feasibility, economic feasibility, and management feasibility of the project to ensure that the budget is actually paid only for projects whose feasibility is above a certain level.

Second, it is necessary to manage the total cost of the project over a certain scale. When a capital expenditure project with a certain amount of total cost over a certain period of years is to be newly introduced, it is necessary to plan the business before the execution and calculate the total cost of the project. A government department pursuing the project must obtain the approval for the total project cost calculated before the execution of the project from the public finance authority or related agencies. In addition, it is necessary to execute the project within the scope of the total cost; in addition, when the total cost should be changed, the changed cost should be re-approved from the public finance authority or related agencies.

Third, there is a need to establish a separate organization to stably and efficiently manage the pre-feasibility tests and total cost management. In Korea, the Private Infrastructure Investment Management Center(PIMAC), an organization affiliated to the Korea Development Institute(KDI), which is one of the think tanks of the Korean public finance authority, and other organizations have been established to do the jobs. It needs a high degree of expertise to do the jobs such that it will be efficient to establish a separate agency under the Vietnamese public finance authority and to take charge of the relevant tasks for the agency. In addition, the total cost management and pre-feasibility tests are systems that are very helpful in raising the effectiveness and efficiency of the projects and improving the financial soundness. Accordingly, specific manuals and practical implementation plans should be prepared in order to introduce the measures in Vietnam in the near future.

Table 4-4 A few points to be considered when introducing project management in Vietnam

• Pre-feasibility tests needed for projects of a certain size or bigger
• Total cost management needed for projects of a certain size or bigger
• A separate organization needed to manage the pre-feasibility tests and total cost management stably and efficiently

3.4. Performance Management

This report recommended that the introduction of performance management in Vietnam should be cautious. However, international organizations have recommended to various countries that the performance management be introduced. It will be probable that the performance management will be introduced in Vietnam within the near future, either due to the independent judgment of the Vietnamese government or by the recommendation of an international organization. Here, we would like to present some points to consider when introducing the performance management in Vietnam at the request of the Vietnamese HCMA.

First, a considerable amount of tangible and intangible costs can be incurred in driving performance management. You will need to design a number of options in advance to minimize the cost. In order to do this, priority should be given to determining which business should be evaluated and how the performance can be evaluated. Performance evaluation for a program level or an activity level is not easy. This is because the evaluation needs to consider whether the activities under the program level and the projects under the activity level are operating well and whether any synergy between the activities and between the projects exists. Considering these difficulties, it is necessary to first evaluate the performance at the project level, which is the lowest level of budget classification.

In principle, when creating performance indicators, outcome or output indicators should be preferred, which is not easy. In reality, there are many temptations to create input or process indicators. It is difficult to avoid this phenomenon at the initial stage of performance management. However, the input or the process indicator cannot represent a goal that the project is intended to pursue. This is one of several factors that detract from the effectiveness of performance management.

Second, it is not desirable to conduct performance management on all departments at once. It is desirable to conduct a pilot system by selecting some departments or agencies that need higher performance results or in which it is relatively easy to implement the performance management. It is also desirable to evaluate the performance of the piloting, and gradually to expand the performance management if necessary. A department or an agency with big capital expenditure projects or projects with some problems would be good for the piloting in that the organizations can get the external jurisdiction for the performance management.

Third, it should be considered that a very long time is required for effective performance management. The international organizations such as the OECD and the World Bank are evaluating that Korea's performance management is very good, but Korea is not satisfied with its performance management internally. The Vietnamese government should not be impatient for performance management, considering that Korean's evaluation on the performance management is not positive even after 50 years, since the start of performance management in the 1960s. It is important to improve the system of performance management, but it is more important to change the mindset of public officials regarding performance management. However, it is not easy to change the people's minds. Therefore, if performance management is introduced in Vietnam in the future, it is better to carry out the phased strategy or action plans of the performance management step by step.

Table 4-5 A few points to be considered when introducing performance management in Vietnam

• To evaluate the performance of a project, which is the lowest level in budget classification, before evaluating an activity or a program level
• Not to conduct performance management in all departments at once ⇨ Piloting by selecting some departments or agencies that may need higher performance results
• Step-by-step approach needed

4. Organization and Capacity Building Needed for PEM Reforms in Vietnam

4.1. Organization Needed for the PEM Reforms

An organization for the PEM reforms will be needed in Vietnam. A task force team (TFT) composed of Vietnamese top PEM experts should be formed. It should be noted that a few TFTs have been established to reform Vietnam in the past, but the result was not so positive. Considering this, it is necessary to include foreign PEM experts when establishing the new TFT, if needed. In addition, it will be necessary to have an organization capable of carrying out the PEM reforms.

Depending on the size of future PEM reforms, the size and mission of the organization may differ. If the Vietnamese government undertakes several important PEM reforms separately in the future, the organization should be at a small scale. The organization will also be tasked with drawing the grand strategy of each PEM reform or monitoring the progress of the PEM reform. In this case, the organization can be established as a division of the existing related organization.

However, if the government of Vietnam is to carry out PEM reforms on a large scale, as Korea fully implemented the four major PEM reforms, it would be appropriate to make a separate organization. In the case of Korea, a separate organization, the Budget and Accounting Reinvention Office(BARO),was formed to implement the task. The BARO was composed of a public official group comprised of the best experts in public finance fields, and an advisory committee composed of the best private experts. The BARO has designed, implemented, and managed various PEM reforms, operating as a task force team for about 10 years. The Vietnamese government currently lacks an efficient financial information service. Accordingly, they can refer to the Korean case.

4.2. Capacity Building Needed for the PEM Reforms

In order to successfully complete the PEM reforms in Vietnam, Vietnam's capacity building should be considered at the same time. Although there are a few government finance related academies, a few PEM training centers with full understand of the purpose and details of all PEM reforms are needed. Alternatively, an advanced PEM training center for instructors who can instruct government officials can be established.

An existing agency or a subordinate organization may take on this task, or the new organization may take on this task. If it is difficult for the Vietnamese government to establish an organization dedicated to capacity building, it may be possible to carry out the capacity building in an organization that is set up to implement the PEM reforms mentioned above.

5. A Suggestion on Phased Schedule for the Implementation of PEM Reforms

PEM reforms cannot be completed at once; a step-by-step approach is required. At this time, considering the reality of Vietnam, it is necessary to carry out the action from a basis reform to a complicated reform as well as from an individual reform itself to link with PEM reforms.

The step-by-step approach to Vietnamese PEM reforms can be divided into two categories. One is to implement comprehensive PEM reforms, like the four major PEM reforms in Korea; and the other is to implement individual PEM reform separately without pursuing the comprehensive PEM reforms. Each phased schedule is provided below.

5.1. A Suggestion on a Phased Schedule for the Implementation of Comprehensive PEM Reforms

Phase 1 - Preparation Period: It is necessary to establish a TFT separated from existing organizations. An organization like BARO in Korea can be a reference point for Vietnam. At this time, the TFT should be composed of top experts in public finance in Vietnam, regardless of public fields or private fields. Foreign public finance experts can be included in the TFT if necessary. In addition, any law or rule for the TFT and the PEM reforms can strengthen the justification.

Vietnam can draw up four or five major PEM reforms and provide concrete reform measures, like Korea performed the four major fiscal reforms. MTEF, rearrangement of public finance statistics, project management, and an integrated (advanced) budget information system, which will help improve the transparency and efficiency of the PEM reforms, will be the five candidates.

Phase 2 - Establishment Period: This is a period when more concrete reform results will be seen and an integrated (advanced) budget information system will be established based on the four or five major PEM reforms determined in Phase 1. During the period, the MTFF can be introduced as a basis of the MTEF. In case of rearrangement of financial statistics, it is possible to set up a rearrangement plan on macro-financial statistics such as government debt or liability statistics, fiscal expenditure statistics, and public-sector employee statistics. In case of project management, a total cost management and a pre-feasibility test plan may be prepared. During this period, an integrated (advanced) budget information system will actually be established.

Phase 3 - Upgrade Period: During this period, the MTEF can be upgraded from MTFF to MTBF. The introduction of program budgeting can be considered for efficient conversion. The rearrangement of public finance statistics can be performed in micro-financial statistics following the rearrangement of macro-financial statistics in Phase 2. A necessary organization (such as Korea's PIMAC) that can actually manage project management can be established during this period. During this period, Vietnam can upgrade the integrated (advanced) budget information system while actually operating it.

Table 4-6 A suggestion on phased schedule for the implementation of comprehensive PEM reforms

Phase	Period	Contents
Phase 1	Preparation Period	- To establish a TFT separated from existing organizations (comprised of top Vietnamese experts in public finance fields, and foreign experts) - Law or rule for the TFT and the PEM reforms needed - To draw up four or five major PEM reforms and to provide concrete reform measures
Phase 2	Establishment Period	- MTFF introduced as a basis of the MTEF - Rearrangement of macro-financial statistics performed - Total cost management and a pre-feasibility test introduced - To pilot a few departments or agencies for performance management - Integrated(advanced) budget information system established, if needed
Phase 3	Upgrade Period	- Upgrade MTEF from MTFF to MTBF - Rearrangement of micro-financial statistics performed - To expand the departments or agencies for performance management - To establish an organization (such as Korea's PIMAC) to manage project management, if possible - To upgrade the integrated (advanced) budget information system while operating the system, if established - Program budgeting introduced, if needed

5.2. A suggestion on a phased schedule for the separate implementation of an individual PEM reform without a comprehensive plan

Table 4-7 A suggestion on phased schedule for the separate implementation of an individual PEM reform without a comprehensive plan

Phase	Period	Contents
Phase 1	Preparation Period	- To establish a small division within a relevant existing organization - MTFF introduced as a basic of MTEF
Phase 2	Period for introducing new PEM reforms	- Rearrangement of macro-financial statistics performed - Total cost management and a pre-feasibility test introduced (Under an assumption that the new PEM reforms will be these two) - To pilot a few departments or agencies for performance management, if needed
Phase 3	Period for performing comprehensive PEM reforms	- To carry out the tasks suggested in the preparation period for the implementation of comprehensive PEM reforms - Tasks of next periods performed sequentially - To expand the departments or agencies for performance management, if needed

Phase 1 - Preparation Period: It is necessary not to establish a new separate organization, but to establish a small division within the relevant existing organization, which is in charge of planning and monitoring the individual PEM reform. Relevant laws or rules can be made if necessary. The MTFF can be introduced as a basis of the MTEF.

Phase 2 – Period for introducing new PEM reforms: During this period, it is assumed that the new PEM reforms will be the rearrangement of public finance statistics and project management. In the former case, macro-finance statistics can be rearranged. In the case of project management, there may be a plan to introduce total cost management and pre-feasibility test. If other PEM reforms are introduced, then there should be a suitable introduction measures.

Step 3 – Period for performing comprehensive PEM reforms: Vietnam can carry out the tasks of the Phase 1 period when implementing the comprehensive PEM reforms. The tasks of Phase 2 and 3 in implementing the comprehensive PEM reforms can be performed sequentially.

V. Conclusion

This research analyzes the reality of public expenditure and PEM in Vietnam before recommending strategies and action plans applicable to Vietnam. In order to solve fiscal problems such as steady fiscal deficit, sharp increase in government debt, and inefficiency of public expenditure, the Vietnamese government should prioritize PEM reforms. However, the Government is just considering to introduce MTEF or to increase the effectiveness of MTEF among various PEM reforms. The Government has not confirmed whether it will introduce other PEM reforms such as rearrangement of public finance statistics and project management other than MTEF. However, based on the political and economic importance of, and concerns over Vietnamese government debt, it is requested that the rearrangement of government debt statistics be carried out as soon as possible. In addition, considering that all PEM policies are interlinked, it is desirable for the government to perform PEM reforms comprehensively. However, the government is not considering introducing the PEM reforms.

However, academic research has not cast light on the strategy, action plans, and methods in the PEM reform field. There is also a lack of detailed experience-sharing in the field. Fortunately, Korea has a long history in the PEM reform and has received positive response from international organizations for its PEM reform. This research does not emphasize the positive response to the Korean PEM reform. Rather, the research introduces Korean cases selectively, carefully judging the applicability to Vietnam. Based on an author's experience as a core practitioner in the Korean government, the authors analyze the contribution as well as limitation and difficulty of the Korean PEM reform cases. This can help the Vietnamese government make appropriate policy decisions on PEM reform.

This study recommends selected strategies and action plans to minimize uncertainty, difficulty, and resistance caused by PEM reforms in Vietnam. First, Vietnam's unconditional introduction of various PEM reforms proposed or introduced by foreign governments or international organizations could lead to considerable confusion or resistance. This study analyzes the PEM reality and criteria that should be considered when introducing various PEM reforms in Vietnam. Based on that, we propose a few PEM reforms that should be introduced and others that should not. In addition, we suggest the introduction methods in the PEM reforms in order to increase the likelihood of PEM reform success in Vietnam. In particular, the study suggests action plans divided into two types: action plans applicable when introducing an individual PEM reform sporadically and action plans applicable when introducing all core PEM reforms comprehensively. The study recommends a method to comprehensively introduce a few core PEM reforms at a shot, taking into account the linkages among the PEM reforms. This approach could be successful with aggressive support from the top political party in Vietnam. However, the support, a prerequisite for the success, may not be provided. In the case, an individual PEM reform could be introduced sporadically. An alternative for that has also been proposed in the study. In addition, we propose to establish a separate TFT composed of top Vietnamese and overseas experts, and an advanced public finance academy. The TFT will be able to prepare PEM reforms and to provide advanced education and training for instructors who will teach PEM reforms in the future. These measures could minimize the uncertainty, difficulty, and resistance caused by the future Vietnamese PEM reforms.

When analyzing government reforms, we should also analyze the dilemmas or issues which may arise between central and local governments, if any. However, the coverage of this study focuses on the central government, as mentioned in the first section. The Vietnamese government can analyze and complement the results and limitations of the PEM reforms for the central government, before the PEM reforms performed in the central government can be applied to local governments and SOEs.

The research suggests strategies and concrete action plans for PEM reforms applicable in Vietnam. When the Vietnam government follows these suggestions, expected consequences or outcomes can be as follows.

Firstly, the Vietnamese government needs a swift PEM reform. Considering the rapid increase in the fiscal deficit and the government debt, and inefficient expenditure management, Vietnamese PEM reform is an essential aspect that can no longer be delayed. Our strategies and action plans can be used as an accelerator for the Vietnamese PEM reforms.

Secondly, our research could minimize any uncertainty, difficulty, and resistance caused by the future PEM reforms. Korea has experienced some limitations in that the government did not take into consideration the linkages among PEM reforms and outcomes from a PEM reform has not been achieved as expected. By taking these into consideration, Vietnam will be able to overcome the limitations that Korea experienced.

Thirdly, our research could greatly enhance the prospect of Vietnamese PEM reforms. For example, rearrangement of public finance statistics suggested could enhance the objectivity in the government debt statistics. In addition, efficient project management will enhance value for money in an individual project. A series of PEM reforms will ultimately improve the contribution of public finance to Vietnam's economic growth.

Table 4-8 Expected consequences or outcomes from the strategies and action plans suggested in this research

	As-is	To-be (Consequences or Outcomes)
Swift PEM reforms	- Vietnam has not prepared a strategy or action plans for the PEM reform	- Our strategy and action plans can be used as an accelerator for the Vietnamese PEM reforms
Any limitations caused by PEM reform	- Vietnam does not consider them	- With our strategy and action plans, Vietnam could overcome some limitations which Korea experienced before
Prospect of Vietnam PEM reforms & contribution to Vietnam economic growth	- Low efficiency in public finance - Low contribution to economic growth	- Our research could enhance the prospect of Vietnam PEM reforms - High contribution to economic growth

CHAPTER FIVE :

Conclusion

Yeonseob Ha

Professor, Department of Public Administration, Yonsei University

CHAPTER FIVE:

Conclusion

This report recommends specific reform measures in the areas of institutional and administrative reforms, governance reform, human resource management reform, and public expenditure management reform.

In the area of institutional and administrative reform, the Vietnamese Government will need to address the issue of how to sequence several actions as both the order in which actions are developed and the timing of each must be set in a specific manner; we suggest three policy recommendations for the three stages of reform with which to realize Vietnam's successful administrative reforms and further the Vietnam Vision of 2035.

In the PLAN stage, establishing empowered "reform units" would be necessary to render networks effective among units. Only when empowered units exist can networks exist among independent "reform units" that are responsible for making coherent and systematic reforms. Regarding South Korea, the Economic Planning Board (EPB) was created in 1961 and orchestrated the overall economic reforms of President Park Chung-hee as a means of promoting economic development. This coordinating unit drafted and executed the Five-year Plans of Economic Development and led both national reform and economic growth. Moreover, several other effective reform bodies were established with which to manage national reforms over several decades. For instance, the Government Reform and Decentralization Committee was one of the key units entrusted with the role of pushing government reform forwards in the Roh Moo-Hyun administration. The committee was highly significant for addressing and resolving regional disparities as one of the main initiatives during his term. Given the complexity of values that Vietnam must pursue, creating fully empowered, well networked reform units is markedly significant. Those units will support the ongoing execution in Vietnam to ensure the achievement of sustainable development.

In the DO stage, Vietnam needs sound umbrella organizations that coordinate think tanks to enhance the coherence and systematics of reform strategies, initiatives, and actions. The benefits of having multiple policy research institutes and think tanks lie in the fact that each institute can focus on producing relevant policy recommendations on subjects related to their own expertise while others pay attention to policy issues in their own arenas. Thus, it is critical to facilitate a research environment in which each think tank can work proactively with a proper degree of autonomy and responsibility. However, given that many think tanks exist that support the Vietnamese government, building orchestrating organizations that can formally coordinate the dispersal of policy support for think tanks at the ministry level is necessary. In Korea, the National Research Council for Economics, Humanities and Social Sciences (NRC) and the National Research Council of Science & Technology (NST) are known national umbrella organizations that support and promote government-funded research institutes in corresponding sectors. The Vietnam Chamber of Commerce and Industry (VCCI) has been noted for its great influence as a leading policy think tank for the Vietnamese government, emerging as a medium with which to identify policy problems and put pressure on changes in governance. Settling and reinforcing institutes with a coordinating organization would contribute to creating a sustainable foundation of national governance under such a vision and philosophy.

In the CHECK&ACT stage, there should be evaluation and feedback systems that can monitor national reform processes. Vietnam does have highly utilized government performance and reform indices with which it can enhance organizational effectiveness; for example, SIPAS and the PAR Index bring in policy implications that asks the government at all levels to open up for greater information access and transparency, simplify of administrative processes, increase the use of ICT when organizing public service works, reduce fees, and improve public ethics and behavior. However, these tools are not fully utilized, in that their results are merely considered when designing future incentives or goals. To take the example of Korea, performance evaluation in Korea aims to evaluate performance in three dimensions: individual, organizational, and project, the results of which are routed back to the inputs used to redirect the organizational structure. Gathering evaluation results from all levels allows Vietnam to create a comprehensive evaluation system in which information is properly reflected when designing budgets and organizing personnel and incentives. Furthermore, Vietnam's numerous tools need to be further developed and refined to accurately measure objectives. Tools constantly evolve to meet the system's current policy demands and these efforts can be expected to preserve their objectivity and credibility. These steps in the feedback system will ultimately be reflected to enhance the organization's performance. Adapting knowledge to local context requires complicated but constant efforts. Vietnam needs to take a long-term perspective to adopt the full-fledged feedback loop system. Officials need to develop the policy agenda with exhaustive efforts built on well-supported research and studies. If required, launching a more complete performance management program is highly viable with the collaboration of international organizations such as KOICA. Based on the cooperation with expert organizations, Vietnam would be able to further enhance its extant instruments to manage performance.

Reform has reached a critical point in Vietnam and the three aforementioned suggestions at each stage can help reflect concrete actions in the near future. Materializing the Vietnam Vision for 2035 will require considering these suggestions as high-priority when designing the Vietnam Socio-economic Development Strategy for 2021–2030.

Governance reform touches upon very broad areas. It is virtually impossible to draw a specific action plan that covers all the government reform issues discussed thus far in a single set of policy recommendations. It would be practically useful for the Vietnamese government to first identify any significant barriers it must overcome. We believe that three issues should be carefully addressed that are not limited to specific subjects of governance reform, but rather are associated with government culture, overall governance structure, and the characteristics of political leadership in Vietnam.

First, the Vietnamese government must be well prepared for dealing with resistance from people with vested interests in maintaining the status quo; the people who benefit the most from the existing management system tend to have strong political influence. A high ranking official of Vietnam's Communist Party stated, "the threat from vested interests is the biggest threat among all threats" (translated from Vu Ngoc Hoang, "Nguy cơ "lợi ích nhóm" bao trùm lên mọi nguy cơ khác", Nhân dân Newspaper, 28/07/2016). Since governance reform pays attention to how to change existing mechanisms and remove policy loopholes, vested interests will use all resources to resist changes. Such resistance is further strengthened by Vietnam's collective political leadership principle in decision making: decisions will be only adopted with a clear majority, some must even be unanimously agreed. If different opinions still exist , the status quo will be preserved until an absolute majority can be achieved. Hence, attempts to block governance reform efforts will find it easier to succeed than attempts to promote them.

The next issue is the public administration inertia that has accumulated in the Vietnamese bureaucratic culture and in the fragmented Vietnamese administrative system. Public administration inertia is embedded in the administrative system as most people tend to feel comfortable with old administrative routines and procedures. Moreover, public bureaucrats are those who implement reform, but they are also the targets of said reforms. As analyzed above, the fragmentation of government authority also contributes to administrative inertia as achieving coordination in implementing processes is very difficult. Therefore, strengthening the mechanisms that control and monitor public bureaucrats is important. It is noteworthy that the current prime minister has established a special task force (Tổ công tác của thủ tướng, Decision No 1642/QĐ-Ttg, 8/2016) to inspect the implementation of PM orders and instructions in many branches and provinces to overcome administrative inertia.

The lack of strong and cohesive leadership created by Vietnam's political system is an ongoing dilemma that increases the difficulty of achieving successful reform. The Communist Party of Vietnam and the government have both expressed the clear will to affect reform in many important documents, but the speed of reform remains very slow. Furthermore, cohesion among leaderships at various government levels is also weak, especially between the two most important leadership positions: the head of the party and the head of People Committee.

We can imagine several conditions that could help the Vietnamese government overcome its barriers or minimize the negative effects that arise from its challenges. First, significant efforts should be made to promote the development of a civil society. If the success of governance reform depends on the good will of the political leadership and government bureaucrats, Vietnamese governance reform initiatives might not reach the desirable future. Organized citizens' pressure on reform will mobilize political support for such reforms and provide ideas for reforms that the government bureaucracy may not have considered.

Second, Vietnam must drastically improve the capacities of national think tanks that specialize in key governance areas. Think tanks staffed with top-notch experts have been a key success factor in Korea's development. Making investments for policy-oriented research agencies with a certain degree of independence from the executive power to investigate and publish governance reports is a precondition for harnessing the accountability of central and local government agencies. Think tanks should be considered a critical asset in the state's capacity to set up development priorities. Besides, the presence of such institutions provides objective professional policy recommendations and guidelines, which are important political instruments with which to secure political justifications for governance reform.

For better results with Human Resource Management (HRM) reform, we provide a sequence of reforms in three stages. If six HRM initiatives discussed above are conducted simultaneously, that might lead to unexpected negative results and the effects of the reform might not be fully realized. Accordingly, this chapter illustrates which initiatives should be prioritized and which initiatives serve as a foundation for others to demonstrate their full potential. As a preliminary prescription, we provide three steps with which to conduct HRM initiatives as follows: 1) the stabilization of the career civil service system, 2) the establishment of evidence-based management, and 3) the full implementation of performance management and the adoption of position classification system (open system) elements. Practically, the first and second steps work as the foundation for the third step. That is, the first and second steps can be conducted simultaneously. However, when resources are constrained, one may delay the establishment of evidence-based management systems while prioritizing the stabilization of the career civil service system.

First, achieving stabilization in the career civil service system should be prioritized. Management based on merit is required, and assuring a high standard of administrative ethics is necessary for successfully adopting other reform initiatives. Providing a competitive salary to public personnel is also important when asking for a high standard of morale. Currently, the Vietnam government implements the cut-back of public officials to enhance its efficiency and performance. When considering that current salary levels are not sufficiently high, the Vietnam government may want to use the budget it has saved by making cutbacks to increase salary levels. Finally, making public services attractive, giving pride to existing public personnel, and developing public personnel who are respected by citizens for their high moral standards and competence are critical to establishing an effective civil service.

Second, the Vietnamese government must establish a system with which to regularly collect data about public personnel, which will make grounds for evidence-based management. Understanding the distribution of public officials and evaluating their current statuses will help make future recruitment plans. For example, the database will clarify what types of expert the government currently requires, which professionals will be needed in the next 10 years, etc. Further positive steps include the classification of major tasks for public personnel and the preparation of specific job descriptions for each Ministry.

Related to the current cutback efforts, each Ministry must prepare job descriptions to justify their personnel, which will also help in other areas. For example, one can systematically classify the tasks an organization requires to successfully conduct its mission. The job description also illustrates each job holder's core competences. Such information will serve as a basic standard with which to evaluate the performance of public personnel, and becomes a basis for effective performance management. In addition, introducing some elements of a position classification system is a pre-condition .

Finally, after stabilizing the career civil service system and achieving sufficient preparation for the evidence-based management and detailed job descriptions, it will be possible to adopt a performance management system and introduce some executable elements of a position classification system. When accompanied with sophisticated performance measurements, performance management can be a quite useful tool for enhancing individual and organizational performance. Some elements of a position classification system will be helpful for increasing expertise in the public sector, which will supplement the civil service career system's shortcomings.

Keeping this sequence is desirable to maximize the effectiveness of HRM reform. For example, performance management (third phase) may not achieve its expected effects when the job descriptions (second phase) are poorly prepared. As discussed, if job descriptions are not prepared, designing proper performance measurements becomes difficult. Without stabilizing the career civil service system (first phase), introducing an open system (position classification system) (third phase) will cause confusion among public officials. For example, introducing an open position recruitment system may not attract competent personnel from the private sector if the salary level is not competitive. Likewise, unless a merit-based system is well established in the first phase, public officials are unlikely to accept performance evaluation results in the third phase. Finally, the effectiveness of reforms will be maximized when the sequence is well maintained.

Selected strategies and action plans are recommended to minimize uncertainty, difficulty, and resistance caused by Public Expenditure Management (PEM) reforms in Vietnam. First, if Vietnam were to introduce various PEM reforms that are proposed or introduced by foreign governments or international organizations unconditionally, this could lead to considerable confusion or resistance. This study analyzes the PEM reality and criteria that should be considered when introducing various PEM reforms in Vietnam. Based on this, we will propose several PEM reforms that should be introduced and others that should not. In addition, we will suggest introduction methods in PEM reforms to increase the likelihood of successful PEM reform in Vietnam. In particular, the study suggests differentiated action plans that are divided in two: action plans that are applicable when sporadically introducing individual PEM reforms and action plans that are applicable when introducing all core PEM reforms comprehensively. The study recommends a method for comprehensively introducing a few core PEM reforms together by taking into account linkages among the PEM reforms. This approach could be successful with aggressive support from Vietnam's top political party. However, there is a chance that the support that is a prerequisite of success may not be met; if so, individual PEM reforms should be introduced sporadically. An alternative has also been proposed in the study. In addition, we propose establishing a separate TFT that is composed of top Vietnamese and overseas experts, and an advanced public finance academy. The TFT will be able to prepare PEM reforms and provide advanced education and training for instructors who will teach

PEM reforms in the future. These measures could minimize the uncertainty, difficulty, and resistance caused by future Vietnamese PEM reforms.

When analyzing government reforms, we should also analyze the dilemmas or issues that may arise between central and local governments, if any. However, the coverage of this study focuses on the central government, as mentioned in the first section. The Vietnamese government can analyze and complement the results and limitations of PEM reforms for the central government, before the PEM reforms applied to the central government can be applied to local governments and SOEs.

This research suggests strategies and concrete action plans for PEM reforms that are applicable in Vietnam. If the Vietnamese government uses these suggestions, the expected consequences or outcomes will be as follows.

First, the Vietnamese government needs swift PEM reform. Considering the rapid increase in the fiscal deficit and government debt and the inefficiencies in expenditure management, Vietnamese PEM reform is an essential aspect that can no longer be delayed. Our strategies and action plans can be used as accelerators for Vietnamese PEM reforms.

Second, our research could minimize the uncertainties, difficulties, and resistances caused by future PEM reforms. Korea has experienced some limitations, in that the government did not consider linkages among PEM reforms and outcomes from PEM reforms as they have not been achieved as expected. Vietnam will be able to overcome the limitations that Korea has previously experienced.

Third, our research could greatly enhance the prospect of Vietnamese PEM reforms. For example, the suggested rearrangement of public finance statistics could enhance objectivity in the government debt statistics. In addition , efficient project management will enhance value for money in individual projects. A series of PEM reforms will ultimately improve public finance contributions to Vietnamese economic growth.

APPENDIX

APPENDIX

Government Structure and Number of Organizations

		The Chun Doo-hwan Government (1980.09-1988.02)			The Roh Tae-woo Government (1988.02-1993.02)		
		The early period	the middle period	the last period	the early period	the middle period	the last period
Govern -ment Structure	Board	2	2	2	2	2	2
	Ministry	14	16	16	16	16	16
	Lower-level Ministry	6	4	4	4	6	6
	Agency	15	14	13	13	12	15
Number of organiza -tions	Board, Ministry, Lower-level Ministry and Agency	35 (-)	36 (+1)	35 (-1)	35 (0)	36 (+1)	39 (+3)
	Board, Ministry and Lower-level Ministry	20 (-)	22 (+2)	22 (0)	22 (0)	24 (+2)	24 (0)
Public Servants		471,438	454,046	477,146	492,466	539,869	565,115

		The Kim Young-sam government (1993.02-1998.02)			The Kim Dae-jung government (1998.02-2003.02)		
		the early period	the middle period	the last period	the early period	the middle period	the last period
Govern-ment Structure	Board	2	2	2	-	-	-
	Ministry	14	13	14	17	17	18
	Lower-level Ministry	6	5	5	2	4	4
	Agency	15	15	14	16	16	16
Number of organiza-tions	Board, Ministry, Lower-level Ministry and Agency	37 (-2)	35 (-2)	35 (0)	35 (0)	37 (+2)	38 (+1)
	Board, Ministry and Lower-level Ministry	22 (-2)	20 (-2)	21 (+1)	19 (-2)	21 (+2)	22 (+1)
Public Servants		492,466	558,489	561,952	555,501	545,690	562,373

		The Roh Moo-hyun Government (2003.02-2008.02)			The Lee Myung-bak Government (2008.02-2013.02)		
		the early period	the middle period	the last period	the early period	the middle period	the last period
Govern-ment Structure	Board	-	-	-	-		
	Ministry	18	18	18	15		
	Lower-level Ministry	4	4	4	4		
	Agency	16	18	18	18		
Number of organiza-tions	Board, Ministry, Lower-level Ministry and Agency	38 (0)	40 (+2)	40 (0)	17 (-5)	-	
	Board, Ministry and Lower-level Ministry	22 (0)	22 (0)	22 (0)			
Public Servants		579,448	571,982	604,714	605,924		

Source: Moon (2009)

REFERENCES

CHAPTER ONE: Institutional and Administrative Reforms

Ali, I., & Son, H. H. 2007.Measuring inclusive growth. *Asian Development Review*, 24(1): 11-31.

Andrews, R., & Boyne, G. 2012. Structural change and public service performance: The impact of the reorganization process in English local government. *Public Administration*, 90(2): 297-312.

Association for Progressive Communications. 2009, *ICTs for Democracy: Information and Communication Technologies for the Enhancement of Democracy – with a Focus on Empowerment*, Swedish International Development Cooperation Agency, Stockholm

Axelrod, B., Handfield-Jones, H., & Michaels, E. 2002. A New Game Plan for C Players, *Harvard Business Review*, 2002: 80-88.

Barker, J. R., & Cheney, G. 1994.The concept and the practices of discipline in contemporary organizational life, *Communication Monographs*, 61(1).

Beblavy, M. 2001. Understanding the waves of agencification and the governance problems they have raised in Central and Eastern European Countries. *OECD Journal on Budgeting*, 2(1): 121-139.

Christensen, T., &Lægreid, P. 2007. The whole-of-government approach to public sector reform. *Public administration review*, 67(6): 1059-1066.

Doan TrongTruyen. 1996. An Overview on Public Administration Reform in the Socialist Republic of Vietnam. Presented at the International Colloquium on

Public Administrative Reform. Hanoi, Vietnam.

Eckardt, S., Demombynes, G., &Chandrasekharan, B. D. 2016. *Vietnam - Systematic Country Diagnostic*. Washington, D.C., World Bank Group.

El-Erian, M. A., & Spence, A. M. 2008.Growth strategies and dynamics.*World Economics*, 9(1): 57-96.

Foucault, M. 1980. *Power/knowledge* (G. Gordon., I. Marshal., J. Mepham& K. Soper) New York: Pantheon.

Fung, A. 2006. Varieties of Participation in Complex Governance," *Public administration Review*, Special Issues: 66–75

George, G., McGahan, A. M., & Prabhu, J. 2012. Innovation for inclusive growth: Towards a theoretical framework and a research agenda. *Journal of management studies*, 49(4): 661-683.

Han, C. H. 2004. Public Management Reform and The Legacy of Developmental State in Korea. OECD World Forum Statistics, *Knowledge and policy.*

Han, I. S., & Shin, Y. 2006. Implication of Customer Satisfaction Survey in Local Public Enterprises, *The Korea Local Administration Review*, 20(3): 105-132.

Henry, P. B. 2013. *Turnaround: Third World Lessons for First World Growth.* Basic Books.

Hwang, J. Y., Lee, J. W., & K, Y. K. 2014.An Empirical study of Low Performer in Public Sector.*Korean Academy of Management*, 13(2): 113-138,*Korean Public Personnel Administration Review*, 13(2): 113-138.

International Colloquium. 1996. Proceedings of the International Colloquium on PAR , Hanoi: 24-26 September 1996. Steering Committee for PAR, UNDP project Vie/92/2002 (1996)

Ianchovichina, E. and Lundstrom, S.. 2009. Inclusive Growth Analytics: Framework and Application. Economic Policy and Debt Department, The World Bank. Retrieved from http://wwwwds.worldbank.org/external/default/WDSContentServer/IW3P/IB/2009/03/03/000158349_200903 03083943/Rendered/PDF/WPS4851.pdf.

Jang, Y. S & Cho, H. J. 2013. The Paradoxical Hybridization of Public-Private Management Paradigms: Changing Trends and Organizational Responses. *Korean Journal of Management*, 21(3): 69-104.

Kim J. Y. 2012. What Affects the Results of Public-Service Customer Satisfaction Survey for the Public Entities in Korea?.*Korean Journal of Public Finance,* 5(3): 69-97.

Kim, P. S., Pindur, W., & Reynolds, K. 1995.Creating a new organizational culture: the key to total quality management in the public sector. *International Journal of Public Administration*, 18(4): 675-709.

Koo, H. 1993. *The state, Minding, and the Working Class in south Korea*. In H, Koo, ed., State and Society in Contemporary Korea. Ithaca: Cornell University Press.

Korea Institute of Public Administration (KIPA). 2013. *Administrative environment and Characteristics of government* VI*: Vietnam*. Seoul: Korea Institute of Public Administration.

Lao Động. 2016.*Giảm 7 đầumốitrựcthuộc, BộCôngThươngsẽgiảm 1,5% sốcánbộ, côngchứ* (November 25, 2016). Retrieved from http://laodong.com.vn/kinh-te/giam-7-dau-moi-truc-thuoc-bo-cong-thuong-se-giam-15-so-can-bo-cong-chuc-614397.bld

Lee, S. M. 2016. Characteristics of Public Services and Customer Satisfaction: Searching on Improved Customer Satisfaction and Its Application to Performance Evaluation. *Modern Society and Public Administration,*26(2): 179-202.

Mai May HtarPhwy, Bob., Won, Sung-soo., & Park, chi-hyoung. 2013. Lessons from Korea SaemaulUndong for the Community Development of Myanmar. *Journal of SaemaulUndong& Community Development*, 2013(9): 107-132.

Moore, Mark. 1995.*Creating public value*, Cambridge: Mass: Harvard.

Martin Minogue & Nguyen Khac Hung. 2004.*Public Administration Reform in Vietnam: Experiences from Ho Chi Minh City*. Center on Regulation and Competition Working Paper Series no.84.

Ministry of Strategy and Finance.2009. *Public Service Customer Satisfaction Survey 2009* (July 10, 2009). Retrieved from http://www.mosf.go.kr/com/synap/synapView.do?atchFileId=ATCH_OLD_00004003611&fileSn=412544

Moon, M. J. 2009.A Repetitive Pattern and Reality of Government Reorganization. *Korean Public Management Review*, 23(4): 23-41.

Noh, D. M., Lee, H. J., Kang, S. W., Kang, E. J., Jun, J. H., & Lee, E. H. (2009). Study on Social Cohesion in Korea: Problems and Strategies. *Korea Institute for Health and Social Affairs*.

OECD. 2007. *OECD Reviews of Regulatory Reform: Korea*, OECD Publishing, Paris.

OECD. 2000. *OECD Reviews of Regulatory Reform: Regulatory Reform in Hungary*, OECD Publishing, Paris

OECD. 2010.*Making Reform Happen: Lessons from OECD countries*, OECD

Publishing, Paris

OECD. 2014. *Report on the OECD Framework for inclusive growth*, OECD Publishing, Paris

OECD. 2015. Policy Shaping and Policy Making: THE GOVERNANCE OF INCLUSIVE GROWTH, OECD Publishing, Paris

Overseas Economic Research Institute of Korea Eximbank. 2016. Vietnam country report, Export–Import Bank of Korea.

Palumbo, D. J., & Maynard-Moody, S. 1990. *Contemporary public administration*. Addison-Wesley Longman Ltd.

Part, C. O. 2011.Critical Discussion on governmental reorganization in Korea. *Korean Review of Organizational Studies*, 8(1): 1-30.

Park S. C. 2013. *Capacity Development in ODA Public Administration Sector: ODA Recipient's Human Resource Development*. Korea Institute of Public Administration

Part, C. O. 2011.Critical Discussion on governmental reorganization in Korea. *Korean Review of Organizational Studies*, 8(1): 1-30.

Pollitt, C.2009. 'Structural Change and Public Service Performance: International Lessons', *Public Money and Management,* 29(5): 285–91.

Seong, S. H., Park, H. J., &Ahn, J. T. 2013. How to Manage Low Performer in the Era of Retirement Age Extension?.Presented at 2013 Korean Academy of Management Fall Conference.

Tap ChìCộngSản. 2011.*TìnhhìnhđấtnướcSau 10 nămthựchiệnChiếnlượcpháttriển kinhtế - xãhội 2001-2010*. Retrieved from http://www.tapchicongsan.org.vn/Home/Quan-triet-thuc-hien-nghi-quyet-dai-hoi-dang-XI/Noi-dung-co-ban-van-kien/2011/2121/Tinh-hinh-dat-nuoc-sau-10-nam-thuc-hien-Chien-luoc-phat.aspx

The Korea Herald. 2015. Government Plans to kick out underperforming public workers Retrieved from: http://www.koreaherald.com/view.php?ud=20151005001147

The World Justice Project. 2016. WJP Rule of Law Index 2016.

Thuy, TranThiThanh. 2016. Leading by Strategy: The significance of strategy in public leadership. *Journal of State management*, no. 10/2016.

Tønnesson, S. 2000. Vietnam's Objective in the South China Sea: National or Regional Security?.*Contemporary Southeast Asia*, 199-220.

TrầnThọĐạt&NgôThắngLợi. 2017. National Economics University Annual Report: "Vietnam Economic Report 2016: Restructuring the economy in the link with changing growth paradigm and the role of the enabling state."

UNDP. 2004. Public Administration Reform Practice Note.

Vietnam Business Forum Magazine. 2015. *Administrative Reform for Higher National Competitiveness*. Retrieved from http://vccinews.com/news_detail.asp?news_id=31734

Vietnam Business Forum Magazine. 2017. *Administrative Reform under*. Retrieved http://vccinews.com/news_detail.asp?news_id=33819

Vogelsang-Coobms, V. & Cummins, M. 1999. Reorganization and Reforms: Promises, Promises, in Richard C. K. & Berman, E. V. eds. Public Sector Performance: Management, Motivation and Measurement. 148-162. Boulder, Colorado: Westview Press.

World Bank; Ministry of Planning and Investment of Vietnam. 2016. Vietnam

2035: Toward Prosperity, Creativity, Equity, and Democracy. Washington, DC: World Bank.

World Bank. 2016. *Vietnam Overview* . Retrieved from www.worldbank.org/en/country/vietnam/overview

Government Performance Evaluation Committee (http://www.evaluation.go.kr/)

IBRD (http://www.worldbank.org/)

Ministry of the Interior (http://www.moi.go.kr/)

Ministry of Gender Equality and Family (http://www.mogef.go.kr/)

Ministry of Government Administration and Home Affairs (http://www.moi.go.kr/)

National Archives of Korea (http://www.archives.go.kr/)

PAPI (http://papi.org. vn/)

Presidential Committee on Government Innovation & Decentralization(http://innovation.pa.go.kr/)

Statistics Korea (http://www.kostat.go.kr/)

The office of the President (http://www.president.go.kr/)

The office of the (17th) President (http://17cwd.pa.go.kr/)

CHAPTER TWO: Governance Reform

Anti-Corruption &Civil Rights Commission. (2017). *ACRC 2016 Annual Report.*

e-People. (n.d.-a). Purpose. Retrieved From http://www.epeople.go.kr/jsp/user/

on/eng/intro01.jsp

e-People. (n.d.-b). Keynote of Service. Retrieved From http://www.epeople.go.kr/jsp/user/on/eng/intro02.jsp

Geum, C, H. (2003). *A Study on the Development of the Public Service Charter in Korea*. KRILA Research Report.

Jeong, S. H. (2014). A Study on the Citizen's Participatory Budgeting System of Seoul Metropolitan City: From the Viewpoint of Participatory Democracy. *Civil Society & NGO*, 12(1): 3-34. (In Korean).

Kim, J. H. (1998). A Study on the Organizational Change in the Early D.J. Kim's Government. *The Journal of Social Science*, 16: 131-148. (In Korean).

Kim, K. (2006). The Public Service Charter in the Republic of Korea: A Development Plan for Government Innovation. *Digital Policy Studies*, 4(1): 55-71. (In Korean).

Kim, K. S. (2002). *Government Reform and Civil Service System*. Paper presented at Ahn-min Forum, Seoul. (In Korean).

Kim, M. (2015). Public Participation in the Development of the Budget System Development and Participatory Democracy in Local Government. *Journal of Public Society*, 5(2): 22-56. (In Korean).

Kim, P. S. (2000). Administrative Reform in the Korean Central Government: A Case Study of the Dae Jung Kim Administration. *Public Performance & Management Review*, 24(2): 145-160.

Kim, Y. J. (2014). A Study on Seoul Metropolitan Citizen Participation Budget Governance. *Journal of Policy Sciences*. 23(2): 36-62. (In Korean).

Korea Development Institution. (2016). *National Spatial Strategy for Balanced*

Development - An approach to enhance regional competitiveness and secure sustainable growth potential across South Korea. Economic Bulletin.

KOREA.net. (n.d.). Sharing with the World, Part 6: e-People. Retrieved From http://www.korea.net/NewsFocus/policies/view?articleId=142921

Kwon, O. S. (2015). *A Study of the Effectiveness Evaluation for Participatory Budgeting System in Korea*. KIPA Research Report 2015-26. (In Korean).

Lee, W. (2004). *Balanced National Development Policies of Korea.* Paper presented to 'Partnership Program in Urban Development Policy for Iraqi Officials', organized by Korea Research Institute for Human Settlements (KRIHS) and Korea International Cooperation Agency (KOICA).

Lim, S., Lee, H., & Seo, J. S. (2013). *A New Local Budgeting System*. Seoul: Parkyoungsa. (In Korean).

Ministry of Public Administration and Security & National Information Society Agency. (2014). *e-Government of Korea: Best Practices*.

Ministry of Strategy and Finance Republic of Korea. (n.d.). Special Account for Balanced National Development. Retrieved From http://investpool.go.kr/kor/policy/fiscal_innovation/balance/view03.jsp

Moon, W. (2004). The Performances and Development Strategies of the Public Service Charter Program. *Policy Analysis and Evaluation,* 14(3): 297-321. (In Korean).

OECD. (n.d.-a). Observatory of Public Sector Innovation. Retrieved From https://www.oecd.org/governance/observatory-public-sector-innovation/innovations/page/minwon24.htm#tab_description

OECD. (n.d.-b). Observatory of Public Sector Innovation. Retrieved From https://www.oecd.org/governance/observatory-public-sector-innovation/

innovations/page/minwon24.htm#tab_implementation

Park, H. K., & Nam, H. (2012). A Study of Factors Influencing the Fiscal Innovation of Local Government: Focused on the Citizen Participatory Budgeting. *The Korean Journal of Local Finance*, 17(3): 165-192. (In Korean).

Participedia. (n.d.-a). Participatory Budgeting System in Seoul, South Korea. Retrieved From http://participedia.net/en/cases/participatory-budgeting-system-seoul-south-korea

Participedia. (n.d.-b). e-People. Retrieved From http://www.participedia.net/en/cases/e-people

Participatory Budgeting in Seoul Metropolitan City. (n.d.-a). 2014 Operation of the Citizen Participatory Budgeting System. Retrieved From http://yesan.seoul.go.kr/wk/wkSelect.do?itemId=59198 (In Korean).

Participatory Budgeting in Seoul Metropolitan City. (n.d.-b). 2014 Operation of the Citizen Participatory Budgeting System. Retrieved From https://yesan.seoul.go.kr/ (In Korean).

Presidential Committee on Government Innovation & Decentralization (2008). *Finance Tax Reform of the Roh Moo-hyun Administration: The White Paper Series of Government Innovation & Decentralization 5*. (In Korean).

Presidential Committee on Government Innovation &Decentralization. (n.d.). Pushing ahead with Service Standard. Retrieved From http://innovation.pa.go.kr/briefing/view.htm?id=1125&page=1 (In Korean).

Prime Minister. (2016a). *Decision No.1600/QD-TTg* dated August 16, 2016 on Approving of the National Targeted Program on New Rural Development during the period 2016-2020.

Prime Minister. (2016b). *Decision No.1722/QD-TTg* dated September 2, 2016 on Approving of the National Targeted Program on Sustainable Property Reduction during the period 2016-2020.

Song, S. Y. (2005). Measures to Enhance Consumer Rights and Interests of Customer Service Charter in Public Service: Countering on Administrative and Compensative Action. *Journal of Consumer Policy Studies*. 28: 69-101. (In Korean).

The Korea Institute of Public Administration. (2015). *The Korean Government: Policies and Administration.*

The Presidential Committee on Balanced National Development. (2005). *Introduction Report.*

CHAPTER THREE: Human Resource Management (HRM) Reform

Acuña-Alfaro, J. (2012). *Incentives and salaries in Vietnam's public sector.* In Vietnam Law and Legal Forum (No. January/February, pp. 11-15).

Acuña-Alfaro, J. (2013) *Civil Service Reform, state employment salary and incentives.* Presentation prepared for Ho Chi Minh Academy of Politics and Public Administration (HCMA) Leadership Training Programme.

Adami, S. (2014) book review: Street level bureaucracy: dilemmas of the individual in public services. By Lipsky. (2010). *Street-level bureaucracy: dilemmas of the individual in public service.* Retrieved from https://steveadami.myefolio.com/Knowledgeofpa

Behn, R. D. (2002). The psychological barriers to performance management: Or why isn't everyone jumping on the performance-management bandwagon?

Public Performance & Management Review, 26(1), 5-25.

Bourgon, J. (2008). *The public service of 2025-Themes, Challenges and Trends: Human resources management trends in OECD countries*. Quebec City.

Can, N. T., (2013). Public administration reform in Vietnam: Current situations and solutions. *Scholarly Journal of Business Administration, 3*(5), 110-116.

Cho, I. H. (2016). *Public employee perception survey 2016* (KIPA research 2016-survey02). The Korea Institution of Public Administration. (*In Korean*)

Cho, Y. J., & Lee, J. W. (2012). Performance management and trust in supervisors. *Review of Public Personnel Administration, 32*(3), 236-259.

Cho, Y. J., Ahn, J. S., Song, H. J., & Nho, H. J. (2014) Evaluation of New Personnel System in Seoul Metropolitan Government. *Korean Public Personnel Administration Review, 13*(3), 277-303. (*In Korean*)

Choi, S. O., & Park, S. M. (2013). *The establishment of career civil service system in the Korean government.* Knowledge Sharing Program: KSP Modularization.

Choi, S. Y. (2015). *Policy alternatives for improving civil service system in Korean Government* (KIPA research 2015-14). The Korea Institution of Public Administration. (*In Korean*)

Choson Ilbo. (March, 7. 2009). [Why] Behavioral changes by the Corrective System. Retrieved from http://news.chosun.com/site/data/html_dir/2009/03/06/2009030601118.html. (*In Korean*)

Central Officials Training Institute (National Human Resources Development Institute in present). (2015). *HRD Annual Report 2015* (no. 11-1311127-000001-10). Central Officials Training Institute. (*In Korean*)

G20 ACWG. (2015). *2015-16 G20 Anti-corruption implementation plan.*

Retrieved from http://www.bmjv.de/SharedDocs/Downloads/EN/G20/G20%20ACWG%20Anti-Corruption%20Implementation%20Plan%202015-2016.pdf?__blob=publicationFile&v=1

Gainsborough, M., Dinh, D. N., & Phuong, T. T. (2009). *Corruption, public administration reform and development: Challenges and opportunities as Vietnam moves towards middle-income status.* Reforming Public Administration in Vietnam.

Gerrish, E. (2016). The impact of performance management on performance in public organizations: A Meta-analysis. *Public Administration Review, 76*(1), 48-66.

Hai, H. Nguyen (2016), *Public Administration Reform: Theory and practice*, National Politic Publisher.

Hausman, D. (2010). Policy leaps and implementation obstacles: Civil service reform in Vietnam, 1998–2009. *Innovations for Successful Societies,* Princeton University, accessed at http://www.princeton.edu/successfulsocieties

Homepage of Ministry of personnel Management (2017, August 19) Retrieved from http://www.mpm.go.kr/english/

Homepage of OECD CleanGovBiz (2017, August 19) Retrieved from http://www.oecd.org/cleangovbiz/about/

Homepage of OECD G20 (2017, August 19) Retrieved from https://www.oecd.org/g20/topics/anti-corruption/

Homepage of Office of Personnel Management (2017, August 19) Retrieved from https://www.opm.gov/

Im, S. G., & Lee, G. (2015). A Comparative study of perceptions of public officials and citizens on administrative ethics. *Korean Public Personnel Administration Review, 10*(2): 85-117. (*In Korean*)

JoongAng Ilbo. (Dec, 31, 2007). Seoul Metropolitan City distributed the 'Human Resource Innovation White Paper'. Retrieved from http://news.joins.com/article/print/2995768. (*In Korean*)

Kang, Y. J., & Bae, G. H., (2012). A Study of the effectiveness of Pay-for-Performance in public enterprise: Focusing on stakeholders` perception related to Pay-for-Performance. *The Korean Journal of Public Administration, 21*(2), 199-238. (*In Korean*)

Ketelaar, A., N. Manning & E. Turkisch. (2007). Performance-based arrangements for senior civil servants OECD and other country experiences, *OECD working papers on public governance, No. 5*, OECD Publishing. doi:10.1787/160726630750

Kickert, Walter, & Tina Randma-Liiv. (2015). *Europe managing the crisis: The politics of fiscal consolidation.* New York: Routledge.

Kim, H. G. (2013). System stability function and accountability of the career civil service system. *Korea Public Land Law Association Public Land Law Review, 63*. 345-367.

Kim, J. Y. & Kim, M. S. (2000). *The National Public Service Law.* Pakyoungsa. (*In Korean*)

Kim, P. S. (2003). Strengthening the pay-performance link in government: A Case study of Korea. *Public Personnel Management, 31*(4), 447-446.

Kim, P. S., & Hong, K. P. (2006). Searching for effective HRM reform strategy in the public sector Critical review of WPSR 2005 and suggestions. *Personnel Administration, 35*(3), 199-215.

Kim, P. S. (2009). *Moving forward for better performance management in government: The case of South Korea.* Paper presented at the international conference on Administrative Development: Towards excellence in public sector performance in Riyadh, Saudi Arabia. On November 1-4, 2009. Retrieved Sept. 10, 2012, from http://ipac.kacst.edu.sa/eDoc/2009/182491_1.pdf

Kim, P. S. (2014). Performance appraisal and performance-related pay in government: the case of south Korea. *International Journal of Civil Service Reform & Practice, 4*. 11-31.

Ko, K. K. (2017). Government integrity and future government management. Presentation prepared for special conference by Korean Association for Public Administration (*In Korean*)

Kong, D., Kim, S., & Yang, S. B. (2013). *Individual performance appraisal in the government of Korea*. Knowledge Sharing Program: KSP Modularization.

Koolstra, J. (2016), Integrity: Part of the day-to-day practice in the City of Amsterdam, in Huberts, L. W. J. C., & Hoekstra, A. (2016). *Integrity management in the public sector: The Dutch approach.* BIOS, The Hague.

Lah, T. J., & Perry, J. L. (2008). The diffusion of the Civil Service Reform Act of 1978 in OECD countries: A tale of two paths to reform. *Review of Public Personnel Administration. 28*(3), 282-299.

Lee, G. J., Lee, C. G., Kim, J. S., & Kim, S. S., (2016). *Ten years of SCS: Review and Prospects*. Presentation prepared for International Conference on Senior Civil Service.

Lee, C., Lim, J. W., & Kang, D. C., (2010). Strategies for the improvement of performance management in the public sector using BSC. *Journal of Agricultural Education and Human Resource Development, 42*(2). 243-262.

Lee, D. H. (2007). *Strategic human resource management of government.* Book Korea.

Lee, J. E. & Song, S. J. (2016). Analysis of the 2015 reform plan of GEPS. *Journal of the Korean Data & Information Science Society, 27*(1). 19-32.

Lee, M. H., Ryu, H. S., Yoon, K. S., Im, & S. K. (2011). A Study on the efficiency of the government system for advancing public service. *The Korea Institute of Public Administration (KIPA) Research Report 2011-12.* (*In Korean*)

Lipsky, M. (2010). *Street-level bureaucracy: dilemmas of the individual in public service.* The Russell Sage Foundation: New York, NY

Ministry of Personnel Management (2007). *Introduction of senior civil servant system* (English brochure).

Ministry of Personnel Management (2013). The Analysis of the 10th investigation of public officials in Korea. Retrieved from http://www.mpm.go.kr/mpm/info/infoStatistics/statisticsApprove/?boardId=bbs_0000000000000038&mode=view&cntId=223&category=&pageIdx=

Moon, M. J., & Hwang, C. (2013). The state of civil service systems in the Asia-Pacific region: A comparative perspective. *Review of Public Personnel Administration, 33*(2), 121-139.

Ngoi, T. V. (2016). *Public Administration Reform in Vietnam.* Unpublished manuscript.

Nielsen, P. A. (2014). Performance management, managerial authority, and public service performance. *Journal of Public Administration Research and Theory, 24*(2), 431-458.

Nigro, F.A. & Nigro, L.G., (1986). *The new public personnel administration,* Illinois: F.E. Peacock Publishers, Inc.

OECD (2003). *The new public executive: Reforming the senior civil service in 12 OECD member countries.* GOV/PUMA (2003) 17 OECD Publishing, Paris.

Retrieved from http://www.oecd.org/governance/pem/33708901.pdf

OECD (2005). *Modernising government: The way forward*, OECD, Paris. DOI: http://dx.doi.org/10.1787/9789264010505-sum-en

OECD. (2006). *The OECD Fights Corruption*. Retrieved from http://www.oecd.org/dataoecd/36/51/37418910.pdf

OECD. (2008). *The state of the civil service*. Unpublished paper.

OECD. (2015). Strengthening HRM reforms in the Dominican public administration for more innovative and tangible results, *in Dominican Republic: uman Resource Management for innovation in government*, OECD Publishing, Paris. DOI: http://dx.doi.org/10.1787/9789264211353-10-en

OECD. (2016). *Boosting integrity, fighting corruption*, OECD, Paris. Retrieved from https://www.oecd.org/competition/50350066.pdf

OECD. (2017). *Trust and public policy: How better governance can help rebuild public trust*, OECD Publishing, Paris. DOI: http://dx.doi.org/10.1787/9789264268920-en

Oh, S. H. (2009). *Public personnel administration. the 6th edition.* Seoul: Pakyoungsa. (*In Korean*)

Park, E. Y. (2015). *Anti-Corruption*. Presentation prepared for KDI G-20 Global Leadership Program presentation.

Poon, Y., Hùng, N. K., & Trường, D. X. (2009). *The Reform of the civil service system as Vietnam moves into the middle-income country category.* Reforming public administration in Vietnam.

Schermerhorn, J. R., Hunt, J. G., & Osborn. R. N. (2008). *Organizational behavior (10th ed.)*. New York, NY: Wiley.

Seo, W. S., & Im, J. B. (2015). *Public administration and policies in Vietnam.*

(KIPA research 2015-22-2). The Korea Institution of Public Administration. (*In Korean*)

Seoul Metropolitan Government. (2007). *Performance point system detailed operation plan.* (*In Korean*)

Seoul Metropolitan Government. (2009). *信神新辛 New Personnel System*. Retrieved from https://lib.seoul.go.kr/search/detail/CAT000000059965. (*In Korean*)

Seoul Metropolitan Government. (2012). *The white paper for voluntary personnel transfer.* (*In Korean*)

Shin, D. M., & Kang, D. S. (2003). A study on part-time civil servant: It's aims and measures for extending to the civil service system. *Korean Journal of Public Administration, 41*(1). 1-22.

Transparency International. (1998). *New perspectives on combating corruption, A joint publication of transparency international and the economic development.* Institute of the World Bank.

Transparency International. (2007). *National integrity systems in east and southeast Asia 2006.* Berlin: Transparency International.

Transparency International. (2014). *Corruption perceptions index 2014*. Berlin: Transparency International.

UNDP. (2008*). Tackling corruption, transforming lives: Accelerating human development in Asia and the Pacific.* Delhi: Macmillan

World Bank. (2006). *Anticorruption in transition: Who is succeeding and why?* Washington: World Bank

World Bank& Ministry of Planning and Investment of Vietnam. (2016) *Vietnam*

2035: Toward prosperity, creativity, equity, and democracy. Washington: World Bank

Yang, H-S. (2011). *The Performance management and evaluation system of Korea*. Paper Presented in the Improving the Quality of Public Services. A Multinational conference on public management. June 27-29, 2011, National Research University-Higher School of Economics, Moscow, Russia

Yoo, M. B., & Park, S. M. (2013). *Public personnel administration*. Seoul: Pakyoungsa. (*in Korean*)

CHAPTER FOUR: Public Expenditure Management Reform

Bae, D. & Yu, S. (2014). *Public Budgeting and Financial Management*. Seoul: Parkyoungsa.

Choi, S. D. & Yu, S. (2004). Introduction of program budgeting in Korea: focused on central governments. *Special seminar co-held by The Korean Association for Local Finance and The Korean Association for Government Accounting*.

Ha, Y. S. (2014). *Public Budgeting and Financial Management*. Seoul: Dasan.

Kang, T. H. (2006). A comparative study on the Korean government's top-down budgeting system, *Korean Governmental Accounting Review*, 4(2): 3-33.

Kim, J. M., & Park, C. K. (2006). Top-down budgeting as a tool for central resource management. *OECD Journal on Budgeting*, 6(1), 87.

Oh, Y. (2007). A study on the top-down budget system and budget deliberation by national assembly, *Korean Public Management Review*, 21(3): 91-112.

OECD. *Reallocation: The Role of Budget Institutions*. GOV/PUMA/SBO(2003)15.

Park, N. W., Oh, Y. M. & Weon, J. H. (2015). Assessment of the performance management system of budgetary programs in Korea. *Korea Institute of Public Finance* 15-18.

Pham The Anh (2008), Investigating the Relationship Between Government Expenditure and Economic Growth, *Journal of Economic Research*, Vol. 10/2008, 17-27.

Schick, A. (2003). Does Budgeting have a future? *OECD Journal on Budgeting*, 2(2): 7-48.

Shin, M. S. (1993). Improvement of the Formation and Enforcement System of the Government Budget of Korea, *The Korea Public Administration Journal*, 2(2).

Sung, N. H. & Kim, S. H. (2014). A study on assessment and improvement of Korean top-down budgeting. *Seoul national University requested by Korean Ministry of Finance and Strategy.*

World Bank. (2013). *Beyond the annual budget-Global experience with medium term expenditure frameworks*. The World Bank

Yu, S. (2015). Challenges and improvement devices of Korean program budgeting. *Korean Society and Public Administration*, 26(3)

INDEX

S

T

U

V

W

AUTHORS

Yeonseob Ha

Professor, Department of Public Administration,
Yonsei University
Dean, Graduate School of Public Administration,
Yonsei University

Yong Suk Jang

Professor, Department of Public Administration,
Yonsei University
Deputy Head, Institute for Higher Education Innovation,
Yonsei University
Former Faculty, Department of Sociology, Korea University
and University of Utah

Hyun Joon Kim

Professor, Department of Public Administration,
Korea University
Former Assistant Professor, Department of Political Science,
Texas Tech University

Yoon Jik Cho

Professor, Department of Public Administration, Yonsei University
Director, Social Science Research Institute, Yonsei University
Former Assistant Professor, Andrew Young School of Policy Studies, Georgia State University

Seungwon YU

Professor, Department of Public Administration, Korea National Police University
Chair, Department of Public Administration, Korea National Police University
Former Senior Deputy Director, Ministry of Economy and Finance, Korea